O9-AHW-357

AP® PSYCHOLOGY

2013-2014

Kaplan offers resources and options to help you prepare for the PSAT, SAT, ACT, AP exams, and other high-stakes exams. Go to www.kaptest.com or scan this code below with your phone (you will need to download a QR code reader) for free events and promotions.

snap.vu/m87n

AP® PSYCHOLOGY

2013-2014

Chris Hakala

KAPLAN

PUBLISHING

New York

AP® is a registered trademark of the College Board, which neither sponsors nor endorses this product.

This publication is designed to provide accurate and authoritative information in regard to the subject matter covered. It is sold with the understanding that the publisher is not engaged in rendering legal, accounting, or other professional service. If legal advice or other expert assistance is required, the services of a competent professional should be sought.

© 2012 by Kaplan, Inc.
Published by Kaplan Publishing, a division of Kaplan, Inc.
395 Hudson Street
New York, NY 10014

All rights reserved. The text of this publication, or any part thereof, may not be reproduced in any manner whatsoever without written permission from the publisher.

Printed in the United States of America

10 9 8 7 6 5 4 3 2 1

ISBN-13: 978-1-60978-696-0

Kaplan Publishing books are available at special quantity discounts to use for sales promotions, employee premiums, or educational purposes. For more information or to purchase books, please call the Simon & Schuster special sales department at 866-506-1949.

TABLE OF CONTENTS

ABOUT THE AUTHOR

Chris Hakala is Professor of Psychology at Western New England College in Springfield, Massachusetts. He earned a master's degree and PhD in cognitive psychology from the University of New Hampshire. His areas of interest include the teaching of psychology, reading comprehension, and language development.

Chris has been an Advanced Placement reader for 15 years and has extensive knowledge of test and rubric development.

ACKNOWLEDGMENTS

To write such a book such as this, it took more than just my own effort. I would like to formally acknowledge those who provided assistance, both in terms of the work itself as well as with the time commitment to finishing such a project.

Thanks to Sharon Maiuri, my devoted work-study student, for helping me with some of the clerical work; to Dennis Kolodziejski, my chair, for giving me the freedom from committee work to complete this book; to my colleagues, for giving me advice and emotional support; to Western New England College, for providing me with the flexibility to do this work; and to all my students, for listening to me wrestle with which topics to include in this study guide.

I would like to give a special thanks to Ruth Ault (Davidson College) and Nancy Homb (Cy-Falls High School, Houston, Texas) for their terrific insight on the material in this study guide. The students who use this book should be eternally grateful to these two tremendous people for their effort and diligence.

Finally, I would like to thank my family (my children, Abigail and Lillian) for being patient with me as I worked on this study guide at various hours of the day and night.

I would also like to thank my parents for giving me guidance and support and for always being there for me.

KAPLAN PANEL OF AP EXPERTS

Congratulations—you have chosen Kaplan to help you get a top score on your AP exam.

Kaplan understands your goals and what you're up against—achieving college credit and conquering a tough test—while participating in everything else that high school has to offer.

You expect realistic practice; authoritative advice; and accurate, up-to-the-minute information on the test. And that's exactly what you'll find in this book, as well as every other in the AP series. To help you (and us!) reach these goals, we have sought out leaders in the AP community. Allow us to introduce our experts.

AP PSYCHOLOGY EXPERTS

Ruth Ault has taught psychology for the past 25 years at Davidson College in Davidson, North Carolina. She was a reader for the AP Psychology exam and has been a table leader since 2001.

Nancy Homb has taught AP Psychology for the past seven years at Cypress Falls High School in Houston, Texas. She has been a reader for the AP Psychology exam since 2000, and began consulting for the College Board in 2005.

Barbara Loverich has taught AP psychology for the past 18 years at Hobart High School in Valparaiso, Indiana. She has been an AP reader for nine years and a table leader for six years. From 1996 to 2000, she was a board member of Teachers of Psychology in Secondary Schools and was on the State of Indiana committee to write state psychology standards. Among her distinguished awards are the Outstanding Science Educator Award and Sigma XI, Scientific Research Society in 2002.

Steve Jones has taught AP Psychology for eight years and has been a teacher for 13, all in Durham, North Carolina. He holds a bachelor's degree from the University of North Carolina at Chapel Hill and a master's degree from the University of North Carolina at Greensboro. He is a cofounder of the blog Teaching High School Psychology (http://teachinghighschoolpsychology.blogspot.com/).

Nancy Fenton has taught psychology since 2004, and currently teaches at Adlai E. Stevenson High School, which is located in a suburb of Chicago, Illinois. She has a master's degree in psychology and has been a reader for the AP Psychology exam since 2008.

| Part One |

THE BASICS

CHAPTER 1: INSIDE THE AP PSYCHOLOGY EXAM

CONTENT AREAS

The AP Psychology Exam is divided into two sections. Section I is 100 multiple-choice questions covering a variety of topics from introductory psychology. The topics covered are as follows:

History and Approaches (2–4%)

Research Methods (8–10%)

Biological Bases of Behavior (8–10%)

Sensation and Perception (6–8%)

States of Consciousness (2–4%)

Learning (7–9%)

Cognition (8–10%)

Motivation and Emotion (7–9%)

Developmental Psychology (7–9%)

Personality (5–7%)

Testing and Individual Differences (5–7%)

Abnormal Behavior (7–9%)

Treatment of Abnormal Behavior (5–7%)

Social Psychology (8–10%)

AP EXPERT TIP

Guessing is a wise choice because you do not lose points for incorrect answers.

OVERVIEW OF THE TEST STRUCTURE

Section I allows for 70 minutes to complete the 100 multiple-choice questions. This does not give you a great deal of time per question. However, some of the questions are much easier to answer than others. And then, of course, there will be some questions that you will be unable to answer. Answer the questions that you can and try to deduce the answers for those questions that you are unsure of. Know, however, that for some, you will simply have to guess. That is fine, because there is no penalty for answering a question incorrectly.

Section II is the free-response section. In this part, you will be given two questions. You will have 50 minutes to respond to these questions, so try to develop a strategy for answering both questions well. The questions are focused on methodology across areas and on being able to relate one point to several different approaches in psychology. Thus, to do well on the free-response section, you need to be prepared not only to understand the content but also to generalize the content across various areas of psychology.

HOW THE EXAM IS SCORED

Beginning with the May 2011 administration of AP exams, the method for scoring the multiple-choice section has changed. Scores are based on the number of questions answered correctly. **No points are deducted for wrong answers.** No points are awarded for unanswered questions. Therefore, you should answer every question, even if you have to guess.

To prepare for the free-response section, one of the first steps is to review released test materials on the College Board website. The released free-response items have sample answers that will help you learn how to focus your answers on the information that is essential. The free-response section is important (it will count for 1/3 of your final score), so you want to have a complete understanding of the way that the questions are structured and the way that the answers are scored.

The key to answering free-response questions well is to understand that they are written to allow you to demonstrate breadth of knowledge across a variety of areas of psychology. Thus, when answering the question, make sure you provide the reader with enough context to demonstrate complete understanding. A second important point to consider is that each response is worth a certain number of points, and each point is associated with different aspects of the question. As the questions are written with a main question and several subquestions, a good strategy is to answer the question in the same format as the question itself. Organize it in the same way it is written. Don't answer the question in the order that you know things.

The free responses are scored by human readers. Thus, handwriting is important. Take your time answering the question, but not too much time. Just realize that if someone can't read your answer, it won't score—even if it's great. Answers to the free-response section are scored according to a rubric. A rubric is an agreed-upon scoring guideline that all readers use. Typically, a rubric is generated by the people who construct the question. Then, every June, a group of high school and college psychology teachers are brought together at a site in the United States for the AP reading. There, the rubric is refined, and samples are created by the group to provide the readers with training essays. There is a great deal of concern over providing each essay with a fair read; thus, readers are constantly checked to ensure reliability.

The scores from the performance assessment (1/3 of the score) and the multiple-choice (2/3 of the score) are then combined, and the Chief Reader sets the criteria for the final score. Scores range as follows:

> 5 = Extremely well qualified
>
> 4 = Well qualified
>
> 3 = Qualified
>
> 2 = Possibly qualified
>
> 1 = No recommendation

Most colleges will accept an AP score of 3 or higher to award college credit.

> **AP EXPERT TIP**
>
> You don't need a perfect score on both test parts to achieve a 5, so don't stress too much.

REGISTRATION AND FEES

To register for the exam, contact your school guidance counselor or AP Coordinator. If your school does not administer the AP exam, contact the College Board for a listing of schools that do.

As of the printing of this book, the fee for the exam is $87. For those qualified with acute financial need, the College Board offers a $26 credit. In addition, most states offer exam subsidies to cover all or part of the remaining cost for eligible students. To learn about other sources of financial aid, contact your AP Coordinator.

ADDITIONAL RESOURCES

For more information on the AP Program and the Psychology Exam, contact:

AP Services
P.O. Box 6671
Princeton, NJ 08541–6671
Phone: (609) 771–7300 or 888-225-5427
Email: apexgrams@info.collegeboard.org
Website: collegeboard.com/student/testing/ap/about.html

CHAPTER 2: STRATEGIES FOR SUCCESS

Even non-psychologists know that human behavior is hard to predict. Students today live in a world that could not have been predicted 20 years ago. Cell phones, the Internet, and so on have changed the way we live. Where we will be in the next 20 years remains to be seen.

Similarly, psychology has changed over recent years. Advances in biological psychology and research methodology have led to the development of a field that is different than it was 20 years ago.

This book is designed to help you understand not only the current state of the field of psychology but also the unpredictable nature of both human behavior and where the field of psychology may go. It will concentrate on how the standardized test will assess your knowledge of psychological principles.

HOW TO APPROACH THE MULTIPLE-CHOICE QUESTIONS

Because you can't go two weeks as a psychologist without using "the scientific method" in some form or another, let's apply it to the test. Our hypothesis is that you can achieve a higher score by attacking the 100 multiple-choice questions in a specific order. Other students will just turn the page once the test begins and start with question 1. Let these drones be the control group.

All 100 questions are multiple-choice with five answer choices, but there are two distinct question types.

> **AP EXPERT TIP**
>
> Master the key terms, psychologists, and experiments you learned throughout your AP Psych course, and you'll do well on the multiple-choice questions. Making your own flashcards is a great way to study these.

Type 1. Stand-Alone Questions

This type of question makes up most of the exam. The words in the stem provide you with the information you need to answer the question. Each question covers a distinct topic, with easy, medium, and hard questions scattered throughout. (There is no order of difficulty on the exam.)

Here's an example:

A graphical representation of correlational data is called a

(A) bell curve.
(B) chi square.
(C) scatterplot.
(D) bimodal distribution.
(E) skewed distribution.

(The answer is (C), by the way.)

It's easier to talk about what is *not* in the Stand-Alone questions than what is in them.

- There's no order of difficulty; that is, questions do not start out easy and then gradually become tougher.
- No two questions are connected in any way.
- There is no system to when and how the psychology concepts appear.

The Stand-Alones look like a bunch of disconnected psychology questions one after the other, and that's just what they are. A statistics question is followed by a question on personality, which is followed by a question about the brain.

There's no overall pattern, so don't bother looking for one. But just because the section is random doesn't mean you have to approach it on the same random terms. Instead, draw up two lists right now using the exam topics covered in chapter 1. Label one list "Concepts I Enjoy and Know About in Psychology" and label the other list "Concepts That Are Not My Strong Points."

When you get ready to tackle the Stand-Alone section, keep these two lists in mind. Then, take two passes through the exam. On your first pass, answer the questions you find to be easy. None of the question stems contain a lot of text, so you should be able to figure out quickly whether you can tackle them. If you think you can solve a question, answer it and move on. If you're not sure, skip it and come back later. The first pass is about picking up easy points.

Once you have gone through and completed all the easy questions, go through the test a second time. This time, you're facing the tougher questions. Odds are high that you won't know the answer to some of these questions, but whatever you do, don't leave them blank. Guess if you must, but to try eliminate some obvious incorrect answer choices beforehand.

TYPE 2. GROUPED QUESTIONS

Grouped questions provide you with a stimulus (sentences or a graph, for instance) that helps you to answer a set of questions. To attack these questions correctly, you will need to understand the stem and then attack the easiest questions first. You can typically deduce the answer from using all available information.

Make sure you *completely* understand the stem before you attempt to answer the question. Here is an example of a set of Grouped questions:

For the following experiment, answer the questions below.

A researcher is interested in determining if the amount of caffeine students consume influences the number of hours they study. To do this, he varies the amount of caffeine among three groups of students: group 1 drinks 0 servings of caffeine a day; group 2 drinks 3 servings; and group 3 drinks 8 servings. Students keep a log tracking how long they study each day. After the study is over, the researcher collects the logs and obtains an average number of hours studied per group.

In this experiment, _____ is the independent variable.

(A) Group 1
(B) Group 3
(C) number of hours studied
(D) amount of caffeine consumed
(E) number of students per group

In this experiment, _____ is the dependent variable.

(A) Group 1
(B) Group 3
(C) number of hours studied
(D) amount of caffeine consumed
(E) number of students per group

(The answers here are (D) and (C), respectively.)

MULTIPLE-CHOICE STRATEGIES

Admittedly, the AP Psychology test is a test of specific knowledge, so picking the right answer from the wrong answer choices is harder to do than it is on other standardized tests. Still, it can be done. If you don't have enough time to get to all the questions, skip the longest, most involved ones. That's a great use of your limited resource: time.

You don't have much time to ponder every tough question, so trusting your instincts can keep you from getting bogged down and wasting time on a problem. You might not get every educated guess correct, but again, the point isn't about getting a perfect score. It's about getting a good score, and surviving hard questions by going with your gut feelings is a good way to achieve this.

On other problems, though, you might have no inkling of what the correct answer should be. Look at our trusty Stand-Alone question from before:

> A graphical representation of correlational data is called a
>
> (A) bell curve.
> (B) chi square.
> (C) scatterplot.
> (D) bimodal distribution.
> (E) skewed distribution.

Even if you don't know what the problem is asking, look at (D) and (E). Both terms include the term *distribution*. A graph might be a distribution but that isn't *always* the case, so you know that these answers are probably not correct. Thinking "good science" has just helped lead you, at the very least, to eliminate some poor answer choices.

Thinking about good science in terms of the AP Psychology can help you in two ways:

(1) It helps you cross out extreme answer choices or choices that are untrue or out of place.

(2) It can point you to the correct answer, because the correct answer will be a factual piece of information sensibly worded.

Neither of these strategies is 100 percent effective every time, but they do help more often than not. On a tough Stand-Alone problem, these techniques can make the difference between an unanswered question and a good guess.

HOW TO APPROACH THE FREE-RESPONSE QUESTIONS

For Part II, you'll have 50 minutes to answer two questions. That's essentially 25 minutes per question. You might finish faster than that, but try not to speed through Part II in 10 minutes. That's not enough time to answer the questions completely. Take the time to make your answers as precise and detailed as possible.

There are three things to remember about the free-response questions.

1. MOST QUESTIONS ARE STUFFED WITH SMALLER QUESTIONS

You won't get one broad question like "How do psychologists treat depression?" Instead, you'll get an initial setup followed by subquestions labeled (a), (b), (c), and so on. Expect to spend about one half page writing about each letter question.

2. WRITING SMART THINGS EARNS YOU POINTS

Each subquestion has key ideas worth a certain number of points. If you write about one of those ideas, you earn yourself a point. (Remember, the people who score the exam follow a rubric, which acts as a blueprint for what a good answer should look like.)

There's a limit to how many points you can earn on a single subquestion, and there are other strange regulations, but it boils down to this: Writing smart things about each question will earn you points toward that question.

So don't be terse or in a hurry. Use your 25 minutes to be as precise as you can for each subquestion. Doing well on one subquestion can earn you enough points to cover up for another subquestion you're not as strong on. And when all the points are tallied for that free-response problem, you come out strong on total points, even though you didn't ace every single subquestion.

3. MIMIC THE QUESTIONS

Use the format of the question to help you write your answer. That is, follow the structure you are presented on the exam. As we explained, that's usually with (a), (b), and (c) breakdowns.

The free responses are scored by individual readers as opposed to computers. So that points can be assigned in a consistent fashion among all test takers, readers follow the scoring rubric with strict guidelines. To make their job easier, make sure to write out the information in a clear, organized way.

As you prepare for this standardized test, here are some general strategies to keep in mind.

STRESS MANAGEMENT

1. PACING

Because the test is timed, proper pacing will ensure that you will get to every question. Don't get yourself into a situation where you run out of time before seeing each question at least once. Use your time wisely and don't dawdle. Make sure you take the time now to familiarize yourself with the style of questions that will be asked so you can get going right away on test day.

AP EXPERT TIP

As you read each question, try to determine the approximate point value and plan your answer accordingly. Remember: Adding more information than you need will not give you extra points!

AP EXPERT TIP

You don't have to write a lengthy introduction or conclusion. In your essay, address *only* the salient points of each question.

AP EXPERT TIP

Be sure to bring two pencils for the multiple-choice questions and two pens for the free-response questions, just in case.

2. PROCESS OF ELIMINATION

For the multiple-choice questions, the answer is listed. The difficulty resides in the fact that it is hidden among incorrect choices. If you can eliminate answer choices you know are incorrect, you'll be in better shape to guess if necessary.

3. PATTERNS AND TRENDS

Standardized tests don't change much from year to year. Yes, questions themselves change, but the format and the general content remains constant. That's the nature of standardized testing—if the test changed wildly each time it came out, it would be useless as a tool for comparison.

Learn what you can about the previous test administrations of AP Psychology to understand the test you are about to take. Use the trends and patterns to your advantage.

4. THE RIGHT APPROACH

Having the right mindset can play a bigger role than you might think in a test. Those who are nervous about an exam and hesitant to guess often fare much worse than those bearing a proactive, confident attitude.

And students who start with question 1 and plod on from there tend not to score as well as those who carefully pick and choose their questions. Tackle the easy questions first before you take on the harder ones.

COUNTDOWN TO THE TEST

Planning your time before test day is essential. The study schedule presented here is the ideal. Compress it to fit your needs. Do keep in mind, though, that research in cognitive psychology has shown that the best way to acquire a great deal of information about a topic is to prepare over a long period of time.

Because you have several months to prepare for this exam, it behooves you to use that time to your advantage. This book, along with your text, should be invaluable in helping you prepare for this test.

If your course is a full year in length, the following schedule is recommended:

September:

Take the Diagnostic Test in this book and isolate areas in which you need help. Assuming this is your first introductory psychology course, the Diagnostic will serve to familiarize you with the type of material you will be asked about on the AP exam.

Begin reading your introductory psychology text along with the class outline.

October–February:

Continue reading this book and use the summaries at the end of each chapter to help guide you to the most salient information for the exam.

March and April:

Take the two Practice Tests and get an idea of your score. Also, identify the areas in which you need to brush up. Then go back and review those topics in both this book and your introductory psychology text.

May:

Do a final review and take the exam.

If your course is only one semester in length, you will need to prepare along a more expedient path:

January:

Take the Diagnostic Test in this book.

February–April:

Begin reading your introductory psychology text along with this book and identify areas of strengths and weaknesses.

Late April:

Take the two Practice Tests and use your results to guide you in your preparation.

May:

Do a final review and take the exam.

| Part Two |

DIAGNOSTIC TEST

This Diagnostic Test is a brief multiple-choice exam to help you identify your strengths and weaknesses in the area of AP Psychology. The goal is to help you determine the areas that you should focus on while studying. The questions are drawn from all areas covered on the actual AP Psychology exam.

To score your Diagnostic Test, go through the answers once you have completed the exam. Add up the number of questions you answered correctly and those you answered incorrectly.

If you score well (that is, answered 18–20 questions correctly) you are in terrific shape. Keep doing what you are doing. If you didn't score that high, you have some studying to do. This book should help a great deal.

Diagnostic Test Answer Grid

To compute your score for the Diagnostic Test, calculate the number of questions you got right, then divide by 20 to get the percentage of questions you answered correctly.

The approximate score range is as follows:

5 = 80–100% (extremely well qualified)
4 = 60–79% (well qualified)
3 = 50–59% (qualified)
2 = 40–49% (possibly qualified)
1 = 0–39% (no recommendation)

A score of 49% is a 2, so in this case, you could definitely do better. If your score is low, keep on studying to improve your chances of getting credit for the AP Psychology exam.

1. Ⓐ Ⓑ Ⓒ Ⓓ Ⓔ   11. Ⓐ Ⓑ Ⓒ Ⓓ Ⓔ

2. Ⓐ Ⓑ Ⓒ Ⓓ Ⓔ   12. Ⓐ Ⓑ Ⓒ Ⓓ Ⓔ

3. Ⓐ Ⓑ Ⓒ Ⓓ Ⓔ   13. Ⓐ Ⓑ Ⓒ Ⓓ Ⓔ

4. Ⓐ Ⓑ Ⓒ Ⓓ Ⓔ   14. Ⓐ Ⓑ Ⓒ Ⓓ Ⓔ

5. Ⓐ Ⓑ Ⓒ Ⓓ Ⓔ   15. Ⓐ Ⓑ Ⓒ Ⓓ Ⓔ

6. Ⓐ Ⓑ Ⓒ Ⓓ Ⓔ   16. Ⓐ Ⓑ Ⓒ Ⓓ Ⓔ

7. Ⓐ Ⓑ Ⓒ Ⓓ Ⓔ   17. Ⓐ Ⓑ Ⓒ Ⓓ Ⓔ

8. Ⓐ Ⓑ Ⓒ Ⓓ Ⓔ   18. Ⓐ Ⓑ Ⓒ Ⓓ Ⓔ

9. Ⓐ Ⓑ Ⓒ Ⓓ Ⓔ   19. Ⓐ Ⓑ Ⓒ Ⓓ Ⓔ

10. Ⓐ Ⓑ Ⓒ Ⓓ Ⓔ   20. Ⓐ Ⓑ Ⓒ Ⓓ Ⓔ

DIAGNOSTIC TEST

1. Which of the following disorders involves a patient having more than one personality?

   (A) Bipolar disorder
   (B) Antisocial personality
   (C) Borderline personality
   (D) Schizophrenia
   (E) Dissociative identity disorder

2. A clinician is interested in helping someone overcome a phobia of crossing a bridge. To do this, she asks the client to imagine himself driving near a bridge. When the client gets near the bridge in his imagination, he should stop and use progressive relaxation techniques. Eventually, the client will be able to use these techniques to help himself to cross bridges. This kind of therapy is called

   (A) client-centered therapy.
   (B) psychodynamic therapy.
   (C) learned helplessness.
   (D) systematic desensitization.
   (E) Gestalt therapy.

3. Which definition of *psychology* is most representative of the modern understanding of psychology? Psychology is the science of

   (A) the study of the mind.
   (B) the study of the behavior and mental processes of organisms.
   (C) human behavior.
   (D) the study of the brain and behavior.
   (E) thought and the mind.

4. Freud claims, in his theory of personality, that we often push unwanted ideas or urges into our unconscious to protect our ego. This defense mechanism is called

   (A) repression.
   (B) regression.
   (C) reaction formation.
   (D) sublimation.
   (E) projection.

5. Our tendency to infer causes of behavior in others is called

   (A) attribution.
   (B) socialization.
   (C) maturation.
   (D) diffusion.
   (E) formalization.

6. The part of the eye that responds most to changes in amounts of light is the

   (A) cornea.
   (B) pupil.
   (C) retina.
   (D) lens.
   (E) sclera.

GO ON TO THE NEXT PAGE

7. Abby is interested in determining if music helps people study. To do this, she enlists the help of the 30 students in her psychology class. Half the people study with music in the background for an hour, and the other half study with no music for an hour. The students then take an exam on that material. In this example, the independent variable is the

   (A) group that studies with music.
   (B) music versus no music.
   (C) group that studies with no music.
   (D) scores on the exam.
   (E) students in the class.

8. While sleeping, we pass through a series of stages. Which stage is considered to be the deepest stage of sleep?

   (A) REM sleep
   (B) Stage 1
   (C) Stage 2
   (D) Stage 3
   (E) Stage 4

9. A research method that measures the relationship between two variables is a(n)

   (A) experiment.
   (B) correlational study.
   (C) case study.
   (D) naturalistic observation.
   (E) longitudinal study.

10. After a head injury, a patient has experienced a range of problems including difficulty with muscle coordination and maintaining balance. Which of the following areas was most likely damaged?

    (A) Thalamus
    (B) Parietal lobe
    (C) Amygdala
    (D) Cerebellum
    (E) Hypothalamus

11. Which of the following is NOT considered an anxiety disorder?

    (A) Depression
    (B) Obsessive-compulsive disorder
    (C) Post-traumatic stress disorder
    (D) Agoraphobia
    (E) Panic disorder

12. In Stanley Milgram's landmark studies on obedience, in which of the following situations were the teachers MOST likely to comply with the experimenter's request to shock the learners?

    (A) When the subject and the learner were in the same room
    (B) When the experiment was performed at Yale University
    (C) When no other teachers were observed administering high levels of shock
    (D) When the testing administrator failed to wear a white lab coat
    (E) When the student asked to be shocked by the teacher

GO ON TO THE NEXT PAGE ⟩

13. A rat presses a bar. As it is pressed, a shock is delivered to the rat's brain. The rat then begins to press the bar at a faster rate. In this example, the shock serves as

    (A) positive reinforcement.
    (B) negative punishment.
    (C) unconditioned stimulus.
    (D) positive punishment.
    (E) conditioned stimulus.

14. Which part of the brain appears to be most responsible for vision?

    (A) Temporal lobe
    (B) Occipital lobe
    (C) Limbic system
    (D) Cerebellum
    (E) Hippocampus

15. A solution that guarantees a correct answer to a problem is called a(n)

    (A) heuristic.
    (B) algorithm.
    (C) shortcut.
    (D) divergent thought.
    (E) convergent thought.

16. According to Jean Piaget, what stage of cognitive development would a child be in if she were unable to conserve, to think concretely, to solve simple problems, or to make logical connections?

    (A) Preoperational
    (B) Sensorimotor
    (C) Formal operational
    (D) Concrete operational
    (E) Latency

17. Short-term memory (STM) seems to be limited in its capacity. In fact, most people would argue that the limit of STM is

    (A) 5 ± 2.
    (B) 9 ± 2.
    (C) 7 ± 2.
    (D) 4 ± 3.
    (E) 6 ± 5.

18. In general, IQ is used as a generic measure of intelligence. If someone were believed to have an IQ better than at least 85 percent of the population, he would have an IQ of at least

    (A) 85.
    (B) 100.
    (C) 105.
    (D) 115.
    (E) 130.

GO ON TO THE NEXT PAGE

19. A rat that is being reinforced with a pellet of food for every fifth time it presses a bar is on which of the following schedules of reinforcement?

    (A) Continuous
    (B) Variable interval
    (C) Variable ratio
    (D) Fixed interval
    (E) Fixed ratio

20. Which of these is the best example of a homeostatic behavior?

    (A) A woman forgets the names of two neighbors she just met at a party.
    (B) A dog hears its owner's voice and bounds to the door to greet him.
    (C) A teenager gives in to her peers and goes out to dinner at a restaurant she doesn't like.
    (D) A little boy shivers from the cold air and puts on a sweater to warm himself.
    (E) A toddler cries when his mother leaves him alone with a new babysitter.

IF YOU FINISH BEFORE TIME IS CALLED, YOU MAY CHECK YOUR WORK ON THIS SECTION ONLY. DO NOT TURN TO ANY OTHER SECTION IN THE TEST.

STOP

ANSWER KEY

1. E	11. A
2. D	12. B
3. B	13. A
4. A	14. B
5. A	15. B
6. B	16. A
7. B	17. C
8. E	18. D
9. B	19. E
10. D	20. D

DIAGNOSTIC TEST: ASSESS YOUR STRENGTHS

Use the following tables to determine which topics (chapters) you need to review most.

Chapter and Topic	Question
Chapter 3: History and Approaches	3
Chapter 4: Research Methods	7, 9
Chapter 5: Biological Bases of Behavior	10, 14
Chapter 6: Sensation and Perception	6
Chapter 7: States of Consciousness	8
Chapter 8: Learning	13, 19
Chapter 9: Cognition	15, 17
Chapter 10: Motivation and Emotion	20
Chapter 11: Developmental Psychology	16
Chapter 12: Personality	4
Chapter 13: Testing and Individual Differences	18
Chapter 14: Abnormal Behavior	1, 11
Chapter 15: Treatment of Abnormal Behavior	2
Chapter 16: Social Psychology	5, 12

Chapter and Topic	Number of Questions on Test	Number Correct
Chapter 3: History and Approaches	1	
Chapter 4: Research Methods	2	
Chapter 5: Biological Bases of Behavior	2	
Chapter 6: Sensation and Perception	1	
Chapter 7: States of Consciousness	1	
Chapter 8: Learning	2	
Chapter 9: Cognition	2	
Chapter 10: Motivation and Emotion	1	
Chapter 11: Developmental Psychology	1	
Chapter 12: Personality	1	
Chapter 13: Testing and Individual Differences	1	
Chapter 14: Abnormal Behavior	2	
Chapter 15: Treatment of Abnormal Behavior	1	
Chapter 16: Social Psychology	2	

ANSWERS AND EXPLANATIONS

1. E

Dissociative identity disorder was formerly called multiple personality disorder. The most common mistake would be to choose (D), schizophrenia, because of popular culture, but do not be swayed by that. The other answers are disorders but involve different behaviors.

2. D

The question is designed to identify your ability to determine which techniques are utilized with different forms of therapy. The kind of therapy in this scenario is called systematic desensitization. All of the other forms of therapy involve a cognitive component that is not directly connected to behavior. Choice (C), learned helplessness, might give rise to depression, but it is not a therapeutic technique.

3. B.

The goal here is to determine if you have a good idea of what modern psychologists believe to be an accurate definition of *psychology*. The other definitions are close, but they do not include all that is necessary. You need to have both behavior and mental processes, and you need to include all animals to make the definition complete.

4. A

Each answer choice here is a defense mechanism, so it's tricky. The correct answer is (A), repression. The others involve some form of active (typically unconscious) protection of the ego, but they are against specific fears or anxieties. Repression helps in general, according to Freudian psychology, by protecting the ego from harm.

5. A

Here, you are being challenged to pick a term from several that look similar. (B), (C), and (D) are used in social psychology, but they are not correct in this context. (E) is used in measurement theory, not social psychology.

6. B

The cornea, (A), and lens, (D), bend light, the sclera, (E), provides structure for the eye, and the retina, (C), contains the photoreceptors.

7. B

Questions like this appear frequently on the AP Psychology exam. They measure your knowledge of research methods. Answer (A) is the experimental group, (C) is the control group, (D) is the dependent variable, and (E) is the sample.

8. E

Often, students assume REM sleep (A) is the deepest stage of sleep, but it is not. In fact, in some ways, it is the lightest form of sleep. Stage 4 sleep is the stage when your brain waves are going the slowest.

9. B

All of the answers are types of research methods, so read the question carefully to make sure you understand it. In this case, research that compares the relationship between two variables is the definition of (B), correlation. You might be tempted by choice (A), the experimental method, but experiments allow researchers to determine if there is a cause-and-effect relationship while a correlation does not do this. Remember, a correlation is not the same as causation.

10. D

This type of question is common on the AP Psychology exam, so it's important to know the functions of various parts of the brain and also what the effect would be if these parts did not function properly. Choice (D), the cerebellum, is the region in which voluntary motor movements and balance are coordinated. Damage to the thalamus and parietal lobe, (A) and (B), would result in a loss of sensory perception, damage to the amygdala, (C), would affect the experience of fear, and damage to the hypothalamus, (E), would alter the body's ability to regulate hormonal production and many internal processes.

11. A

A common question about abnormal behavior is the identification of not just a particular disorder but the group to which that disorder belongs. In this case, choices (B), (C), (D), and (E) are all examples of anxiety disorders, but depression (A) is categorized as a mood disorder.

12. B

Stanley Milgram performed a number of variations on this experiment to determine what qualities affected the level of obedience. He found that, as in choice (B), the prestige associated with Yale University led to higher levels of cooperation, whereas moving the experiment to a warehouse in a nearby town yielded less compliance from the subjects. In each of the other conditions, Milgram found that compliance from the "teachers" actually increased.

13. A

Be careful here. Read the question completely. Positive reinforcement is correct because the result of the shock is an *increase* in bar-pressing behavior. Because it is an increase, it is reinforcement, and because it is due to something being given, it is positive.

14. B

With the increasing emphasis on brain and behavior, such a question is very common. The other structures control, in order, auditory processing and language, emotional response, autonomic response, and memory.

15. B

An algorithm is a step-by-step solution to a problem that guarantees the correct answer. The other terms are important in problem solving, but they do not guarantee a correct response.

16. A

If a child were not able to conserve, to think concretely, to solve simple problems, or to make logical connections, she would be in a preoperational stage. (B), (C), and (D) do not show those characteristics, and (E) is not a stage.

17. C

This question could be considered a history or a cognition question. Essentially, you just have to know that the capacity is (C), 7±2, which was described by Miller in 1956.

18. D

This question requires some knowledge of both IQ and statistics. This is the answer because we know that average IQ is 100 with a standard deviation of 15.

19. E

In this question, (A) can be eliminated first, because all reinforcement schedules are forms of partial and not continuous reinforcement. The rat has to do a behavior a set number of times to earn the reinforcement, so the combination of an active respondent performing a fixed number of repetitions makes this an example of a fixed ratio schedule. A variable ratio schedule, (C), would provide reinforcement after an unknown number of repetitions. The interval schedules provide reinforcement based not on the number of repetitions but on time: fixed interval schedules, (D), after a set amount of time, and variable interval schedules, (B), after a varied amount of time.

20. D

Homeostasis is a key concept in motivation that refers to the internal forces that regulate an animal's behavior so that it maintains a constant balance. While all of these choices reflect ordinary behaviors, only choice (D) is an example of an organism seeking to return to a balanced state, as the child who is cold shivers and puts on clothes in an effort to return his body temperature to a normal level.

| Part Three |

AP PSYCHOLOGY REVIEW

CHAPTER 3: HISTORY AND APPROACHES

IF YOU LEARN ONLY FOUR THINGS IN THIS CHAPTER . . .

1. Wilhelm Wundt is credited with being the founder of modern experimental psychology when he founded a lab at the University of Leipzig in 1879.

2. Titchener, Watson, James, and Skinner are all important early psychologists.

3. Understanding the differences between the different approaches or perspectives—behavioral, biological, cognitive, humanistic, psychoanalytic, and sociocultural—is the key to understanding psychology.

4. The modern definition of psychology combines the scientific study of behavior and mental processes in humans and other animals.

INTRODUCTION

The history of psychology is not limited to psychologists. It has been said that psychology has a short history and a long past. This is in part because psychology has been a separate discipline for only the past 110 years. Prior to that, psychology was essentially a subdiscipline of philosophy. Though intellectuals have been interested in understanding the "workings of the mind" or behavior for centuries, it took Wilhelm Wundt to recognize and formalize the discipline that we now know.

ANCIENT TIMES

However, most historians of psychology trace the roots of the discipline back to the ancient Greek philosophers. For example, both Plato and Socrates described human knowledge as being innate. This idea is reminiscent of modern thought that humans are born with the ability to perform specific behaviors.

Other ancient Greeks disagreed. Aristotle, for example, believed that to understand something, one must directly observe that phenomenon. Aristotle's idea is an early example of what scientists now call **empiricism**. Empiricism means that to understand something, we need to be able to observe the phenomenon in question directly. Modern behaviorists (and most psychologists) today believe this to be one of the essential components of the science of psychology.

Throughout much of recorded history, philosophers have talked extensively about issues that are psychological in nature. For example, René Descartes was very interested in understanding the causes of human behavior. He was influenced by watching some automatons perform mechanical behavior in a garden. Descartes reasoned that because the cause of those behaviors was mechanical, perhaps human behavior is similar. His theory posited that humans behavior is very much like this but is driven by "animal spirits" that make contact with the "mind" at the pineal gland. Philosopher John Locke, on the other hand, believed that humans were born *tabula rasa*—that is, as a "blank slate," with no inborn knowledge. To Locke, the most important thing was to understand how experience shaped human behavior instead of focusing on innate ideas that emerged over time.

1850–1920

In more modern times, the aforementioned Wilhelm Wundt, of the University of Leipzig, had been interested in understanding the biological causes of behavior. He realized, however, that it would be difficult to study the brain of a human directly while the human was using it! He devised, therefore, a technique that would allow him to observe causes of behavior indirectly. Wundt called his approach *introspection,* and it involved an attempt to understand the concept of consciousness by having a trained researcher observe an object and report the thoughts, sensations, and feelings he experienced while perceiving the object. Through introspection, Wundt believed, a psychologist would be able to distill the structure of consciousness. This theory of psychology is called **structuralism**.

While Wundt was developing his theory in Germany, William James was developing his own theory of human behavior in the United States, at Harvard College (now Harvard University). James believed that understanding the structure of consciousness was useful, but it wasn't enough. He felt that we needed to understand not just how consciousness was structured but the purpose for consciousness. That is, what is the function of conscious activity? James's theory became known as **functionalism**.

During this time, E. B. Titchener, who had previously been a student of Wundt in Germany, came to the United States and began applying Wundt's theories at Cornell University. Titchener became convinced that unless we taught students *how* to do psychology, psychology as a scientific discipline would never develop the way biology, physics, and chemistry had. So he set up a lab at Cornell for the express purpose of teaching students how psychology works.

EARLY 20TH CENTURY

All three of the previously mentioned psychologists influenced modern psychology in innumerable ways. They laid the groundwork for a discipline that developed into modern psychology. Along the way, psychology split along the lines of being either an *applied discipline* (such as clinical psychology) or a *basic discipline* (such as behaviorism or cognitive psychology). Noted clinical psychologists include Sigmund Freud (founder of the psychodynamic or psychoanalytic movement), Carl Rogers, Alfred Adler, Carl Jung, and Aaron Beck. Noted experimental psychologists include B. F. Skinner, John Watson, Jean Piaget, Stanley Milgram, Phil Zimbardo, Michael Gazzaniga, Roger Sperry, E. C. Tolman, Lev Vygotsky, and Albert Bandura.

Each psychologist contributed to the discipline in ways that have helped shape what we currently think of as psychology. Watson and Skinner, for instance, used the work of Ivan Pavlov and Edward Thorndyke to develop the area of **behaviorism** in the early part of the 20th century. According to behaviorists, things such as memory, language, and thinking are not viable topics of study because they are not directly observable. Behavior, however, is observable, and because of that, behavior should be the only topic psychologists should examine experimentally. The behaviorist movement was powerful throughout the 20th century and influenced generations of psychologists.

Also during the early part of the 20th century, clinical psychologists were refining their techniques. Freud and his colleagues (e.g., Jung, Adler) believed that the reason people suffered from anxiety was due to conflicts that were unresolved in their unconscious. The claim was that people suffered because they were influenced by thoughts, or conflicts, that were outside of their awareness. Psychodynamic psychologists developed techniques to help people deal with these anxieties through therapy that came to be known as "talk therapy."

A final movement in the 20th century was the development of humanistic psychology. Led by Abraham Maslow and Carl Rogers, humanists saw people as basically good and focused on an individual's ability to grow and achieve his or her full potential. Humanistic psychology is often referred to as the "third wave," as it was an alternative to the psychoanalytic and behavioral approaches.

LATER 20TH CENTURY AND 21ST CENTURY

As the 20th century progressed, psychologists began to study internal events such as memory and thoughts. The belief was that if internal events could be turned into behavior, they could be observed. So if someone could report memory in some objective way, we could actually study memory. Psychologists such as George Miller led

> **AP EXPERT TIP**
>
> It is common for AP essays to be framed around the various approaches, so you should be familiar with each approach.

this line of thinking, and they worked to make the field of **cognition** into one of the most influential areas for the last part of the 20th century.

Coupled with cognition, the study of biological psychology dominated the end of the 20th century (and current study). Biological psychologists study the influence of biology on human behavior. The belief is that internal causes might be inferred from behavior.

Because psychology is such a diverse field, there is no *one* agreed-upon method for studying human behavior. The AP Psychology exam asks questions on the different areas of psychology that fall under the following broad approaches:

- Biological
- Behavioral
- Cognitive
- Humanistic
- Psychoanalytic
- Sociocultural

The areas discussed here are essentially umbrella terms for smaller areas of psychology. The discipline is fractured to some extent, yet the goals remain the same: the prediction and control of human behavior.

BIOLOGICAL APPROACH

The biological approach to psychology focuses on the physiological bases of behavior. Specifically, it is based on the assumption that to understand human behavior, the physiological underpinnings must be understood. Such structures include the brain and the central nervous system.

Biological psychologists are also interested in the role of drugs on human behavior; as such, they often use animal models as a means of understanding human behavior. Animal models, they believe, are good vehicles for determining the effects of various substances on the human body. Rats, for example, are used as the subjects to study drugs such as THC (the active ingredient in marijuana). Researchers do this because (1) it is illegal to test such substances on humans and (2) the rats' brains are similar enough to humans' brains to be able to make leaps of logic from the animal to the human.

Other areas of biological psychology involve the role our senses play in our overall experience as humans. Sensation psychologists study the various sense organs to understand how they gather information from the environment to allow us to perceive the world.

Biological psychologists also explore the role of the endocrine system in influencing human behavior. The glands in the endocrine system secrete slow-acting hormones that move throughout the body and are involved in processes like the fight-or-flight response and homeostasis.

BEHAVIORAL APPROACH

Many psychologists, such as John Watson and B. F. Skinner, believe that to refer to the "behavioral approach" as an *area* of psychology seems inappropriate. Behavioral approaches, they believe, are the *only* way to understand humans. To these psychologists, behavior and the surrounding environment are the only topics worth studying to understand humans.

In a landmark paper in 1913, for instance, John B. Watson wrote, " . . . give me a dozen healthy young infants. . . . I will take any one and create . . . a doctor, a lawyer, and yes, even a beggar man thief. . . ." According to Watson, if one is interested in controlling human behavior, one needs only to develop a set of environmental conditions that give rise to the desired behavior.

B. F. Skinner took a different perspective. According to him, behavior isn't controlled so much by the precursors of behavior but rather by the history of what has occurred when the behavior was performed previously. The consequences of behavior have a small, continuous influence on behavior, until the behavior is under the control of the environmental consequence. If a child is rewarded for taking his clothes to the hamper at night, the child will continue to bring his clothes to the hamper. And even if the child is not rewarded once, he will still bring his clothes there, so long as the reinforcement has been well-established. (Casino and card players can vouch for the fact that one doesn't need constant reinforcement to continue playing! A reward once in a while will do the trick.) Rewards are called **reinforcement** in behaviorism.

Proponents of the behavioral approach argue, essentially, that observable behavior and the environment are all that is needed to form a science of psychology.

COGNITIVE APPROACH

Cognitive psychologists and those who subscribe to the cognitive approach believe that internal mental events are essential aspects of human behavior and are clearly worth examination. Cognitive areas include the study of memory, language, thought, and attention. In these areas, psychologists try to make predictions about behavior by measuring changes in behavior (reaction time, typically) and then to infer internal mechanisms that control such behavior.

A large body of literature exists that demonstrates the connectedness of ideas in memory; in these studies, participants are presented with a word and then have to say that word out loud. In one condition, the first and the second words are related. In a second condition, they are not. The amount of time it takes people to say the second word is faster when the words are related than when the words are not related. This suggests that the ability to say these words is influenced by the relationship between these words in memory. Cognitive psychologists claim that this demonstrates the phenomenon of semantic relatedness in memory.

The cognitive approach is very popular today in many areas of psychology, including social, developmental, personality, and clinical psychology. The overriding idea is that to understand the individual, one must understand the way that people think, remember, process information, and reason about the world.

HUMANISTIC APPROACH

The humanistic approaches to psychology focus on people as being goal directed and driven. According to humanistic psychologists, humans are driven to achieve all that they can achieve and to work toward the goal of **self-actualization** in all that they do. Abraham Maslow defined a self-actualized person as someone who has reached his or her own unique potential.

Humanistic theories have been around for thousands of years and have gone in and out of fashion, but essentially, the issue has always been one of free will and motivation. Humanistic psychologists believe that we are completely in control, and in fact, some would argue that the only reality that matters is subjective reality. People create their own view of the world, and that view shapes their interactions with others.

Humanistic approaches can take the form of a theory or a form of psychotherapy. In humanistic therapy, psychologists attempt to help individuals see the misconceptions they hold in their subjective view of reality. If those views can be corrected, the individual will often feel better about herself.

PSYCHOANALYTIC APPROACH

Psychoanalytic approaches to human behavior are some of the more controversial approaches. According to proponents of the psychoanalytic approach, humans are controlled by forces that are out of their control. Specifically, humans are controlled by forces buried deep in their unconscious. According to people like Sigmund Freud, people have a great many unconscious conflicts that cause them discomfort. They are unable to verbalize these conflicts, however, because they are outside of their consciousness. That is, people feel stress, but they don't know why they feel stress. To help people overcome this anxiety or stress, psychoanalytic psychologists encourage lots of free association and "talk therapy" to help people come to understand the roots of these anxieties. Dream analysis, at one time, was considered to be vital to the process.

Unfortunately, and no doubt disappointingly to students, little evidence supports the psychoanalytic approach to psychology. This doesn't mean that this approach is not potentially valuable to psychology. But as a science, psychology is interested in developing theories that are theoretically sound and testable, and psychoanalytic approaches are not, to date.

SOCIOCULTURAL APPROACH

Sociocultural approaches to psychology focus on the diversity of the human experience and attempt to explain human behavior by focusing on the **context** in which one develops (i.e., developmental psychology), the **influence** of groups (i.e., social psychology), or some *applied* aspect of psychology (i.e., forensic psychology). These areas all operate on the assumption that human behavior doesn't occur in a vacuum and that groups, cultures, and situations all have an impact on human behavior.

Social psychology deals with the influence of groups on an individual's behavior. To understand social psychology completely, one must understand the context in which one exhibits behavior. To a social psychologist, behavior is predicted in part by the presence or absence of another person.

THE APPROACHES IN SUMMARY

While it is important to be able to see each of these approaches as a distinctly different perspective, it is also vital to see how they interact. A psychologist who studies sensation and perception would, for example, need to see how these systems work from both a biological approach, which would focus on the mechanics of how sensations are detected by the senses, and a cognitive approach, which would examine how these sensations are interpreted and understood through perception. A psychologist using the sociocultural approach would look at the social surroundings of a student who is struggling in school, while a behaviorist would focus on how the student's behaviors are being punished or reinforced. The AP Psychology exam often poses questions that ask the student to examine problems using these multiple approaches.

MODERN AREAS OF PSYCHOLOGY

The major areas of psychology have been covered in this book. Below is a summary:

Area	What the Area Covers
History of Psychology	Historical roots of the discipline, including the influences before psychology became a separate discipline
Research Methods and Statistics	How to do research in psychology; what to do with the results once they are obtained; role of statistics in science
Biopsychology	The interaction of biology and behavior; the study of the brain and the neuron
Sensation and Perception	How the sense organs receive information and transform it into a code our brains can understand
Motivation and Emotion	What motivates us to begin or continue behavior and how our emotions work
Consciousness	Our ability to focus on information (the way our awareness varies at different times of the day)
Learning	How the environment influences behavior. How an individual's history can predict future behavior
Cognition	How humans process information; specifically, memory, attention, comprehension, and problem solving
Language	The development and use of language as a uniquely human process
Development	How we change over the life span: physical, social, and cognitive forms of development
Personality	How we differ from each other: theories of personality
Psychological Disorders	Disorders of behavior as defined by the *Diagnostic and Statistical Manual of Psychiatric Disorders*
Therapy	How to treat psychological disorders, including therapeutic techniques of Freud, Skinner, etc.
Social Psychology	How people interact in groups; the power of the situation

REVIEW QUESTIONS

1. Which of the following psychologists started the first psychology lab in Germany?

   (A) William James

   (B) Wilhelm Wundt

   (C) John B. Watson

   (D) Ivan Pavlov

   (E) Sigmund Freud

2. Of the following approaches to understanding behavior, which will most likely focus on the way that adults process information?

   (A) Biological

   (B) Cognitive

   (C) Sociocultural

   (D) Psychodynamic

   (E) Humanistic

3. Which philosopher discussed the mind–body problem?

   (A) Plato

   (B) Socrates

   (C) Kant

   (D) Freud

   (E) Descartes

4. What is the difference between cognitive psychology and behavioral psychology?

   (A) Behavioral psychology deals with reinforcement and punishment, while cognitive psychology deals with information processing.

   (B) Cognitive psychology focuses only on observable behavior, while behavioral psychology focuses on internal processes.

   (C) Both focus on observable behavior; there is no difference.

   (D) Cognitive psychology focuses only on the ego, while behavioral psychology focuses on the id.

   (E) Behavioral psychology focuses on the superego, while cognitive psychology focuses on the ego.

5. Of the following approaches to psychology, which area would be most concerned with the idea that people strive toward self-actualization?

   (A) Biological

   (B) Cognitive

   (C) Social/cultural

   (D) Psychodynamic

   (E) Humanistic

6. Which of the following approaches to psychology is most likely to have a paper entitled "The role of the endocrine system as a secondary neurotransmitter"?

   (A) Biological

   (B) Cognitive

   (C) Social/cultural

   (D) Psychodynamic

   (E) Humanistic

7. In early psychology, Wilhelm Wundt developed a technique for doing research that involved having people describe their thoughts as they observed an object. This technique is called

   (A) dream analysis.
   (B) mind/body analysis.
   (C) behavior analysis.
   (D) introspection.
   (E) algorithm.

8. Watson and Skinner both believed that _____ was/were the biggest predictor of future action.

   (A) inborn tendencies
   (B) temperament
   (C) environment
   (D) thoughts
   (E) memory

9. The paper "The role of imagery in memory processes" would most likely be written by someone who subscribes to

   (A) biological psychology.
   (B) cognitive psychology.
   (C) social/cultural psychology.
   (D) psychoanalytic psychology.
   (E) humanistic psychology.

10. The person who is most responsible for developing the school of thought called *functionalism* is

   (A) James.
   (B) Wundt.
   (C) Skinner.
   (D) Watson.
   (E) Miller.

11. A psychologist who is researching the impact of peer pressure on the behavior of adolescents would most likely be a

   (A) clinical psychologist.
   (B) social psychologist.
   (C) cognitive psychologist.
   (D) biological psychologist.
   (E) humanistic psychologist.

12. Those who believe that the most important key to understanding behavior is to understand the role of the environment in shaping organisms are called

   (A) cognitive psychologists.
   (B) humanistic psychologists.
   (C) biological psychologists.
   (D) developmental psychologists.
   (E) behavioral psychologists.

13. Which of these would a social psychologist be MOST likely to investigate?

   (A) The amygdala's role in the fight-or-flight response
   (B) The effects of giving monetary rewards for academic success
   (C) How the size of a group influences decisions made by group members
   (D) Why humans often make irrational financial decisions
   (E) How unresolved internal conflicts affect one's personality

14. According to operant conditioning, the_____ of behavior are the best predictor of whether or not that behavior is performed again.

    (A) derivatives

    (B) consequences

    (C) antecedents

    (D) causes

    (E) contexts

15. Which of the following approaches focuses on free will and personal growth?

    (A) Biological

    (B) Cognitive

    (C) Sociocultural

    (D) Psychoanalytic

    (E) Humanistic

16. The psychoanalytic approach to understanding personality was described by

    (A) Freud.

    (B) Descartes.

    (C) Kant.

    (D) Hobbes.

    (E) Miller.

17. Which philosopher is responsible for the concept of *tabula rasa*?

    (A) Descartes

    (B) Darwin

    (C) Locke

    (D) Wundt

    (E) James

18. Which area of psychology is most concerned with understanding the internal works of the "mind," such as memory and thought?

    (A) Biological

    (B) Cognitive

    (C) Social/cultural

    (D) Psychoanalytic

    (E) Humanistic

19. Both Plato and Socrates saw knowledge as

    (A) complete.

    (B) innate.

    (C) learned.

    (D) incomplete.

    (E) reflexive.

20. Which area of psychology is most often criticized for offering theories that are not supported by evidence and testable theories?

    (A) Cognitive

    (B) Biological

    (C) Behavioral

    (D) Sociocultural

    (E) Psychoanalytic

ANSWERS AND EXPLANATIONS

1. B

Though there is some dispute in the literature, Wundt is credited by most as starting the first lab in psychology in 1879. This is mostly because Wundt began training his first graduate student that year.

2. B

The cognitive approach would most likely look at how adults process information. It attempts to understand human behavior by examining the ways that people process information in order to deal with the stimuli they encounter in the world.

3. E

René Descartes was very concerned with the mind–body problem. In fact, it consumed much of his energy as he tried to wrestle with this debate. The issue, by the way, continues to be of interest to psychologists.

4. A

Behavioral psychology deals with reinforcement and punishment, while cognitive psychology deals with information processing. Note the similarity among the answer choices; this is a common format on the AP exam, so be careful that you are selecting the one that you intend.

5. E

Humanistic psychologists would be concerned with the idea that people strive toward self-actualization. In fact, they state the development of self-actualization as a goal of human behavior.

6. A

"The role of the endocrine system as a secondary neurotransmitter" deals with a biological process of the endocrine system. Therefore, the only appropriate type of psychology would be biological psychology.

7. D

All the areas mentioned are valid in psychology. The key is to know that Wundt's early approach was most concerned with determining the *structure* of consciousness. To do that, people had to describe their consciousness. That is introspection.

8. C

Both Watson and Skinner were behaviorists and, as such, were concerned with understanding the role of the environment on behavior. They, like Locke, believed that children are born with no knowledge and all they know is acquired from the environment.

9. B

"The role of imagery in memory processes" would be written by a cognitive psychologist. The cognitive approach centers on the notion that to understand behavior, we need to understand the way humans process information. Memory is one of the key concepts in this area.

10. A

William James and Wilhelm Wundt disagreed on how to study humans. Wundt believed we should study the structure of consciousness, while James believed we should study its function. Hence, his area is called *functionalism*.

11. B

Although each of these types of psychologist may study adolescents, only (B), a social psychologist, focuses on the influence of groups on human behavior. Be sure to recognize that a phrase like "peer pressure" refers to how a group may sway an individual to change his or her behavior.

12. E

This is a tough question. All of the mentioned areas of psychology are concerned with the environment, yet behavioral psychologists are *most* concerned with it. They argue that nothing else influences behavior the way the environment does.

13. C

The sociocultural approach is interested in the interplay between groups and individuals, so the answer here must also reflect the influence of groups. While all of the answers are psychological concerns, only choice (C) explores how groups can affect the behavior of individuals.

14. B

According to operant conditioning, the consequences of behavior are the biggest predictors of whether or not a behavior reoccurs. If we do not control the consequences, we do not control behavior.

15. E

Humanists are concerned with free will, while the other areas of psychology do not emphasize it or do not believe it exists.

16. A

Freud's approach was groundbreaking in that he attempted to explain all of human behavior using one unifying theory.

17. C

Locke is famous for many of his thoughts, though he is most well known for arguing one thing—that people are born as blank slates and experience is written on them. That experience, then, goes on to determine behavior.

18. B

Cognitive psychologists argue that by using creative research techniques, we can study memory well.

19. B

Plato and Socrates were both nativists and argued that we are born with all the knowledge that we need. We spend our lives trying to "discover" what we already know.

20. E

The psychoanalytic approach is the oldest of the approaches and is often criticized by modern psychologists as not offering testable hypotheses, so (E) is the correct answer. Psychologists who are involved in the other areas listed use the scientific method and statistical analysis to examine human behavior and mental processes.

CHAPTER 4: RESEARCH METHODS

IF YOU LEARN ONLY EIGHT THINGS IN THIS CHAPTER . . .

1. Observation is the most important aspect of psychological research.

2. Operationalism means to define our variables in the manner in which we are going to measure them.

3. Correlation measures degree of relationship between variables and ranges from −1 to +1.

4. Correlation does not imply causation.

5. Independent variables are controlled by researchers, while dependent variables are what researchers are measuring.

6. Experimental, correlational, and descriptive methods all have strengths and weaknesses in describing human behavior.

7. Descriptive statistics describe the data gathered in research, while inferential statistics allow us to draw conclusions about how this data can be generalized to a larger population.

8. Following ethical principles is vitally important in any kind of psychological research.

INTRODUCTION

In psychology, we are interested in understanding human behavior and mental processes. To do that, we need an organized set of methods that will allow us to ask questions and provide coherent explanations about the "whys" of human and animal behavior. This chapter will help you understand the role that research plays in psychology.

OBSERVATION

It is essential to understand that psychology is an empirical discipline. *Empirical* means that we use observation as a means of understanding questions about behavior. It is not enough simply to *believe* that something (a behavior, say) is true. A technique is needed to allow for the direct observation of that behavior under a variety of conditions.

The discipline of psychology relies heavily on well-established empirical techniques. For example, psychologists are often interested in questions about behavior in specific contexts. Suppose a psychologist is interested in the seating arrangement in a college class. To be able to answer questions about why students choose to sit where they do, he could simply observe several classes and try to determine how students made their seat selection. Such a technique, called *naturalistic observation,* is a common method of investigation by psychologists.

Naturalistic observation involves going out to the location where the behavior of interest occurs and observing it as it unfolds. This can occur either with intervention (such as participating in the situation to be observed) or without (such as observing from a separate location). Both scenarios have advantages and disadvantages.

To observe accurately, one must first define the variables. A variable is any observable phenomenon that can take on more than one value. Income, number of credits in psychology, and height are all variables that would be of interest to a psychologist, as would other, less easily quantifiable variables. To solve this problem with quantification, psychologists will often operationalize their variables. To operationalize a variable, one must define the variable in such a way that it can actually be measured.

Suppose a psychologist is interested in the construct of aggression. Aggression cannot be measured directly, so there is no way to come to any objective definition. Thus, the researchers must state how they intend to measure aggression and what behaviors they plan to use as a proxy for aggression. A researcher interested in aggression might measure the number of aggressive words (such as swearing) one uses or the number of times a participant hits another person. In such a way, the researcher is stating in clear and defendable terms what she is going to use to identify aggression.

Once an observational study has been completed, a researcher needs to understand what it is she has found. If she used a survey to gain attitudinal data about a particular phenomenon, for example, she might then use a correlation to understand the data more completely. A correlation is a statistical technique that allows us to understand the degree to which two variables are related.

ON CORRELATION

Remember: Just because two variables are related doesn't necessarily mean that one causes the other. *Correlation* is not *causation*.

A correlation coefficient can range only from −1 to +1, and it tells us two things about a relationship. First, the sign indicates the direction of the relationship. That is, it tells us if the relationship is one in which the numbers vary *together* (as one increases or decreases, the other does the same, etc.) or in which the variables vary *inversely* (the numbers go up or down in opposite directions).

Second, the number tells us the strength of the relationship. **The closer the number is to 1, the stronger the relationship**.

Let's say we want to determine the correlation between IQ and income. We would collect survey data examining the variables of interest. Then, we would rank order IQ and rank order income (that is, put the data in order from greatest to least) and determine if the ranks of the two variables are similar or not. If IQ and income are related such that the higher the IQ, the higher the income, the correlation would be positive (say, +0.75). If the relationship is inverse— that is, as IQ increases, income decreases—the correlation would be negative (say, −0.60).

The correlation is often depicted by a scatterplot, which plots one score against another. By understanding the correlation, we have some idea of how variables relate. We don't, however, know which variable caused which outcome. Thus, we cannot claim a cause-and-effect relationship from correlation.

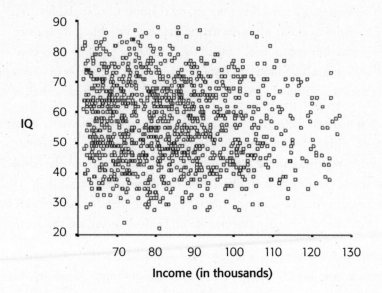

EXPERIMENTAL TECHNIQUES

Observational techniques are very good at helping researchers gain some idea about a particular phenomenon. However, the goal of psychology is often to predict and

AP EXPERT TIP

Remember: The dependent variable is dependent upon the independent variable.

control behavior, and observational techniques do not allow this to happen. What they allow, rather, is a **description of behavior**. The lack of control one has over the variables of interest makes it difficult to draw strong conclusions about data. So researchers often attempt to answer questions about behavior by manipulating variables to measure how they are influenced by environmental factors.

Suppose we wanted to understand the influence of a drug on the ability of a rat to run a maze. We could take two groups of rats and inject one group with the experimental drug and the second with a placebo (an inert substance designed to not cause a change in behavior). Both groups of rats would then run the maze while we measured their speed in seconds. We could compare the results and attempt to determine if the running speed was influenced by the drug.

In this experiment, whether or not the rat gets the drug is the **independent variable**. The speed that the rat runs the maze is the **dependent variable**.

In psychology, this type of experiment is common. One variable is manipulated in a variety of ways to determine its effects on an outcome variable. Such an experimental procedure allows for **cause-and-effect relationships** to be established. We will talk about different aspects of research methodologies later in this book.

EXPERIMENTAL DESIGN

To do an experiment in psychology, we must first understand the notion of **variables** and **experimental control**. Experiments occur when we manipulate one variable and measure the outcome of that variable in multiple conditions. One of the benefits of psychology is that we can manipulate multiple variables at any one time and not only determine the effects of one variable on another but also measure the interaction of variables as they combine to determine their effects.

Studying experimental design allows us to understand how we design experiments to determine causes of behavior. There are different ways to do this, but the most common is to develop **a variable with two or more conditions and then to measure an outcome from the conditions to determine if the independent variable had an impact on the dependent variable**. If it did, there should be differences in the performance of our participants on those conditions. If it did not, there should be no difference, and the same performance will be observed across the conditions.

If we wanted to understand memory, we would set up two conditions: In one condition, participants might be given a word list to memorize in the presence of music, while in the other condition, participants might learn the list in silence. Memory can then be tested by having participants recall the information.

If the students are not all run through the experiment at the same time of day, we may have a confounding variable. A **confounding variable** is a variable other than an independent variable that completely explains the results. Assume a few participants run through the experiment at

7:30 A.M. while they are still sleepy, while others run it at 12:00 noon when they are hungry. The problem lies in the fact that participants' level of arousal—and, therefore, their ability to perform the task—is unsystematically influenced by the time of day the participants ran through the experiment. To control for this, we need to make sure all participants run through the experiment under conditions that are as similar as possible.

The key to doing good experimental research is to **control confounding variables** as much as possible. One must always ensure that in an experiment, there is no other explanation for differences between conditions besides the independent variable.

STATISTICS

Statistics traditionally falls into two categories: *descriptive* and *inferential*. **Descriptive statistics** is that used to describe a sample. If we have a set of data, such as scores on an exam (80, 90, 100, 80, 95), we can describe that data in a few ways. First, we can tell what the *most common score* is (80). This concept is called the **mode**. Second, we can tell which score is in the *middle of the distribution* (90). This is the **median** (like a median strip on a highway divides the highway, the median in a distribution divides the distribution).

Third, we can add all the numbers and divide by the number of scores (89). This is called the **mean**, and it is the most common measure of *central tendency*. Another important descriptive statistic is the **standard deviation**, which is the amount, on average, that each score differs from the mean. Thus, the standard deviation tells us about how much each score is different from the average score. The bigger the standard deviation, the more spread out the scores are.

When we measure a population on variables of interest to psychologists (IQ, speed of processing information, aggression), we find that scores are often normally distributed. The **normal distribution** looks like this:

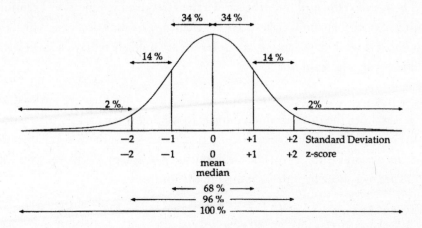

One reason we use the normal curve so much is that we know so much about it. See the information on the graph for how the normal curve is divided out. We know, for example, that if we select a random point on the curve, we'll most likely get a score that falls between −1 and +1 standard deviations from the mean. Essentially, we can predict there is a 68 percent chance we will get a score from that section of the curve. That is enormously helpful when it comes to inferential statistics.

INFERENTIAL STATISTICS

While descriptive statistics allow us to fully understand the behavior of the subjects in our research, psychologists need a way to suggest that what is true of these subjects might also be true for an entire population. **Inferential statistics** are used to make generalizations from a research sample to a population.

To really understand statistics, you must be familiar with the concept of **probability**. Probability is essentially a theory that suggests that things will sometimes happen by chance. One goal of using probability in psychology is to determine the chance that something might happen randomly versus the chance that it happened because of some manipulation. Statistics allows us to evaluate the probability of an outcome to determine if there is any reason we should assume it happened by chance.

In the study previously described, after we collected our data, let's say we found a difference in memory performance (on a 10-point test) of about 3 points (the people studying without music answered 3 more questions correctly). We can use statistics to evaluate if that difference of 3 points is meaningful or not. We use the term *statistically significant,* but essentially, we are seeing if we could expect a difference of 3 by chance or if it is not likely due to chance.

In statistics, we operate under the assumption that there are no differences between groups or conditions. This is called the **null hypothesis**. We then test this hypothesis by examining if there are in fact differences that are unlikely to occur by chance. Our statistical tests will allow us to reject our null hypothesis if we find evidence that our results are unlikely to have occurred by chance (the probability is less than, say, 5 percent).

This is, to say the least, a different way of thinking about the world than we are used to. The best advice for you is to learn the rules of which statistic to use and when and try to practice as much as possible. In the appendix of most introductory psychology texts, there is a chapter devoted to statistics and practice problems. If you choose to pursue psychology as a career, you will have ample opportunity to practice more hypothesis testing in the future.

ETHICS

Because psychology deals with living organisms, we need to be careful about the ethics of doing research. Contrary to popular belief, psychologists do not torture animals (human or otherwise) or purposefully create situations that give rise to emotional or psychological harm in experimental participants. In fact, psychologists are guided by ethical principles set forth by the American Psychological Association (APA) to ensure that they follow the rules of decorum when running experiments.

For experiments involving humans, participants are entitled to both **informed consent** and full debriefing following the experiment. Participants are not allowed to be coerced into taking part in the experiment and should know that they can leave at any time. In addition, all proposals that involve experiments are typically reviewed for ethical standards by an Institutional Review Board (IRB) prior to the beginning of the experiment. The IRB reviews the proposal to ensure that the research is not going to cause the participants any undue harm. It operates on a cost–benefit analysis. If deception must be used, the participants need to be debriefed immediately.

If animals are going to be used, researchers have the responsibility to ensure the proper care of the animals. That is, the temperature must be controlled, the animals must be fed, cages must be cleaned, and the holding rooms need to be secured. The minimum number of animals should be used to achieve interpretable results, and if the animals are to be sacrificed, they need to be done so humanely.

Essentially, any research that is psychological in nature needs to be done with the best interests of the participants in mind.

> **AP EXPERT TIP**
>
> Ethical guidelines have been emphasized on recent AP Psych exams, so make sure you keep them in mind as you study.

REVIEW QUESTIONS

1. Suppose a study finds there is only a small correlation between IQ and the ability to solve word problems in math. The correlation shows that a very weak relationship demonstrates that the higher the IQ, the better the ability to solve word problems. A correlation that would demonstrate such a relationship could be

   (A) 0.00.
   (B) +0.99.
   (C) +0.10.
   (D) −0.98.
   (E) −0.56.

2. A teacher wants to determine the impact of teaching style on quiz scores. To do this, she divides a class into two groups and teaches one group using one style and the other group using a second, different style. She then measures the scores on the quizzes. The independent variable here is

   (A) group 1.
   (B) group 2.
   (C) teaching style.
   (D) scores on quizzes.
   (E) the teacher.

3. In the experiment just described, which is the dependent variable?

   (A) Group 1
   (B) Group 2
   (C) Teaching style
   (D) Scores on quizzes
   (E) Teacher

4. If José were to do a study that involved using two groups that already existed, and he simply measured an aspect of their behavior, he could determine how the groups are related on a particular measure of behavior. Such a study would typically involve statistics. If he didn't want to infer causation but rather was just interested in the relationship between the variables, he would be using which statistic?

   (A) Mean
   (B) Standard deviation
   (C) T-test
   (D) F-test
   (E) Correlation

5. If Sarah scored 1 standard deviation above the average, _____ of the population scored higher than she did.

   (A) 15 percent
   (B) 25 percent
   (C) 50 percent
   (D) 65 percent
   (E) 95 percent

6. A researcher decides to study how students in a classroom respond to positive feedback from their teacher by watching them via a two-way mirror. This method of unobtrusive viewing of behavior in its usual setting is referred to as

   (A) a longitudinal study.
   (B) a case study.
   (C) an experiment.
   (D) remote viewing.
   (E) naturalistic observation.

7. Suppose a psychologist wants to study the effect of caffeine on happiness. Which of the following would be an appropriate operational definition of happiness?

(A) The number of times a subject smiles during the experiment

(B) Whether or not the subject seems happy during the experiment

(C) The names of comedians that the subject likes

(D) The number of times that a subject smiles before the experiment

(E) Whether or not the subject seems happy before the experiment

8. If a teacher gives a test in two different classes and has a much larger standard deviation for the scores in the second class, which of these MUST be true?

(A) The test was equally hard for both classes.

(B) The scores in the first class are closer to the mean.

(C) The scores in the second class are closer to the mean.

(D) Students in the first class performed just as well as in the second class.

(E) No one in either class did well on the test.

9. A correlation of +0.90 would probably indicate

(A) a very weak negative relationship between two variables.

(B) that variable *a* caused variable *b* to occur.

(C) that variable *b* caused variable *a* to occur.

(D) a strong positive relationship between two variables.

(E) no relationship between two variables.

10. Control is essential in psychological research. Which of the following research methods procedures has the most control?

(A) Correlational study

(B) Experiment

(C) Observational study with participation

(D) Observational study without participation

(E) Operationalization

11. According to the ethical principles of doing psychological research, which of the following would not likely be allowed?

(A) Participants are deceived but eventually debriefed.

(B) Participants are given informed consent but are deceived.

(C) Participants are not given informed consent but are debriefed.

(D) Participants are given full disclosure but are not able to tell the independent from the dependent variable.

(E) Participants are not told what to expect but are given informed consent and debriefed.

12. Suppose a researcher finds the correlation between two variables to be −0.98. Which of the following is an accurate statement?

(A) There is a very weak relationship between the variables.

(B) There is a very strong relationship between the variables.

(C) Because the number is negative, there is almost no relationship between the variables.

(D) Because the number is so close to 1, we can say that one variable causes the other variable.

(E) One of the variables must be a dependent variable and the other an independent variable.

13. The term *operationalize* means to

    (A) utilize more than one independent variable.

    (B) create an experiment.

    (C) define a correlation.

    (D) define variables clearly.

    (E) define the statistical procedures.

14. A confounding variable is one that causes

    (A) unsystematic variation.

    (B) systematic variation.

    (C) unreliable data.

    (D) participants to feel deceived.

    (E) an experiment to be valid.

15. Whose job is it to review research proposals and determine whether experimenters are allowed to deceive subjects during an experiment?

    (A) An institutional review board (IRB)

    (B) The American Psychological Association (APA)

    (C) The experimenters themselves

    (D) A review panel made up of former subjects

    (E) The American Ethical Association (AEA)

16. Which of the following is the most commonly used measure of central tendency?

    (A) Correlation

    (B) Mean

    (C) Median

    (D) Standard deviation

    (E) Mode

17. Which of the following is the most commonly used measure of variability?

    (A) Correlation

    (B) Mean

    (C) Median

    (D) Standard deviation

    (E) Mode

18. Inferential statistics is used to

    (A) establish strength of relationship.

    (B) establish cause and effect.

    (C) generalize to the population.

    (D) describe a data set.

    (E) formulate hypotheses.

19. A negative correlation typically means that

    (A) variables are related inversely.

    (B) variables are related directly.

    (C) variables are unrelated.

    (D) variables are only weakly related.

    (E) variables are strongly related.

20. Suppose you wanted to study the effects of dopamine on the amount of exercise in a rat. In such an experiment, the dependent variable would be

    (A) the amount of dopamine.

    (B) the rat.

    (C) the groups of rats.

    (D) the amount of exercise.

    (E) the number of rats in the groups.

ANSWERS AND EXPLANATIONS

1. C

Because we're looking for a weak, positive correlation, +0.10 is correct. (A) is incorrect because a 0.00 correlation shows no relation between the variables. (B) is a very strong correlation, and (D) and (E) are both negative.

2. C

You're being asked for a description of the independent variable (IV), not its levels. If you remember that an IV is what the experimenter manipulates or what differs between the groups, then teaching styles, (C), stands out as correct. Choice (D) is the dependent variable (DV), and (E) is irrelevant.

3. D

The other choices are either levels of the IV or the IV itself. This is an important distinction.

4. E

If José were interested in the relationship between the variables, he would use correlation. The study described is designed to measure how related two variables are. The only statistic that does that is the correlation. The other answers are statistics, but they are not the correct answers here.

5. A

Here, you have to know that between the mean and 1 standard deviation from the mean is 34 percent of the scores. So roughly 84–85 percent of the scores are below that; therefore, 15 percent or so are above that.

6. E

This method is an example of naturalistic observation, choice (E). The cardinal rule of naturalistic observation is to observe participants in their natural environment without the participants being aware of your presence, so that they will not alter their behavior. A longitudinal study, (A), would study participants over time, a case study, (B), would get in-depth information, and an experiment, (C), is a form of research that allows for the study of cause and effect. Remote viewing, (D), is a term associated with psychic abilities, not with psychological science.

7. A

An operational definition is a way of quantifying the dependent variable; that is, a way to measure the dependent variables in a numerical manner so that the data can be recorded and statistics can be used to interpret the data. Only choice (A) operationally defines happiness in a way that can be measured as an effect of the independent variable. While choice (D) also is measurable, be aware that it happens before the experiment, not during it. Note that variables can be operationally defined in different ways by different researchers.

8. B

Standard deviation is a measure of how far data spreads out from the mean (average) of the data. The smaller the standard deviation, the closer the data is to the mean, and vice versa. Because the second class's standard deviation was much larger, this means that these scores deviated from the mean more so choice (B) must be correct.

9. D

A +0.90 correlation is a very strong, positive correlation demonstrating that two variables probably vary in the same direction. The other choices do not indicate either the appropriate direction or strength of relationship. To answer this question, you must know what both parts of the correlation coefficient, the sign and the number, show.

10. B

Experiments have the most control. In fact, the other forms of research here are all criticized for *not* having enough experimental control.

11. C

Informed consent is essential in psychological research today. Without it, an experiment should not be performed. Deception is possible as long as there is informed consent and full debriefing afterward.

12. B

A correlation coefficient is a way to indicate both the strength of the relationship between two variables and whether that relationship is direct (+) or inverse (−). The closer the coefficient is to 1 or −1, the stronger the relationship is. A correlation of −0.98 is a very strong relationship, so (B) is the correct answer. Be careful, though, to not assume that because two variables have a strong relationship, one variable causes the other; correlation does not equal causation.

13. D

Operationalizing variables is a very important concept that you need to know. To operationalize is to state your variables so clearly that anyone can know exactly what it is you are measuring.

14. B

A confound occurs when a situation is created that causes systematic variance, making it impossible to determine the reason for an outcome.

15. A

While the APA sets the ethical guidelines that researchers must follow when using humans as participants, it is the job of local institutional review boards to determine whether individual requests can be approved. The IRB's role is to evaluate the cost and benefit of temporarily deceiving participants, for example, by deciding whether the long-term benefits of learning more about human behavior would outweigh the short-term anxiety or even pain to participants.

16. B

Mean is most commonly used. The other measures of central tendency—mode and median—are used as well but only when the mean does not work. The other choices are not measures of central tendency.

17. D

Standard deviation is the most commonly used measure of variability. The other statistics are not measures of variation.

18. C

Inferential statistics is used so that we can draw conclusions about populations from a sample.

19. A

A negative correlation is one in which the variables go in opposite directions. As one variable increases in value, the other decreases.

20. D

The dependent variable is the variable that is measured, or the outcome. Here, that's the amount of exercise. The other choices are not measured outcome variables.

CHAPTER 5: BIOLOGICAL BASES OF BEHAVIOR

IF YOU LEARN ONLY FIVE THINGS IN THIS CHAPTER . . .

1. There are different methods for peering into the human brain, including CT scans, PET scans, MRIs, and fMRIs.

2. The three regions of the brain (hindbrain, midbrain, forebrain) control different parts of the body.

3. The structure of the neuron is important to understand when studying the correlation between the brain and behavior.

4. A neuron can fire an action potential, or message.

5. Neurotransmitters go across the cell membrane and cause the next cell to change its permeability and the whole neuron process begins again.

INTRODUCTION

Psychologists are very interested in understanding the relationship between the brain and behavior and, at the cellular level, the role of certain substances (i.e., drugs) on the activity of neurons. Both issues are very important in psychology as we attempt to understand the biological nature of behavior.

Understand that other systems can also cause behavior to occur. The endocrine system, for instance, can act as a secondary messenger to cause behavior to occur. The entire system is based on small amounts of biological changes giving rise to behavioral outcomes.

RESEARCH METHODS IN BIOPSYCHOLOGY

Biological psychology (or physiological psychology) is concerned with understanding the role of the brain on behavior. It is very difficult, however, to do research on this topic unless we do invasive surgery. Seriously, doing research in physiological psychology is not easy. One thing that makes this easier is the assumption that we can use animal models as a proxy for human biology. The most commonly used animal is the rat, because the brain of the rat is very similar to the brain of a human in many ways. It is smaller, obviously, but many of the pathways and tracks are very similar. Thus, we can use the animal as a model to provide us with an approximation of what might happen in the human body.

If we must use human models, one of the advantages of modern times is the variety of imaging techniques that allow us to peer inside the human body without invasive surgery. A **CT scan** (computer axial tomography) was one of the earliest techniques. In this procedure, X-rays are taken from a variety of angles, and from that, we are able to develop a structural image of the brain. The CT scan is really a detailed X-ray. The technology is improving, however. Recently, 4-D CT technology has advanced, and the images it creates are as detailed as many MRI images.

PET scans (positron emission tomography) use a radioactive dye that is eventually absorbed by the brain. A trace of that activity is recorded by the PET scanner; that image is then transformed into a computerized image that will show the parts of the brain that are more active. The resulting image allows researchers to know the parts of the brain that are active during different activities, thus allowing them to assume that those areas are important for performing that activity.

The **MRI** is a newer technique that uses nuclear technology to develop a detailed image of the brain. It has an advantage over both the PET scans and the CT scans because the level of detail is dramatically improved. An **fMRI** is an even more detailed technique. It works like an MRI but provides detailed images of both the structures and the parts of the brain that are active (essentially, an MRI and a PET scan combined).

THE BRAIN

Typically, the brain is divided into three regions: hindbrain, midbrain, and forebrain. The **hindbrain** is the first part of the brain to develop during gestation. This region consists of parts of the brain such as the cerebellum (coordination of motor movements and regulatory functions), the medulla (habitual, automatic

AP EXPERT TIP

A helpful way to remember the various imaging techniques is to think of which ones are designed to examine the brain's structure (CAT, MRI), which ones examine the brain's function (PET, EEG), and which do both (fMRI).

behaviors), and the reticular formation (controls the flow of sensory information from the lower part of the body up to the brain). Much of what happens in the hindbrain revolves around the regulation of normal body functions.

The **midbrain** contains the sensory pathways that carry visual information from the eyes back to the part of the brain that processes visual information.

Finally, the **forebrain** is probably the most complex of all the regions. It is composed of the limbic system and the cortex. The limbic system is the part of the brain that is responsible for our emotional response to stimuli. For example, the hypothalamus, a structure located in the limbic system, is responsible for the motivation of what has been called the **four F's** (feeding, fighting, fleeing, and sexual reproduction). That is, the limbic system controls motivation for some of the basic processes in life.

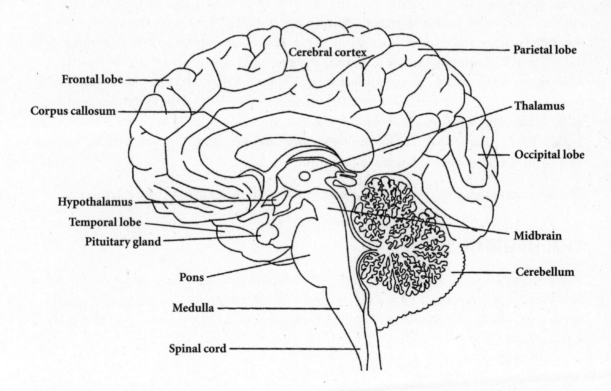

The cortex is the part of the brain that is responsible for higher-order cognitive functioning. It controls memory, thought, and so on. Much has been made about the different functions controlled by each half of the cortex; it is actually not as simple as some believe. The cortex is an integrated set of structures that controls the behavior that makes humans human.

The cortex is composed of four lobes, each with its own set of cells designed to carry out different functions.

- The **occipital lobe** is located at the rear of the cortex (the back of your brain) and is responsible for vision.
- The **parietal lobe,** on the top of your brain, is responsible for processing much of the sensory information that we are able to understand.
- The **temporal lobe** is located on the side of your brain (in both hemispheres) and is responsible for processing auditory information as well as language information.
- The **frontal lobe** is located in the front of your brain and is responsible for many higher-order cognitive processes, such as memory, thought, and so on.

The somatosensory cortex is a strip across the very front of the parietal lobe that receives information from other areas of the body. There is a relationship between the amount of cortex devoted to a region and the level of sensitivity of that area. For example, a great deal of cortex is devoted to the fingertips, because those areas are much more sensitive than, say, the back. In addition, on the frontal lobe side of a fissure (a large "valley" in the brain) that separates the frontal from the parietal lobe is the motor cortex. The motor cortex works similarly to the somatosensory cortex in that there is an amount of cortex that is directly proportional to the ability of that area to perform complex motor acts. The tongue, for example, requires very complex movements to speak. Thus, a great deal of cortex is devoted to that organ.

Each lobe works along with the others to give rise to the experience that we have every day.

THE NEURON

The most important set of cells in the brain are the neurons. By one estimate, we have in the order of 1.5 trillion neurons at birth, though some claim that this is a gross underestimation. Regardless of the actual number, it is an indisputable fact that humans have many more neurons than they will ever need.

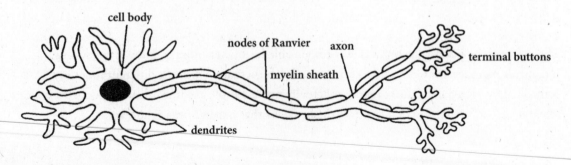

The neuron functions like a gun. One can squeeze on the trigger gently (accumulating action potential) and the gun will not fire, but past a certain point, the bullet is ejected. (The neuron fires, and the potential moves down the axon like the bullet moves down the barrel of the gun.) Different neurons fire at different speeds (just as bullets and guns have different calibers and barrel-lengths, respectively), but the same gun always fires at the same speed, just as one neuron always fires at one speed.

Similarly, a neuron can either fire a message (called an action potential) or not fire a message. When a neuron fires a message, it is said to depolarize. The method of firing an action potential is actually the accumulation of several hundred (and in many cases, thousand) small potentials that take place around the neuron's dendrites.

Dendrites are branchlike structures in cells that receive information from neighboring cells. At rest, because the membrane of the cell is semipermeable, dendrites carry a −70 millivolt charge. When the cell receives a message from another cell, the membrane becomes more permeable to allowing in the ion sodium (NA+) and releases a tiny bit of the ion potassium (K+). When that happens, the cell becomes much more likely to fire an action potential. The reason is that when NA+ enters the cell and only a bit of K+ leaves the cell, the inside of the cell becomes less negative (or depolarized). If enough depolarization occurs in a cell (called the threshold of excitation, or −65 millivolts), the cell will fire an action potential.

When a cell fires an action potential, a message is sent down an axon to the axon terminal, where it releases neurotransmitters into the synapse. Those neurotransmitters go across the cell membrane and cause the next cell to change its permeability, and the entire process starts again. Common neurotransmitters are acetylecholine, dopamine, serotonin, gamma amino butyric acid (GABA), and norepinephrine. Hormones can also cause behavior changes, but their effect is much more subtle.

If an axon is covered in myelin, the axon is insulated and will speed the action potential down the axon to the next cell. Myelin is important for providing fast action potentials so we can perform some of our fine motor movements.

These small changes in electrochemical charges give rise to all the complex behavior that humans perform at any given time. One of the most important issues to consider when discussing these small electrochemical charges is the influence of small amounts of psychoactive substances on behavior. We will return to this issue in the chapter on consciousness, where we discuss the role of drugs on behavior.

GENETICS

One of the most interesting debates in the way we view human behavior is the debate over genetics. Of course, there really is no controversy over the fact that genes seem to control our physical characteristics. Yet there is a question about whether or not genes control our behavior. Most psychologists argue that genes code for predispositions but do not code for behavior. Thus, we are not genetically predetermined to become one way or another. Rather, our biology plays a role in the development of who we become. The environment works on the biology to give rise to human behavior.

Humans have 23 pairs of chromosomes that code for our biological traits. Of those 23 pairs, 22 are identical: Half of the genes come from the mother and half from the father. On the 23rd pair, however, we see some differences. In some cases (about half), the 23rd pair is comprised of an X and a Y chromosome. That condition produces a male. In other cases, the 23rd pair is an XX pair, and that condition produces a female.

An understanding of genetics has helped psychologists understand more completely the complex interaction between the environment and our biology. Some things are fixed in our genetic endowment—typically, physical characteristics. Some are more malleable—alcoholism, mental illness, or temperament. Studies with twins have helped to clarify these issues, but we are still years away from a complete understanding of the role of genetics in all of the behavior we produce.

EVOLUTIONARY PSYCHOLOGY

Many psychologists have begun to see a seventh approach to understanding human behavior in addition to the ones we explored in chapter 3. The evolutionary approach is the application of the principles of Charles Darwin's theories of evolution and natural selection to the study of psychology. Evolutionary psychologists look at the interaction of genetics and the environment and how changes in genetics over time make individuals more fit for their surroundings. For example, they might look at what characteristics humans choose when selecting a mate, or why humans tend to be universally afraid of spiders and snakes. This approach helps us to think about not only how humans behave in the present, but also how those changes over time may alter human behavior.

REVIEW QUESTIONS

1. The area of the brain responsible for controlling motor movements is the

   (A) hindbrain.
   (B) temporal lobe.
   (C) frontal lobe.
   (D) midbrain.
   (E) occipital lobe.

2. The area of the brain responsible for controlling vision is the

   (A) hindbrain.
   (B) temporal lobe.
   (C) frontal lobe.
   (D) midbrain.
   (E) occipital lobe.

3. There are several techniques for peering inside the brain. Which of the following provides a detailed image only of the structure of the brain?

   (A) MRI
   (B) fMRI
   (C) CT scan
   (D) X-ray
   (E) PET scan

4. The most commonly used animal model in physiological psychology is the

   (A) dog.
   (B) rat.
   (C) cat.
   (D) monkey.
   (E) dolphin.

5. Because of the complex movements that it does when speaking and eating, there is a great deal of the _____ devoted to the tongue.

   (A) temporal lobe
   (B) motor cortex
   (C) hypothalamus
   (D) cerebellum
   (E) occipital lobe

6. The area of the brain most responsible for controlling motivation for fighting, fleeing, feeding, and sexual reproduction is the

   (A) thalamus.
   (B) hypothalamus.
   (C) hippocampus.
   (D) pons.
   (E) medulla oblongata.

7. The process of a neuron firing is called

   (A) action potential.
   (B) inhibitory potential.
   (C) excitatory potential.
   (D) graded potential.
   (E) neuron potential.

8. During a softball game, you are hit in the head with the ball. Your vision becomes blurred. What region of the brain was MOST likely involved?

   (A) Hindbrain
   (B) Occipital lobe
   (C) Temporal lobe
   (D) Midbrain
   (E) Parietal lobe

9. The chemical messengers that cross synapses to "send a message" from one neuron to the next are called

   (A) action potentials.

   (B) hormones.

   (C) neurotransmitters.

   (D) genes.

   (E) chromosomes.

10. The _____ seems to be responsible for motivation in actions such as eating and sexual activity.

    (A) occipital lobe

    (B) temporal lobe

    (C) thalamus

    (D) hypothalamus

    (E) cerebral cortex

11. Which of the following imaging techniques provides a detailed impression of the activity of the brain?

    (A) MRI

    (B) PET scan

    (C) fMRI

    (D) CT scan

    (E) X-ray

12. The _____ is the area of the brain that seems to be responsible for language comprehension.

    (A) limbic system

    (B) occipital lobe

    (C) temporal lobe

    (D) parietal lobe

    (E) hypothalamus

13. The part of the brain that seems to be responsible for receiving sensory information from the environment is called the

    (A) motor cortex.

    (B) somatosensory cortex.

    (C) sensory memory.

    (D) receptive field.

    (E) limbic system.

14. If an axon of a neuron is covered with myelin, which one of the following is TRUE?

    (A) The action potential will move much slower down the axon.

    (B) The action potential will move much faster down the axon.

    (C) The neuron must be a sensory neuron.

    (D) The threshold of excitation will increase.

    (E) The threshold of excitation will decrease.

15. The part of the neuron that receives information from neighboring cells is called the

    (A) membrane.

    (B) axons.

    (C) vesicles.

    (D) nucleus.

    (E) dendrites.

16. The part of the neuron that sends information to neighboring cells is called the

    (A) membrane.

    (B) axons.

    (C) vesicles.

    (D) nucleus.

    (E) dendrites.

17. What ion is concentrated outside the cell membrane when a cell is at rest?

    (A) Oxygen
    (B) Nitrogen
    (C) Potassium
    (D) Sodium
    (E) Chloride

18. Which is the correct path that the action potential moves across a neuron?

    (A) Axon → Cell Body → Dendrite
    (B) Dendrite → Axon → Cell Body
    (C) Cell Body → Axon → Dendrite
    (D) Dendrite → Cell Body → Axon
    (E) Axon → Dendrite → Axon

19. The _____ pair of chromosomes controls the sex of the infant.

    (A) 21st
    (B) 32nd
    (C) 13th
    (D) 22nd
    (E) 23rd

20. Which psychological approach looks at both genetics and the changes in human behavior over time?

    (A) Cognitive
    (B) Humanistic
    (C) Psychoanalytic
    (D) Sociocultural
    (E) Evolutionary

ANSWERS AND EXPLANATIONS

1. C

The frontal lobe controls motor movements. The hindbrain, (A), is mostly responsible for regulatory function, the temporal lobe, (B), is mostly responsible for language and audition, the midbrain, (D), passes information from the eyes to the visual cortex, and the occipital lobe, (E), is responsible for vision.

2. E

The occipital lobe is essential in vision. The eye projects its cells back toward that region of the brain, and along the way, several processes are added to the image (color from the thalamus, etc.). The occipital lobe contains seven layers of cells, which provide for the detailed images that we see.

3. A

The fMRI displays both function and activity, the CT scan, (C), is not very detailed, the X-ray, (D), mainly shows bone, and the PET scan, (E), shows function.

4. B

The rat is most often used in physiological psychology. The other animals have been used by psychologists, but for a variety of reasons, they are not used as much—particularly the dog and cat, (A) and (C), because they are household pets. The monkey, (D), and the dolphin, (E), are too expensive.

5. B

More space is assigned in the frontal lobe's motor cortex to parts of the body whose movement requires the most control, regardless of size. Here's a memory tip: Motor cortex, muscles, and movement all start with the letter *M*. The other choices are all parts of the brain, but they are not associated with the motor movements of speaking and eating.

6. B

The hypothalamus is most responsible for controlling motivation for fighting, fleeing, feeding, and sexual reproduction. The thalamus, (A), is responsible for sensory information, the hippocampus, (C), is responsible for encoding memory, and the pons and the medulla, (D) and (E), are responsible for regulatory functions such as breathing and heart rate.

7. A

Action potential is the name assigned to the firing of a neuron. The other choices are all potentials that give rise to small changes in permeability of the membrane, except for (E), neuron potential, which is a concept not used often.

8. B

The occipital lobe was most probably affected. If you were hit in the hindbrain, (A), you might lose your ability to breathe. If you were hit in the temporal lobe, (C), you might have a language or hearing problem. As for the midbrain, (D), that is too deep in the brain to be affected, and the parietal lobe, (E), would give rise to sensory experiences that mimic parts of your body being stimulated.

9. C

The chemical messengers are choice (C), neurotransmitters. Note that as a chemical, the neurotransmitter is slower than its electrical counterpart, the action potential. Messages are sent along the neurons as electrical energy, converted to chemical energy to cross the synapse, then converted back to electrical energy along the next neuron. Choice (B), hormones, are also chemical in nature, but effect change much more slowly than neurotransmitters. Hormones also travel long distances in the bloodstream instead of the brief distance across the synapse.

10. D

The hypothalamus is responsible for motivation. The occipital lobe, (A), is responsible for vision, the temporal lobe, (B), for language and hearing, and the thalamus, (C), for sensory information. The cerebral cortex, (E), is the entire external part of the brain.

11. B

The PET scan gives a detailed impression of the activity of the brain. An MRI, (A), gives detailed structure, an fMRI, (C), gives detailed structure and function, a CT scan, (D), gives a less detailed image, and an X-ray, (E), shows detail about bone.

12. C

The temporal lobe is responsible for language. The limbic system, (A), controls emotional response, the occipital lobe, (B), controls vision, the parietal lobe, (D), controls sensory information, and the hypothalamus, (E), controls motivation.

13. B

The somatosensory cortex receives sensory information from the environment. The motor cortex, (A), causes motor responses. Sensory memory, (C), is responsible for storing sensory information for a short period of time, while the receptive field, (D), is a component of vision. The limbic system, (E), controls emotional response.

14. B

When myelin is found along an axon, the action potential "jumps" from one unmyelinated section (called a node of Ranvier) to another, thus greatly increasing the speed at which the action potential moves along the axon. Thus, choice (B) is correct. Note that certain diseases such as multiple sclerosis are caused by the breakdown of these myelinated sheaths, resulting in a loss of dexterity and difficulty with the coordination of muscle movements.

15. E

Dendrites receive information from other cells nearby. The membrane, (A), is the outside of the cell, axons, (B), send messages to other cells, vesicles, (C), carry neurotransmitters, and the nucleus, (D), contains the genetic code.

16. B

Axons send information to neighboring cells. The axon is typically depicted in traditional introductory psychology books as one long, branchike structure, yet axons can take many forms and can project to many different cells. The simplistic depictions you see in those books are merely to help you understand the basic structure.

17. D

Sodium is concentrated outside the cell membrane when a cell is at rest. The other ions are important in cellular transmission, but they are not located outside the cell membrane.

18. D

Action potentials always begin at the dendrite and are transmitted through the cell body and then to the axon, where they stimulate the production of neurotransmitters capable of crossing the synapse. Dendrites are the receivers and axons the transmitters. To help you remember, note that this pattern is in reverse alphabetical order: D, C, B, A.

19. E

The 23rd chromosome pair is either XX or XY. If you are an XX, you are a female. If you are XY, you are a male. The difference is controlled by the father (because he is the only one with a Y chromosome). There are cases of XXY or XYY, but these are relatively rare and, in most cases, not apparent to the naked eye.

20. E

The approach that combines genetics and the change in behavior over time is (E), evolutionary psychology. This is one of the newest approaches to understanding human behavior, but the theories of Darwin are 140 years old. The cognitive perspective, (A), is involved with thinking and memories, humanistic, (B), with personal growth and free will, psychoanalytic, (C), with the unconscious, and sociocultural, (D), with the effects of the culture on individuals.

CHAPTER 6: SENSATION AND PERCEPTION

IF YOU LEARN ONLY FOUR THINGS IN THIS CHAPTER . . .

1. Perception is the interpretation of sensory information; it relies on experience.

2. There is a difference between sensation and perception.

3. It is important to understand the structure and function of the eye.

4. It is important to understand the structure and function of the ear.

INTRODUCTION

Sensation and perception are areas that have been of interest to psychologists for most of the history of psychology. As we sit here, our senses receive literally thousands of messages. We need to make sense of this information. Our senses take in the information, and they do so from birth. Yet the interpretive part—perception—requires knowledge.

In this chapter, we will discuss first two senses and then how those senses pass the raw data on to the perceptual processes we have developed over time.

SENSATION

The process of **sensation** is that of **receiving information from the environment**. Humans have five senses—vision, hearing, smell, touch, and taste—and some argue that we have a sixth sense—the vestibular sense.

AP EXPERT TIP

Sensation is receiving raw data; perception is how the brain interprets the data.

Each sense has a system that allows for the reception of information from that system. The sense organs receive information mechanically, and the information is passed on for further processing. The process of transforming physical energy into neural impulses is called sensation.

Typically, two main systems are described when discussing sensation: **vision** and **hearing**. In the first section of this chapter, we will discuss the two organs that are involved in this process. In the second section, we will discuss how the brain seems to work to interpret the sensory information that is gathered.

VISUAL SYSTEM

Of course, the primary organ involved in vision is the eye. The eye is a fairly simple organ, but it is capable of amazingly complex processing. Use the image below to guide you through the description of the different parts.

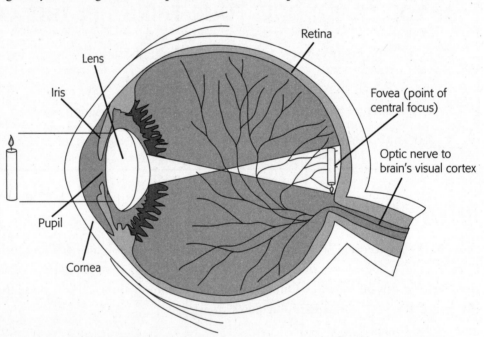

Working from the inside out, the first structure of the eye is the **cornea**. The cornea is responsible for bending light waves to help focus those waves on the back of the eye. The cornea, in fact, is the part of the eye that is most responsible for bending light. The relatively new laser surgery that has become so popular works by reshaping the cornea to allow for the proper bending of light into the eye.

The white part of the eye is called the **sclera**. The sclera is filled with blood vessels to provide nutrients to the eye. In addition, the sclera provides structure to the eye.

In the front of the eye, just behind the cornea, is the **iris**, which surrounds the pupil. The iris is the color of our eyes. The iris does not have an impact on how well we can see, though it does have a job: it is a muscle that controls the size of the pupil.

The **pupil**, on the other hand, is *very* important for vision. The pupil changes size depending on the amount of ambient light present. If there is a lot of ambient light, the pupil constricts to limit the amount of light coming in. If there is a lot of surrounding darkness, the pupil dilates to allow in as much ambient light as possible. In this way, we are able to adapt to the ever-changing amount of ambient light that is available at any given time.

Just behind the pupil lies the **lens**. The lens is a structure that works in conjunction with the cornea to bend light so that it falls on the appropriate space in the rear of the eye. The lens is the secondary structure in the focusing process. The lens changes shape as a means of helping to focus.

At the back of the eye lies the **retina**, the structure most responsible for visual acuity. The retina stretches across the back half of the eye, with a differential distribution of types of cells across the structure. Two types of photoreceptor cells directly receive light stimulation: rods and cones. **Rods**, more likely found in the periphery, are more important in processing darks and lights. **Cones**, found mostly in the center of the retina, code more for color and are concentrated in a region called the **fovea**. When we look at something in the environment, that object is falling directly on the fovea. This is our area of **greatest visual acuity**.

Directly in front of the retina are two layers of cells that help code for visual information. **Bipolar cells** in the first layer translate the information from the rods and cones back out to the ganglion cells. **Ganglion cells** then transfer the information down toward the optic nerve. The point where the optic nerve exits the eye is the **blind spot**. You cannot see anything because there are no photoreceptors at the point at which those cells exit the retina.

The information is carried down the optic nerve, where it undergoes additional processing. Color information is added at the **thalamus**. At the end of the optic nerve is the **occipital lobe**, the structure most responsible for visual processing.

AUDITORY SYSTEM

Like the visual system, the auditory system is a mechanical system designed to translate external stimuli into a code that is understandable by the brain. The mechanical process of audition is very interesting, and in many ways, it is amazing that it works as well as it does. The main goal of the auditory system is to **translate**

> **AP EXPERT TIP**
>
> Quick trick for differentiating rods and cones: Cones Code for Color and Clarity.

acoustic energy into sound. It does this by passing sound waves down through the ear until specialized cells are able to translate this sound into a code that is interpretable.

The first structure in the auditory system is the **pinna**, or **external ear**. The pinna is the part of the ear that we see. The pinna, composed of cartilage and fat deposits, serves to funnel sound into the ear. The pinna is not essential—if you don't have one, you can still hear—yet the pinna helps us determine the location of sound in space by providing us with a more efficient collection of sound from the front than from the back.

Inside the pinna is the **auditory canal**. At about 2.5 centimeters in length, this canal is the longest depression in the skull. Its purpose is to focus the sound waves toward the tympanic membrane or eardrum. The **tympanic membrane**, a thin tissue stretched over a bone, vibrates in sympathy with the sound waves, creating a message of the same amplitude as the original sound waves. Sound waves are physical features. For all of us to hear sound the same way, we need a system by which to take in and then translate the sound waves. The tympanic membrane allows for this, in part, because it is able to respond at the same rate as the sound waves.

After the sound waves cause the tympanic membrane to vibrate, the vibrations are carried further into the ear via three ossicles (or small bones): the **malleus** (hammer), the **incus** (anvil), and the **stapes** (stirrup). These are the three smallest bones in the human body; they work together to move the sound from the tympanic membrane into the inner ear. The bones vibrate in sympathy with the sound waves that are causing the tympanic membrane to vibrate.

The bones end at the beginning of the inner ear. The **inner ear** is the location of the cochlea, which is where the auditory receptors are located. These auditory receptors operate as follows:

- In the middle of the cochlea is the basilar membrane. The cochlea is fluid filled, and the basilar membrane floats in this fluid.

- The stapes presses against the fluid in the cochlea and causes waves to flow in the fluid.

- The waves cause the basilar membrane to vibrate. On the basilar membrane are receptor cells called hair cells.

- The hair cells are stimulated by the vibrations of the basilar membrane. These patterns of stimulation are then transmitted along the basilar membrane and out the auditory membrane along the auditory nerve to the auditory cortex (the temporal lobes of the brain).

PERCEPTION

The goal of **perception** is essentially to **interpret the visual world into a form** that makes sense to us. Visual perception is organized according to several principles. We tend to organize our perception of form according to the Gestalt principles of proximity, similarity, good continuation, and closure. Each principle provides us with the ability to perceive the world in a way that we can understand.

However, our ability to perceive the world is more than just understanding shape: we also need to perceive motion and color (the eye does much of this work). Each principle that we utilize to understand the world is important, and without experience to develop these skills, we wouldn't be able to have the rich representation of the world that we now have.

An important distinction in the study of perception is the distinction between the proximal stimulus and the distal stimulus. The **proximal stimulus** is the stimulus that is received and transformed by the perceiver, while the **distal stimulus** is the stimulus in the environment. This distinction is important because we do not have direct access to information in the world. Rather, we use what our senses gather to make sense of the world. We use the information gathered from the distal stimulus to generate the proximal stimulus so that we have a representation of the world.

Of course, other perceptual processes also add to the sensory information that people receive. Visual perception is discussed in the greatest depth in textbooks, but auditory perception is also important. For example, we can determine the origin of sound by using several cues. Because we have two ears, we can use the strength and the timing of the sound waves as they hit our ears to determine the direction of the sound. Because the sound waves will hit one ear first and will be stronger in that ear, if the sound is coming from either our right or left, we are able to interpret those differences and determine the direction of the sound.

MEASURING PERCEPTION

One key to understanding perception is the accurate measurement of these processes. Psychologists have worked hard to develop strategies for measuring perception. The concepts are not nearly as clear as other concepts in psychology, but let's address some of these measurement techniques.

Thresholds are the limits of your perception. For example, we all seem to have an absolute threshold for our ability to perceive a stimulus. The **absolute threshold** is the least amount of information that is necessary for you to understand that a stimulus is actually presented.

A **difference threshold** is similar to an absolute threshold. It is the amount of stimulus needed to determine that there has been a change in a stimulus. If you normally drink coffee with one sugar packet in it, how many more granules of sugar are necessary before you notice that there's too much sugar in your coffee? This kind of measurement helps to illustrate how sensitive human perception is. The amount of difference that exists in such a situation is often called the **just noticeable difference**.

Signal detection theory addresses how participants are able to perceive information from the world. It argues that there is either a detected stimulus (hit), a miss, a correct rejection, or a false positive. A participant is presented with a variety of stimuli, and each judgment is recorded. Good ability to detect results in more hits than misses and more correct rejections than false positives.

The study of sensation and perception is as old as the science of psychology itself. To understand it completely, you must immerse yourself in a text that fully explains the concepts described here.

REVIEW QUESTIONS

1. When physical energy is transformed into neural impulses, it is referred to as

    (A) reception.

    (B) transduction.

    (C) perception.

    (D) sensation.

    (E) induction.

2. An object as it appears in the world as a visual stimulus is referred to as the

    (A) distal stimulus.

    (B) proximal stimulus.

    (C) figure.

    (D) ground.

    (E) retinal image.

3. _____ is receiving data from the external environment; _____ is how our brains make sense of that data.

    (A) Induction; reception

    (B) Gestalt; detection

    (C) Comprehension; transduction

    (D) Perception; sensation

    (E) Sensation; perception

4. The amount of stimulus required to determine that a stimulus has changed just a little bit is called the

    (A) difference threshold.

    (B) absolute threshold.

    (C) just noticeable difference.

    (D) just noticeable threshold.

    (E) taste aversion.

5. The part of the eye responsible for receiving photons of light and then translating them into neural messages is the

    (A) sclera.

    (B) lens.

    (C) cornea.

    (D) pupil.

    (E) retina.

6. The part of the ear responsible for translating information into neural impulses is the

    (A) pinna.

    (B) cochlea.

    (C) semicircular canals.

    (D) tympanic membrane.

    (E) incus.

7. The part of the retina in which there are no visual receptors is the point at which the optic nerve exits the eye. What is the term for this point?

    (A) Rod

    (B) Blind spot

    (C) Cone

    (D) Fovea

    (E) Pupil

8. What is the term for the smallest amount of a sensation that is necessary for a person to actually notice that it is present?

    (A) Absolute threshold

    (B) Difference threshold

    (C) Perceptual set

    (D) Perceptual adaptation

    (E) Sensory adaptation

9. The part of the brain responsible for coding auditory information is the

   (A) temporal lobe.
   (B) occipital lobe.
   (C) somatosensory cortex.
   (D) frontal lobe.
   (E) hypothalamus.

10. The part of the brain responsible for coding visual information is the

    (A) temporal lobe.
    (B) somatosensory cortex.
    (C) hypothalamus.
    (D) occipital lobe.
    (E) frontal lobe.

11. The _____ is the first structure involved in focusing photons of light.

    (A) cornea
    (B) lens
    (C) retina
    (D) sclera
    (E) vitreous humor

12. In signal detection theory, when a participant responds that a stimulus was present and it was, the response is called a

    (A) correct rejection.
    (B) ROC curve.
    (C) miss.
    (D) hit.
    (E) false positive.

13. Gestalt principles are used to make order out of perceptions so that we see things as connected and not just random bits of information. Which of these is NOT a common Gestalt principle?

    (A) Similarity
    (B) Localization
    (C) Closure
    (D) Proximity
    (E) Good continuation

14. The structure in the eye that changes shape to accommodate the closeness or distance of an object is the

    (A) cornea.
    (B) retina.
    (C) lens.
    (D) sclera.
    (E) iris.

15. The structure in the ear that is responsible for gathering sound initially is the

    (A) pinna.
    (B) tympanic membrane.
    (C) cochlea.
    (D) semicircular canals.
    (E) stapes.

16. The receptor cells that make the transduction for the auditory system are called the

    (A) basilar membrane.
    (B) hair cells.
    (C) cochlea.
    (D) semicircular canals.
    (E) stapes.

17. The cells responsible for coding for color in the eye are the

    (A) rods.
    (B) iris.
    (C) cones.
    (D) retina.
    (E) fovea.

18. The point of focus for the eye that contains mostly cones is the

    (A) rods.
    (B) iris.
    (C) cones.
    (D) retina.
    (E) fovea.

19. Which part of our auditory system is best able to aid us in the localization of sounds?

    (A) Ossicles
    (B) Pinna
    (C) Tympanic membrane
    (D) Occipital lobe
    (E) Eardrum

20. The structure that contains the main receptor cells in the auditory system is the

    (A) semicircular canals.
    (B) tympanic membrane.
    (C) pinna.
    (D) malleus.
    (E) cochlea.

ANSWERS AND EXPLANATIONS

1. B

Transduction occurs when physical energy is transformed into neural impulses. Reception, (A), does not transform information into neural impulses. Perception, (C), is when information is interpreted. Sensation, (D), is the physical reception of sensory information, and induction, (E), is a process of solving logical problems.

2. A

The distal stimulus describes an object as it appears in the world as a visual stimulus. Proximal stimulus, (B), is the stimulus as it is represented by the brain. The figure, (C), is the object in the foreground, and the ground, (D), is the background in an image. The retinal image, (E), is the image as it is captured by the cells of the retina.

3. E

When looking at the answer choices, it should become clear that only (D) and (E) are possible options. Because getting information into the body is the job of the senses, and understanding that information is the function of perception, choice (E) is correct. Remember that sensation (via the senses) happens first, because one has to sense something before understanding what it is.

4. C

For someone to notice a difference between two stimuli, there must be at least a bit of difference in their energy. A just noticeable difference is the amount the two stimuli need to differ by in order for the person to perceive that difference. A difference threshold, (A), is the ability to detect a difference but not the smallest difference. The absolute threshold, (B), is the lowest detectable stimulus that someone can detect. The just noticeable threshold, (D), is the combination of two other terms. Taste aversion, (E), refers to a learned aversion to a taste.

5. E

The retina receives photons of light and translates them into neural messages. The sclera, (A), provides structure to the eye. The lens, (B), bends light for focusing objects as they move closer to or farther from us. The cornea, (C), is the initial structure in the eye that bends light. The pupil, (D), opens and closes to allow in more or less light, depending on the amount of ambient light present.

6. B

The cochlea translates information into neural impulses. The pinna, (A), collects sound waves, the semicircular canals, (C), help to provide us with the ability to balance, the tympanic membrane, (D), vibrates in response to physical sound waves, and the incus, (E), is one of the ossicles in the inner ear.

7. B

All of these terms are found in the eye, so it is important to read the question carefully. Because the pupil, (E), is not a part of the retina and the rod, (A), and cones, (C), are visual receptors, they can be eliminated. Because there are no receptors where the optic nerve leaves the eye, there is truly no way to get visual information from that place, so it is referred to as the blind spot, (B). Note that we normally are not aware of this, because the visual information in the blind spot of our left eye can be detected by the right eye, and vice versa.

8. A

The smallest information that can be detected by our senses is (A), the absolute threshold. Choice (B), the difference threshold, is the ability to notice an addition to a stimulus. A classic example of the absolute threshold was one drop of perfume diffused in a six-room house. Absolute thresholds can vary from person to person, and can change as one ages. The other terms are all involved with perception, but are not involved with the minimal detection of a stimulus.

9. A

The temporal lobe codes auditory information. The occipital lobe, (B), codes for vision, the somatosensory cortex, (C), helps in the reception of sensory information, the frontal lobe, (D), is important in higher-level cognitive functioning, and the hypothalamus, (E), is important in motivation.

10. D

The occipital lobe codes visual information. The temporal lobe, (A), is responsible for coding for hearing. The somatosensory cortex, (B), is responsible for receiving sensory information, the hypothalamus, (C), is important in motivation, and the frontal lobe, (E), is important for higher-level cognitive functioning.

11. A

The cornea is the first structure involved in focusing photons of light. The lens, (B), helps focus but later in the process. The retina, (C), is responsible for receiving the photons of light, the sclera, (D), provides structure to the eye, and the vitreous humor, (E), is fluid that fills the eye and provides outward pressure.

12. D

A hit is when a participant responds affirmatively to a stimulus that is present. A correct rejection, (A), is when a participant says there is no stimulus

and there isn't. A ROC curve, (B), is a measure of accuracy. A miss, (C), is when a stimulus is present and the participant doesn't perceive it, and a false positive, (E), occurs when a participant claims to have seen a stimulus but one was not presented.

13. B

All of these are Gestalt principles except for (B), localization, which is a method of helping us understand where sounds are coming from. Many designers of web pages and other graphics use Gestalt principles frequently to help viewers understand that certain headings and images are part of the same group.

14. C

The lens changes shape to allow for the distance of an object. The cornea, (A), is the first eye part involved in focusing information, the retina, (B), is the location of the photoreceptors, the sclera, (D), provides structure to the eye, and the iris, (E), is the colored part of the eye.

15. A

The pinna is the structure that initially gathers sounds. The tympanic membrane, (B), vibrates in response to sound in the environment, the cochlea, (C), contains the auditory receptor cells, the semicircular canals, (D), help with balance, and the stapes, (E), is one of the ossicles in the inner ear.

16. B

Hair cells make the transduction for the auditory system. The basilar membrane, (A), is the structure that the hair cells are on. The cochlea, (C), is the structure both are located in. The semicircular canals, (D), are important for balance, and the stapes, (E), is one of the ossicles in the inner ear.

17. C

Cones are responsible for coding the color in the eye. Rods, (A), code for black and white, the iris, (B), is the colored part of the eye, the retina, (D), contains both rods and cones, and the fovea, (E), is the point of focus for the eye (what we are looking at).

18. E

The fovea contains mostly cones and is the point of focus for the eye. Rods, (A), code for black and white, the iris, (B), is the colored part of the eye, cones, (C), code for color, and the retina, (D), contains both rods and cones and collects photons of light.

19. B

Sound localization refers to our ability to tell whether a sound is coming from the left, right, front, or back. Our external ear, the pinna, (B), serves to funnel sound waves into our eardrums. Because we have one on each side of our heads, when we don't know where a sound is coming from, we turn our heads so that one ear is nearer the source and one is farther away. When neurons in one ear detect sound waves faster than the other, we know that sound is coming from the first direction.

20. E

The cochlea contains the main receptor cells in the auditory system. Semicircular canals, (A), help with balance, the tympanic membrane, (B), vibrates in response to sound waves in the environment, the pinna, (C), gathers sound waves from the environment, and the malleus, (D), is one of the ossicles in the inner ear.

CHAPTER 7: STATES OF CONSCIOUSNESS

IF YOU LEARN ONLY THREE THINGS IN THIS CHAPTER . . .

1. People dream during REM sleep.

2. Sleep isn't easy for everyone. There are a variety of sleep disorders that are important to understand.

3. It is important to understand the different stages of sleep.

INTRODUCTION

The topic of consciousness is one that has intrigued psychologists since the beginning of experimental psychology. In fact, the earliest writings in psychology focused on the notion of consciousness. Wundt and James were fascinated with this concept, both from the perspective of how it was **organized** (Wundt) and how it **worked** (James). However, what is consciousness, and how do we understand it in modern psychology? And what does it mean to be in an awakened state of consciousness?

Defined, **consciousness** refers to the active processing of information in the brain. It could be thought of as a form of short-term memory and attention combined. It is the activity that is currently running through our heads or minds. As you sit here, what are you thinking about? This book? Your day? What you are going to have for dinner? All would be part of your consciousness. An altered state of consciousness would be a disruption in normal functioning (e.g., when someone takes drugs).

Studying consciousness is difficult, because we don't have a good definition of it and because we can't really see it. However, techniques have been developed to serve as a *proxy* for consciousness. One of the easiest ways to study consciousness is to examine the process that many high school and college students are interested in: **sleep**.

SLEEP

Sleep is a process that occurs for reasons that are not entirely clear. We do know there is a mechanism that causes us to fall asleep in the brain (two structures, really). And we believe that there is an evolutionary purpose for sleep (at one time, it was dangerous to be active at night). Yet the body does not do as much recuperation during sleep as we might believe, and the brain is active during sleep, so we are not really decreasing activity.

What we do know for sure is that sleep can be measured by tracing the brain waves of someone who sleeps. These brain waves indicate the stage of sleep the person is in.

STAGE 1

In stage 1 sleep, the brain waves are similar to those when someone is awake, where quite a bit of activity occurs. A person in stage 1 sleep is barely asleep; he can be awakened quite easily.

STAGE 2

In stage 2, a person's brain waves slow down dramatically. This is a deeper stage of sleep. Sleep spindles (bursts of neural activity that may be linked to muscle spasms or random neural firings) occur. A person in stage 2 is not so easy to wake up because there is less neural activity.

STAGE 3

This stage is the first of what is called **slow wave sleep**. The brain activity and, hence, the brain waves are very slow. A person in this stage sleeps more deeply and would be difficult to wake up.

STAGE 4

This is the deepest stage of sleep. During this stage, the brain waves are the slowest. In this stage, if a person tried to shut off his ringing alarm, he would remain very groggy. This is because he has to "speed up" his brain activity to engage in that conscious action. So it would take a minute just to get to the point of being able to move toward the clock.

REM SLEEP (OR PARADOXICAL SLEEP)

Rapid eye movement (**REM**) sleep is the stage during which we dream. When we are in REM, our brain waves work almost as fast as they do when we are awake, but the brain causes a decrease in muscle tone and control. The purpose of this is to decrease the likelihood that you might act out your dreams! If it were severed, you would potentially move around and do a variety of activities that might not be appropriate.

One question psychology students always ask is, "When do we sleepwalk?" Not during REM sleep—it isn't possible. Someone might sleepwalk during stage 3 or 4, but not during REM.

The typical person sleeps approximately eight hours a night (though this varies dramatically). Because each set of stages takes around 90 minutes, she will progress through these stages four to six times throughout the night. As the night goes on, more time is spent in REM sleep than in the other stages, which is why we remember dreaming when we awaken. Also, heart rate, blood pressure, and body temperature decrease early in the night but then begin to increase as morning comes. This explains why we cover up at night and then, closer to morning, will kick one leg out of the blankets to cool off.

During REM sleep, we typically experience dreams. Dreams have been of interest to humans for all of recorded history. At one time, they were considered to be messages from others or from evil spirits. But today, our theories of dreaming are much more scientifically based.

Dreams seem to be manifested by our interactions with others or events that occur during the day. When we dream, our brain is as active as it is while we are awake: We experience images, sensations, and so on that we synthesize into dreams. This is called the **activation-synthesis hypothesis**.

Dreams can be frightening, and we all suffer from nightmares occasionally. Yet in rare circumstances, children—boys, in particular—will experience **night terrors**, horrific thoughts that cause a great deal of agitation. Children often cannot describe the image or thought but are very scared by the image. Heart rate is high, and breathing rate increases. Night terrors differ from dreams in that they occur during stage 4 sleep—not REM sleep.

SLEEP DISORDERS

A variety of sleep disorders cause people to suffer.

NARCOLEPSY

Narcolepsy is a condition of excessive sleepiness. A person will fall asleep at unpredictable times and, in fact, cannot control her sleepiness. This type of

> **AP EXPERT TIP**
>
> A good way to help yourself organize the sleep disorders is to list them in order from "least disabling" to "most disabling."

condition significantly affects a person's daily life. People with this disorder go immediately into REM. Narcolepsy is often associated with cataplexy. During cataplexy, a person will fall into REM sleep for reasons that are not clear. With a subsequent loss of motor control, the person will typically fall down.

INSOMNIA

Insomnia is marked by the inability to fall asleep or to maintain sleep during the night. Insomnia has several causes: stress, for one, but also a disorder called sleep apnea.

Sleep apnea occurs when someone stops breathing while sleeping and, thus, wakes up to catch a breath. People with sleep apnea may not know that they are waking up, but interrupted sleep causes them to feel sleepy during the day.

SOMNAMBULISM

Sometimes during stages 3 and 4, people will sleepwalk. They are *not* sleepwalking during dream state but, rather, during a deep stage of sleep.

Sleep is very interesting to discuss. However, we do not have a great deal of knowledge that allows us to fix problems. Medications have been developed, but in general, only symptoms are treated—not the disorders themselves.

ATTENTION

The concept of attention is sometimes discussed in a chapter on cognition. Essentially, **attention** is how we focus our mental energy on any one of a number of possible stimuli. The study of attention can examine either our ability to focus on one task while blocking out other stimuli or our ability to divide our attention among tasks.

SELECTIVE ATTENTION

When we select one stimulus to focus on, this is called **selective attention**. The research on this topic has varied dramatically over the years. Some of the earliest research was done by Cherry and Moray, who utilized the method of dichotic listening to examine the issue. **Dichotic listening** involves wearing headphones and having two different messages coming into your ears. Your task is to listen to one ear and shadow that message while ignoring the other ear.

The research on dichotic listening suggested that we can ignore information in the unattended ear, but some information does get into the unattended channel. Moray demonstrated this via the **cocktail party phenomenon**. In such a situation, you may be focusing your attention on one task, but someone says something that is highly salient to you—things like names, the word *fire* if you are in a movie theater, and so on. When we hear those things, we switch to the unattended ear and pay attention to that information. Thus, we can pay attention to one thing at a time, but we can be distracted by information that seems important.

DIVIDED ATTENTION

By studying divided attention, psychologists have found limits to how much we can divide our attention. Our capacity essentially limits our ability to focus on more than one complex topic at a time.

If we automatize a task (that is, learn it so well that we don't have to pay attention to do it), then we can do more than one task at a time. Just imagine how you can walk and talk to a friend. But if a task isn't automatized, when we try to do it with another task that requires a lot of attention, we fail at one or both of the tasks.

Attention is crucial to understanding human behavior and consciousness. When we are conscious, it is our attention that determines what is part of our short-term memory.

REVIEW QUESTIONS

1. Which stage of sleep is also referred to as paradoxical sleep?

    (A) Stage 1
    (B) Stage 2
    (C) Stage 3
    (D) Stage 4
    (E) REM

2. Difficulty in falling asleep or staying asleep is called

    (A) sleep apnea.
    (B) narcolepsy.
    (C) insomnia.
    (D) cataplexy.
    (E) dichotic listening.

3. Dave has trouble staying asleep because several times during the night, he stops breathing and wakes up for a short time. Dave likely suffers from

    (A) sleep apnea.
    (B) insomnia.
    (C) selective attention.
    (D) narcolepsy.
    (E) cataplexy.

4. Which of the following is the deepest stage of sleep?

    (A) Stage 1
    (B) Stage 2
    (C) Stage 3
    (D) Stage 4
    (E) REM

5. During a typical night, each cycle of sleep lasts

    (A) 8 hours.
    (B) 1 hour.
    (C) 4 hours.
    (D) 90 minutes.
    (E) 30 minutes.

6. Little Tommy is having trouble sleeping. When he first falls asleep, he goes right out. Almost immediately, however, he wakes up screaming and crying uncontrollably, and his heart is racing. Tommy is probably suffering from

    (A) enuresis.
    (B) nightmares.
    (C) cataplexy.
    (D) night terrors.
    (E) sleep apnea.

7. During a typical night's sleep, we go through all the cycles of sleep

    (A) once.
    (B) twice.
    (C) 2–3 times.
    (D) 4–6 times.
    (E) 5–9 times.

8. Lilly is having trouble staying awake during the day. Several times a day, she is overcome with excessive sleepiness—so much so, it is almost impossible for her not to fall asleep. Lilly probably suffers from

    (A) enuresis.
    (B) cataplexy.
    (C) night terrors.
    (D) sleep apnea.
    (E) narcolepsy.

9. A truly automatic task

    (A) uses up most of our available attention.

    (B) allows us to do only one task at a time.

    (C) is beyond the control of the person.

    (D) uses up almost no cognitive resources.

    (E) is possible only under carefully controlled situations.

10. REM sleep is called paradoxical sleep because

    (A) our brains are active even as our muscles are relaxed.

    (B) sometimes we wake up from sleep feeling more tired than before.

    (C) our blood pressure and body temperature are lowest when we wake up.

    (D) our brains shut down and relax even though we are actively dreaming.

    (E) our muscle tone increases during dreams as our brain activity decreases.

11. Abby is having a dream. She is probably in which stage of sleep?

    (A) Stage 1

    (B) Stage 2

    (C) Stage 3

    (D) Stage 4

    (E) REM

12. Another term for sleepwalking is

    (A) cataplexy.

    (B) enuresis.

    (C) somnambulism.

    (D) narcolepsy.

    (E) nightmares.

13. An automatic task

    (A) requires almost no attention to develop.

    (B) requires a great deal of practice to develop.

    (C) works only in selective attention tasks.

    (D) requires one to be asleep.

    (E) works better in children than adults.

14. The idea that a person cannot ignore listening to an important piece of information, even though she is paying attention to something else, is called the

    (A) automaticity effect.

    (B) narcoleptic effect.

    (C) REM sleep effect.

    (D) cocktail party effect.

    (E) hypnotic effect.

15. Tina is walking down the street. All of a sudden, she loses her muscle control and falls to the ground. Tina is most likely suffering from

    (A) narcolepsy.

    (B) night terrors.

    (C) nightmares.

    (D) cataplexy.

    (E) somnambulism.

16. "At one time in our history it was more dangerous for our ancestors to be active at night, so sleeping at night became an advantage for their survival." Which theoretical approach would be MOST supportive of this theory about why we sleep?

    (A) Psychoanalytic

    (B) Evolutionary

    (C) Cognitive

    (D) Behavioral

    (E) Biological

17. The average adult requires _____ hours of sleep per night.

    (A) 8
    (B) 6
    (C) 10
    (D) 4
    (E) 12

18. Which of these is LEAST likely to happen during REM sleep compared to other stages of sleep?

    (A) Dreaming
    (B) Sleep apnea
    (C) Increased brain activity
    (D) Insomnia
    (E) Somnambulism

19. During the night, our body temperature

    (A) drops.
    (B) increases.
    (C) stays the same.
    (D) drops, then increases.
    (E) varies dramatically with time of year.

20. Tom is having trouble sleeping. When he first falls asleep, he goes right to sleep. However, when he wakes up in the morning, he still feels tired. He can't figure out why this happens. Tom is probably suffering from

    (A) enuresis.
    (B) nightmares.
    (C) cataplexy.
    (D) night terrors.
    (E) sleep apnea.

ANSWERS AND EXPLANATIONS

1. E

REM sleep is called paradoxical sleep because during most of the night, our brain waves slow down from stage 1 through stage 4, which is our deepest stage of sleep. But during REM sleep, our brain waves speed up to the rate that they fire during our normal waking state. This is the time of sleep when we are dreaming.

2. C

Someone who has trouble falling or staying asleep has insomnia. Someone with sleep apnea, (A), will stop breathing during the night and wake up to catch her breath. Narcolepsy, (B), is a disorder in which people suffer from uncontrollable sleepiness and, thus, fall asleep several times a day. Cataplexy, (D), is a disorder in which a person falls into REM sleep and, thus, loses muscle control while awake. Dichotic listening, (E), is a task used by cognitive psychologists to test selective attention.

3. A

Sleep apnea is a very dangerous disorder, and it causes a great deal of sleep disruption. Many people who suffer from this disorder don't know that they have it, yet they wake up feeling as though they have not had a good night's sleep and feel drowsy all day. Snoring is a common symptom of someone who has sleep apnea.

4. D

Stage 4 is the deepest stage of sleep. Many people who study sleep believe that REM sleep is the deepest stage; however, we define *deep* by brain wave activity, and during stage 4, our brain waves are firing the slowest. If a person is awoken during stage 4, it takes several seconds for the brain waves to speed up so the person is not disoriented.

5. D

In a normal night's sleep, the cycle that we go through (stage 1–stage 4 and REM) lasts about 90 minutes. The amount of time we spend in each stage varies as the night goes on. During the early cycles, we spend more time in stage 4. However, as the night progresses, we spend more time in REM sleep. By the last cycle, we spend a great deal of the cycle dreaming.

6. D

Tommy likely has night terrors. Night terrors are not dreams but rather scary images that occur to a person when first falling asleep. The person wakes up in a sweat, crying or screaming, and is often inconsolable. Enuresis (bed-wetting) is sometimes comorbid with night terrors. Nightmares, (B), are scary dreams, cataplexy, (C), is a REM sleep disorder, and sleep apnea, (E), occurs when someone wakes up because breathing has stopped.

7. D

Typically, we go through four to six cycles per night, but not everyone experiences this. In fact, recent research has shown that many people in the United States—even children—are not getting enough sleep. If people slept the stated amount each night, they would be more rested overall.

8. E

Lilly has narcolepsy, a disorder that results in an inability to stay awake during the day. Many people with narcolepsy struggle with daily life because of their inability to plan out activities. Their "falling asleep" happens unexpectedly and at inopportune times.

9. D

A task that is automatic is a well-practiced task that, once developed, requires almost no cognitive resources to carry out, as with typing or riding a bike. It is important that we develop automatic skills because they allow us to engage in a variety of tasks at one time.

10. A

In a paradox, one thing is in contradiction to something else. In this case, REM sleep is marked by a very active brain and a very inactive body, because our muscle movements are being suppressed by our brains as described in choice (A). Many people are surprised to learn how active our brains are when we sleep, so choice (D) is incorrect. Choice (E) is the exact opposite of what happens. Choices (B) and (C) may both be true, but they do not evoke the notion of a paradox as in choice (A).

11. E

Abby is likely in REM sleep. REM sleep, or paradoxical sleep, has several features: First, our brain waves are almost as rapid as when we are awake; second, our eyes dart around behind our eyelids; and third, our brains shut off muscle control to keep us from acting out our dreams. REM sleep is very difficult to study because it is not accessible to direct observation.

12. C

Sleepwalking is also called *somnambulism*. This occurs during stage 4. During this stage, a person will move around in unpredictable patterns and do things that may be easily misunderstood. It is important to understand that it *is* appropriate to wake up a person who is sleepwalking. The person may appear to be disoriented, but it is best to get him back to bed so he doesn't hurt himself.

13. B

Automatic tasks require practice and consistent feedback to develop. If the feedback is not consistent, the automaticity will not develop. In 1977, Schneider and Shiffrin showed that if the feedback provided to participants is not consistent, automaticity never develops.

14. D

The cocktail party effect demonstrated that participants could be completely engrossed in a task but be distracted by a small presentation of information that was directly salient to them. So if you are engrossed in a conversation but someone says your name across the room, you will hear it.

15. D

Tina suffers from cataplexy, a REM disorder. During a cataplectic attack, a person will simply collapse. The reason is that during REM sleep, our muscle control shuts off. During cataplexy, we suddenly enter REM sleep, and our muscle control shuts off.

16. B

Be sure that you can recognize the keywords that are associated with each of the approaches; when you see *natural selection*, *adaptation*, or *survival*, you know the answer must be the evolutionary approach. None of the other approaches involves the concepts of our ancestors and survival.

17. A

The recommended amount of sleep is eight hours, though most people do not get that much. If people got enough sleep and made sure that the sleep was consistent each day, they would feel less sleepy.

18. E

By this point you should be very familiar with the fact that REM sleep is paradoxical sleep, which is marked by an active brain and inactive muscles. Even if you don't remember that choice (E), somnambulism, is also called "sleepwalking," you probably know that choice (B) could happen at any time, (B) is defined by wakefulness, and (A) and (C) are *most* likely to happen in REM sleep, so you could eliminate those incorrect options. Somnambulism happens during non-REM stages, typically in stage 3 or stage 4.

19. D

During a typical night's sleep, our body temperature starts out dropping, which is why we need blankets. As the night progresses, our temperature increases slowly as we get closer and closer to waking up. That is why during the early morning hours, we tend to throw off our blankets.

20. E

A person suffering from sleep apnea will probably not remember waking up at night but in the morning will still feel sleepy. All the other disorders will result in some memory of the event.

CHAPTER 8:   LEARNING

IF YOU LEARN ONLY FIVE THINGS IN THIS CHAPTER . . .

1. Learning refers to a relatively permanent change in behavior based on experience.

2. Classical conditioning involves the pairing of one stimulus with another, so that eventually the first neutral stimulus will evoke a reflex.

3. Classical conditioning is associated with Pavlov and Watson; operant conditioning is associated with Skinner.

4. According to operant conditioning, the consequences of a behavior influence whether or not the behavior will be performed again.

5. Reinforcements are used to increase the likelihood a behavior will be repeated and punishments are used to decrease the likelihood a behavior will be repeated.

INTRODUCTION

Psychology is filled with controversies. For example, in the history of psychology, there has long been a debate about the causes of human behavior. Specifically, people have been interested in debating whether human behavior is best captured by understanding people's thoughts (the cognitive approach) or their overt behavior (the behavioral approach).

This debate began with the work of Wilhelm Wundt. Wundt believed that if we could understand human consciousness, we could understand behavior. To gain an understanding of consciousness, Wundt advocated the use of introspection as a research technique. **Introspection** involved having a research participant observe his own thoughts and record them as accurately as possible. The study of introspection went on for several years as people worked feverishly to describe the contents of consciousness.

However, there were rumblings of disagreement among many psychologists over the issue of introspection. Many thought that it did not place enough emphasis on observable behavior.

John B. Watson was one of the psychologists who disagreed with Wundt and his ilk. Watson thought it would be more beneficial to look at the work of **Ivan Pavlov** as a model for understanding humans. Pavlov had recently developed a technique for understanding learned reflexes; the technique demonstrated the notion that reflexes can be brought under experimental control by controlling the association between a reflex-inducing stimulus and a neutral stimulus.

CLASSICAL CONDITIONING

In the classic version of Pavlov's experiment, he noticed that a dog would salivate when presented with food. This is not a surprise. Animals salivate when presented with food. However, Pavlov noticed that if he paired the food enough times with a neutral stimulus, such as a bell, the ring would eventually elicit the salivation by itself. According to Pavlov, the animal learned to associate the ring with the food and, thus, salivated.

In specific language, the food served as the **unconditioned stimulus** (the stimulus that causes a natural response), the salivation as the **unconditioned response** (the naturally occurring response), the ring as the **conditioned stimulus** (the learned stimulus), and, finally, salivation in response to the ring as the **conditioned response** (the learned response). Humans learn their pattern of behavior in the same way, Pavlov believed.

Ordinarily, the sight of food will cause a dog to salivate. The sound of a ring, however, will not.

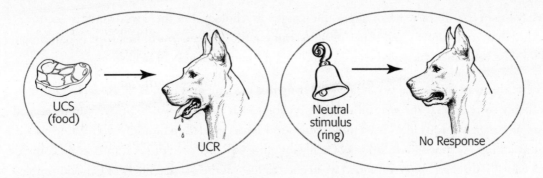

But by pairing the food enough times with the ring, the ring alone will come to produce a conditioned response (CR). The ring, then, becomes a conditioned stimulus (CS).

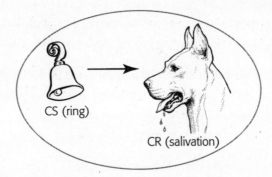

Watson believed this, too, and years later carried it further. He demonstrated that **classical conditioning** (as Pavlovian conditioning was eventually called) can give rise to emotional responses, such as fear, as well. In a study in 1919, Watson, with his colleague (and later wife) Rosalie Rayner, trained a young child (little Albert, age 1) to show a fear response in the presence of a white rat.

The experiment worked in this way: Albert was brought into the lab and showed no fear of the rat. During the conditioning phase, the rat was presented to Albert at the same time a metal bar was struck behind the child's head. The sound made by the metal bar surprised Albert, and he showed a fear response (crying, trying to move away from the rat, whimpering).

After six presentations of the rat and the noise simultaneously, Albert showed fear of the rat alone. In addition, he generalized the fear to include other white or fuzzy things, such as a Santa mask, a fur coat, and a rabbit. According to Watson, all human behavior is acquired in such a manner. In fact, according to Watson's 1913 paper, all that's needed to control human behavior is to control the environment surrounding humans.

OPERANT CONDITIONING

Behaviorism continued to be an important issue in psychology, but there was a shift in focus. Rather than try to understand behavior by examining the **antecedents** of behavior (what came before the behavior), the new direction examined the **consequences** of behavior.

One of the most influential psychologists during this movement was **B. F. Skinner**. In fact, it is probably correct to say the *most* influential psychologist at this time was Skinner. Skinner argued that, although Watson's ideas were important, some issues needed to be addressed. While classical conditioning explained some aspects of behavior quite well, he felt it didn't fully explain complex behavior. To do that, Skinner claimed we needed to look at the consequences of behavior rather than the precursors of behavior. Specifically, we needed to examine how the consequences of behavior serve to shape our behavior in the future.

According to Skinner's theory, two categories of consequences can follow behavior: reinforcement and punishment. **Reinforcement** is designed to increase the probability that a behavior will occur again. **Punishment** is designed to decrease the probability that a behavior will occur again.

Moreover, reinforcement and punishment can be administered in different ways. When something is given to an individual to serve as a reinforcer, it is called **positive reinforcement**. When something is removed from an individual to serve as a reinforcer, it is called **negative reinforcement**. The same is true for punishment.

Let's look at some examples that will clarify Skinner's theory:

	Give	Remove
Increases Behavior	**Positive Reinforcement** Giving stickers for grades Earning money for work Receiving candy for good behavior	**Negative Reinforcement** Taking an aspirin for a headache Putting on a seatbelt to turn off sound Buying a child candy so that she will stop crying
Decreases Behavior	**Positive Punishment** Spanking Verbally lecturing a child Assigning extra chores to a child	**Negative Punishment** Grounding a child Putting a child in "time out" Taking away privileges

Notice that **negative reinforcement** is reinforcement. It is designed to increase the probability of a behavior occurring again. To do this, we **remove an aversive stimulus**. Also, notice that **positive**

punishment is *not* good punishment but, rather, a form of punishment in which we **apply an aversive stimulus** to stop a behavior from occurring.

In addition, Skinner argued that we ought to be careful as to how we administer reinforcement and punishment. One goal of psychology, he felt, should be to predict and control human behavior. To do so, we need to understand completely the influence of reinforcement and punishment on behavior.

Punishment is something that ought to be used either very judiciously or not at all. If one does decide to use it, the punishment must be immediate, consistent, and severe enough actually to be punishing. If it is not, it will not serve as an effective controller of behavior. Punishment has some undesirable consequences as well, he felt. Spanking, for instance, is a popular form of punishment. But some research shows that the aggressive nature of punishment is often imitated by the person being punished. Thus, Skinner says one should use punishment sparingly.

As an alternative, Skinner proposed using reinforcement in an efficient way. Reinforcement does not need to be administered every time a behavior is emitted. If it can be administered on a schedule, people are likely to produce higher levels of behavior.

Let's look at the **schedules of reinforcement** below:

Fixed-Interval: Reinforce after a certain fixed amount of time has gone by	**Fixed-Ratio:** Reinforce after a certain fixed number of behaviors have been emitted
Examples: getting a paycheck every 2 weeks; watching a favorite show at the same time every day	*Examples*: getting paid for every 10 lawnmowers sold; getting money for every five A's on a report card
Variable-Interval: Reinforce after time has gone by, but the amount of time between reinforcers varies	**Variable-Ratio:** Reinforce after a number of behaviors have been emitted, but the number of behaviors required for reinforcement varies
Examples: getting phone calls at random times; getting a verbal reward for talking at unpredictable times	*Examples*: using a slot machine in a casino; getting a bonus based on sales

As you can see, there are many ways one can provide reinforcement for behavior. The schedule of reinforcement determines how resilient a behavior is. If a dog is reinforced on a fixed-ratio schedule and receives a treat every time it performs a behavior, it will perform the behavior until the reinforcement is stopped. Once the reinforcement is stopped, the behavior will stop (**extinction**). But if the dog is reinforced on a variable schedule, it will continue to behave even if the reinforcement is withheld for a fairly long period of time.

To develop behavior, lots of reinforcement should be given immediately and then faded over time. Such a process, called **shaping**, is essential in developing long-lasting behavior. We can also be reinforced vicariously (by watching others). Bandura showed in several studies that both reinforcement and punishment influence an observer's subsequent behavior (called imitative learning or **social learning**).

APPLICATIONS OF LEARNING

Learning theory has been hailed by many as the key to understanding human behavior. And, in fact, learning theory does explain a great deal of human behavior. If we assume these two points as true, then we must also assume that to understand human behavior, we need to understand the context in which behavior occurs. Human behavior does not occur in a vacuum. In fact, the context of human behavior is extraordinarily important in understanding why humans do the things they do.

Applying learning principles has been very helpful in the classroom. We have found that much of human behavior in the learning environment can be improved by controlling the environment in which that behavior occurs. So teachers can improve the learning of their students by controlling the environment in which the learning takes place. As with all other aspects of human learning, we know that if the environment is controlled, we can directly impact human behavior.

In the area of **autism** treatment, applied behavior analysis has been found to be very effective for helping those with this condition function in society more effectively. By doing a detailed analysis of behavior and fully examining the consequences of each individual behavior, we can better control the environment to bring about behavior change. In trying to understand how to develop linguistic skills in an autistic child, for instance, we could start by describing the child's environment in detail. Then, we could modify the environment appropriately to develop basic linguistic skills. This happens by providing small units of reinforcement for general approximations of the desired behavior.

In general, behaviorism or learning forms the basis of much of what we know about psychology. Understanding the basic principles of behaviorism and learning will help you develop a better appreciation for psychology.

REVIEW QUESTIONS

1. Every time a tone sounds, a participant has a puff of air blown into her eye. This causes the person to twitch. After a while, the participant twitches as soon as the tone sounds. The twitching that is caused by the air puff is called

   (A) the conditioned stimulus.
   (B) the unconditioned response.
   (C) the unconditioned stimulus.
   (D) the conditioned response.
   (E) habituation.

2. Every time Reynaldo does well on his report card, his parents take him out for ice cream. This is an example of

   (A) negative reinforcement.
   (B) negative punishment.
   (C) positive punishment.
   (D) habituation.
   (E) positive reinforcement.

3. Tammy is interested in helping her daughter learn manners. Each time her daughter says something that is close to appropriate, she rewards her. Eventually, her daughter should learn good manners. This is an example of

   (A) habituation.
   (B) positive reinforcement.
   (C) priming.
   (D) generalization.
   (E) shaping.

4. If a rat is provided with reinforcement after every 10 bar presses, the schedule is called

   (A) fixed-ordinal.
   (B) fixed-interval.
   (C) variable-interval.
   (D) fixed-ratio.
   (E) shaping.

5. An example of a fixed-interval schedule of reinforcement is

   (A) a dog getting a treat every time it sits on command.
   (B) winning money at a slot machine.
   (C) getting paid for each widget you sell.
   (D) being paid by the week.
   (E) getting a reward for good behavior once in a while.

6. Lilly is eating a hot dog. Shortly after eating the hot dog, she comes down with the flu. After this, Lilly hates eating hot dogs. Even the thought makes her sick. In this example, the flu is

   (A) generalized.
   (B) the unconditioned response.
   (C) the unconditioned stimulus.
   (D) the conditioned stimulus.
   (E) the consequence.

7. A boy is given candy each time he studies for an hour. Eventually, his parents observe an increase in studying behavior. This is an example of

   (A) positive reinforcement.
   (B) negative punishment.
   (C) positive punishment.
   (D) shaping.
   (E) negative reinforcement.

8. The tendency for stimuli similar to a conditioned stimulus to elicit the conditioned response is referred to as

    (A) response bias.
    (B) generalization.
    (C) extinction.
    (D) priming.
    (E) blocking.

9. According to Skinner, punishment is effective only under very specific conditions. Which of the following is one of these conditions?

    (A) The punishment is mild.
    (B) The punishment is delayed.
    (C) The punishment is threatened but not given.
    (D) The punishment immediately follows the behavior.
    (E) The punishment occurs on a variable schedule.

10. An example of positive punishment is

    (A) time out.
    (B) spanking.
    (C) taking away privileges.
    (D) removing chores.
    (E) giving candy.

11. An example of negative reinforcement is

    (A) receiving candy.
    (B) spanking.
    (C) taking away privileges.
    (D) removing chores.
    (E) time out.

12. One of the biggest differences between negative reinforcement and punishment is that

    (A) only punishment involves the use of aversive stimuli.
    (B) only negative reinforcement involves the use of aversive stimuli.
    (C) negative reinforcement increases the likelihood of a desired behavior.
    (D) punishment increases the likelihood of a desired behavior.
    (E) negative reinforcement decreases the likelihood of a desired behavior.

13. According to Skinner, the most important environmental aspect that controls human behavior is the

    (A) antecedents of the behavior.
    (B) consequences of the behavior.
    (C) strength of the behavior.
    (D) amount of punishment.
    (E) amount of reinforcement.

14. Witnessing the reinforcement of someone else's behavior has been found to increase the likelihood of that behavior in the witness. This is referred to as

    (A) visual capture.
    (B) shaping.
    (C) social learning.
    (D) habituation.
    (E) instinctual drift.

15. The person responsible for developing the framework of classical conditioning was

   (A) Pavlov.
   (B) Watson.
   (C) Skinner.
   (D) Bandura.
   (E) Erickson.

16. "One of the major problems with this approach is that it may reduce the likelihood of a behavior, but it doesn't teach the organism what to do instead." What principle is this criticism referring to?

   (A) Negative reinforcement
   (B) Positive reinforcement
   (C) Punishment
   (D) Modeling
   (E) Scaffolding

17. The psychologist who was responsible for developing the framework of operant conditioning was

   (A) Pavlov.
   (B) Skinner.
   (C) Watson.
   (D) Bandura.
   (E) Freud.

18. In a classic study, John Watson demonstrated that he could create fear in a child in response to a neutral stimulus (a rat). By pairing the rat with a fear-inducing stimulus (a loud noise), the child eventually became fearful of related stimuli. This is called

   (A) habituation.
   (B) spontaneous recovery.
   (C) unconditioned stimulus.
   (D) generalization.
   (E) shaping.

19. Classical conditioning and operant conditioning differ in that

   (A) classical conditioning deals with voluntary behavior.
   (B) operant conditioning deals with reflexive behavior.
   (C) classical conditioning deals with shaping.
   (D) classical conditioning deals with reflexive behavior.
   (E) operant conditioning does not work in most situations.

20. Getting paid a piecework at (x dollars per item made) is an example of

   (A) habituation.
   (B) fixed-ratio schedule of reinforcement.
   (C) variable-ratio schedule of reinforcement.
   (D) fixed-interval schedule of reinforcement.
   (E) variable-interval schedule of punishment.

ANSWERS AND EXPLANATIONS

1. B

The twitching that the air puff causes is the unconditioned response. The conditioned stimulus is the tone, the unconditioned stimulus is the puff of air, and the conditioned response is the twitching. Habituation, (E), is a decrease in attention due to a stimulus becoming familiar.

2. E

The ice cream would be considered positive reinforcement. Negative reinforcement, (A), leads to an increase in behavior by removing an aversive stimulus while negative punishment, (B), leads to a decrease in behavior by removing a desirable stimulus. Positive punishment, (C), leads to a decrease in behavior by applying an aversive stimuli.

3. E

This would be an example of shaping. Shaping refers to developing a behavior by reinforcing successive approximations to the target behavior. Habituation, (A), refers to becoming bored with a stimulus, and positive reinforcement, (B), occurs when something is provided that leads to an increase in behavior. Priming, (C), is a concept in cognitive psychology, and generalization, (D), occurs when an organism responds to a stimulus that is not exactly the originally learned stimulus.

4. D

If a rat were given reinforcement after every 10 bar presses, the schedule would be a fixed-ratio. Fixed-interval, (B), refers to receiving reinforcement after a fixed amount of time, and variable-interval, (C), refers to receiving reinforcement of different durations.

5. D

A fixed-interval schedule of reinforcement would be getting paid by the week. A dog getting a treat each time it sits on command, (A), would be a fixed-ratio. The other situations would be variable-ratios.

6. C

The flu is the unconditioned stimulus. Generalized, (A), refers to responding to stimuli that are similar to the original stimulus. The unconditioned response, (B), is getting sick, while the conditioned stimulus, (D), is the hot dog. The consequence, (E), here is getting sick.

7. A

If a boy is given candy for each hour that he studies, that is an example of positive reinforcement. A negative punishment, (B), occurs by removing something to decrease behavior, while positive punishment, (C), occurs by providing an aversive stimulus to stop behavior. Shaping, (D), occurs when we reward successive approximations to the target behavior, and negative reinforcement, (E), occurs when we reinforce by removing an aversive stimulus.

8. B

This would be called generalizaton. A response bias, (A), occurs when we respond only to one stimulus, extinction, (C), occurs when the connection between a behavior and its reinforcement is broken, priming, (D), is a concept in cognitive psychology, and blocking, (E), occurs when one reinforcement blocks another.

9. D

Skinner believed that punishment was effective only if it immediately followed a behavior. The other answer choices would actually *decrease* the effectiveness of the punishment.

10. B

Positive punishment would be spanking. Time out, removing privileges, and removing chores are forms of negative punishment because they remove something. Giving candy, of course, would be a potential positive reinforcement, (E).

11. D

Removing chores is a type of negative reinforcement. Receiving candy, (A), is an example of positive reinforcement, spanking, (B), is a type of positive punishment, taking away privileges, (C), is a negative punishment, and getting a time out, (E), is a type of negative punishment.

12. C

Negative reinforcement increases the likelihood of a desired behavior, while punishment does not.

13. B

Skinner believed that the consequences of a behavior had the most control over how a person behaved. The antecedents of behavior, (A), are important in classical conditioning. The strength of behavior, (C), is insignificant. The amount of reinforcement or punishment, (D and E), has no effect.

14. C

Social learning, often associated with Albert Bandura, means that behavior can be learned and reinforced simply by watching. A student who sees a fellow student get rewarded by a teacher for a particular behavior may then do a similar behavior. Shaping, (B), is a form of operant conditioning, while instinctual drift, (E), occurs when an organism behaves more in line with others of its species than its individual learning. The other terms are not involved with learning: visual capture, (A), is a perception process and habituation, and, (B), is decreased responsiveness after repeated exposure.

15. A

Pavlov developed the framework of classical conditioning. Watson, (B), used classical conditioning but did not coin the concepts. Skinner, (C), was important in the study of operant conditioning, Bandura, (D), described vicarious reinforcement, and Erickson, (E), studied child development.

16. C

Remember that reinforcement—whether positive or negative—makes a behavior *more* likely to occur, so neither (A) nor (B) can be correct. Modeling, (D), is a form of observational learning, and scaffolding, (E), is Vygotsky's term for helping students learn by ensuring that work is challenging but not too hard. Punishment, (C), is often criticized for stopping behavior but not teaching new behaviors; with punishment alone, a child might learn to stop throwing a tantrum for a toy, but not learn a more appropriate way to make that request.

17. B

Skinner developed the framework of operant conditioning. Freud, (E), was not a behaviorist.

18. D

The situation described is an example of generalization.

19. D

Classical conditioning deals with reflexive behavior, while operant conditioning does not. Operant conditioning deals with voluntary behavior.

20. B

Being paid by the item is a fixed-ratio schedule of reinforcement. A variable-ratio schedule, (C), gives reinforcement after a variable number of behaviors occur, a fixed-interval schedule, (D), provides reinforcement after a fixed amount of time goes by, and a variable-interval schedule, (E), provides reinforcement after a variable amount of time goes by.

CHAPTER 9:   COGNITION

IF YOU LEARN ONLY SIX THINGS IN THIS CHAPTER . . .

1. Cognition is the study of mental processes.

2. STM seems to be limited to 7±2 items at any given time.

3. The differences between encoding, storage, and retrieval are important.

4. Models of LTM deal with how we organize information that we know.

5. Problem solving involves applying what we know in an organized way to issues that we face.

6. Language is a complex system of communication that allows us to use complex symbols to talk about things in the past or the future, not just the present.

INTRODUCTION

One of the more recent areas of psychology to attract attention is **cognition**. This area has actually been around for most of the history of psychology, but only in the past 30 years has it taken on its modern form.

Chapter 3 on the history of psychology described the work of Wilhelm Wundt. Wundt was interested in the internal workings of the mind, specifically the way that consciousness is organized and structured. This idea is echoed in modern cognitive psychology as we focus on how our knowledge is organized. However, modern cognitive psychology has developed empirical techniques to study the organization of knowledge and memory.

In this chapter, we will discuss some of the modern conceptions of memory and how we have gone about studying these processes.

MEMORY

One of the early attempts at explaining memory broke the concept down into the following processes:

Sensory memory   Short-term memory (STM)   Long-term memory (LTM)

According to this model (often called the **Atkinson–Shiffrin** model and referred to generally as a **model of information processing**), information enters into a sensory memory for a brief period (typically described as 250 milliseconds). Information that we pay attention to is then moved to short-term memory (capacity about 7±2 items of information), where we elaborate on it, and it stays for only about 30 or 40 seconds. If we elaborate sufficiently, the information is then transferred to long-term memory.

Each process described above was thought to involve some underlying neurological process, but it was not specified at the time how the brain actually created this activity.

ENCODING

Memory involves three processes called **encoding, storage**, and **retrieval**. In short, these are the processes by which we get information in (encoding), hang on to it (storage), and then get it back out when we need it (retrieval).

Information from the environment is encoded when it enters the body through the senses. The three primary ways information is captured are by **visual encoding** (images), **acoustic encoding** (sounds), and **semantic encoding** (meanings). Visual encoding tends to be the most effective of the three, but the most effective way to successfully encode is to combine these: for example, learning the sounds and meanings of new words, or seeing pictures while a storyteller spins a tale. If we want to remember large amounts of information, our recall will be easier if we can use **chunking** to group information together. Remembering a 10-digit phone number is much easier if we remember in the pattern 3-3-4 rather than trying to recall ten unconnected numbers.

AP EXPERT TIP

Incorrect answers on a test can be explained as either encoding, storage, or retrieval problems.

STORAGE

Storage involves the previously mentioned sensory memory, short-term memory, and long-term memory. Short-term memory has a limit not only on the number of items it can hold but also on duration, since it appears to last for about 20 seconds or so. Psychologists today often refer to short-term memory as "working memory." So, when you recall something like a childhood birthday party, those memories are temporarily retrieved from storage and into this working memory. Memories much longer than 20 seconds are part of long-term memory, and we can use **rehearsal** to increase the likelihood that those memories will be recalled. Long-term memory is often divided into **explicit memories**, such as knowing the capital of Brazil, and **implicit memories**, such as remembering how to move your body when you are walking.

RETRIEVAL

When we talk about memory, we can't just talk about encoding. Encoding is, without a doubt, critical; after all, one cannot "remember" without first laying down a clear memory trace. But we must also talk about retrieval—without a good retrieval strategy, we can't get the information back out. The key to accessing information from long-term memory is to have an **appropriate retrieval cue**.

What acts as an effective retrieval cue? For one, what we are currently thinking about. The process has to do with the organization of long-term memory (to be discussed later), but for now, understand that long-term memory *is* in fact organized. We do not simply retrieve information in a happenstance way.

We often want to be more deliberate, rather than just rely on chance to remember things. When we put in a concerted effort to remember things, we often rely on **mnemonics**. A mnemonic is a memory aid. The range of devices that one can rely on is huge, but the one key component of a mnemonic is that it relies on a **reorganization of information** to allow for easier retrieval. Creating a song, for instance, can help us remember things for an exam, or creating a rhyme can help us remember the names of states. By helping us to develop a deeper level of processing, mnemonics allow us to elaborate on what we are trying to remember. The deeper level of processing allows for a better representation of the information.

Evidence also suggests that retrieval is better when the context in which we're trying to retrieve something matches the context in which it was learned. This is called **encoding specificity** or **transfer appropriate processing**. The idea is that when we learn something, the context is part of the overall memory. By reinstating that context when retrieval is occurring, we are creating an **optimal recall situation**.

ORGANIZATION

To understand how encoding, storage, and retrieval work, we must explore how semantic or long-term memory might be organized. It turns out, this is one area in cognitive psychology that has been examined more than most others.

The two biggest assumptions of long-term memory are that

1. capacity is unlimited; and
2. once the information gets into long-term memory, it is there forever.

To accommodate both assumptions, several models have been developed and tested by researchers.

In the most common model of long-term memory concepts are represented as nodes, and relationships between concepts are represented as links. The closer the two concepts are in terms of links, the more related they are.

Activation is the process of "thinking" about a concept. When we activate a node, that activation spreads down the links to related nodes. So if you think about college, classes might be the first thing that comes to mind, and then the other concepts might come to mind later.

Recently, psychologists have divided memory into what has been called explicit and implicit memory. **Explicit memory** is memory for information that you are aware of. **Implicit memory** is memory that influences your behavior but for which you have no conscious awareness. You might remember how to tie your shoes, but you don't necessarily remember when you learned to tie them. The implicit memory is that of the ability to tie the shoes, not the memory of actually learning the process. Implicit memory helps us in a variety of ways from "behind the scenes."

PROBLEM SOLVING

Cognitive psychologists are also interested in the concept of thinking and **problem solving**. In general, the study of problem solving is done by having people solve problems and then studying the strategies they use.

Heuristics are shortcuts to a solution, often used when we have expertise in an area. If we do mental arithmetic, we might rely on shortcuts based on our knowledge of math. **Algorithms** are approaches to problems that will definitely result in a correct solution. They are long—yet certain—approaches to a problem. By studying problem solving, psychologists are able to see *how* we use what we store.

The study of cognitive psychology and memory has come a long way in the past 30 years. We have developed models of memory that help us understand why people remember things, why people forget things, and why, sometimes, we need to work to learn things. In general, it is best to keep in mind that no matter how recent your textbook is, new information is constantly evolving about memory. It is one of the bigger areas of study today, and as we learn more and more about how the brain works, we will develop better and more complete models of memory.

WHAT IS LANGUAGE?

Language is a complex communication system that involves the use of **abstract symbols to convey unlimited messages**. By that definition, then, we have to leave out most of animal communication. There are limits to what animals can communicate to each other.

Human language, however, can convey meaning about things that haven't happened yet, things that happened in the past, and things that may never happen. Because we can transcend time and space with language, we have unlimited ability to communicate ideas.

How is language structured? According to many linguists and psycholinguists, language is a **multi-layered process**. We start with phonemes. A **phoneme** is the smallest unit of *sound* in a language. All the letters of the alphabet are phonemes (though there is some overlap—*c* can make the *k* or the *s* sound, for example). In English, we produce all the unique sounds that we are able to make by combining only about 40–50 unique phonemes. Other languages make do with less. Hawaiian has fewer than 30 phonemes.

The next level of language is the morpheme. According to linguists, **morphemes** are the smallest unit of *meaning* in a language. Small words, such as *cat* or *walk*, are morphemes. If we add the letter *s* to *cat*, we now have two morphemes (*cat*(*s*)), and if we add *-ing* to *walk*, we have two morphemes (*walk*(*ing*)). Many words are composed of a variety of morphemes combined to produce a unique meaning.

To be a language, there must be **grammar**, which refers to the system of rules that are used in a particular language. One of those sets of rules is called **semantics**, which is the way we understand meaning from words by their morphemes and from the context. We know that adding an *-s* to the end of a word means that we are referring to more than one, or we know that words can have different meanings depending on the placement in a sentence or on the context. "I'm dying!" has a very

AP EXPERT TIP

Following a recipe to bake a cake is an example of an algorithm.

different meaning when said by a person who is bleeding on the ground versus an adolescent preparing for her first middle school dance.

Another set of rules is called **syntax**. These rules refer to the way we order words to create meaning. "Your new please away shoes put" makes us confused, whereas "Please put away your new shoes" is quite clear. Different languages use syntax in different ways, so speakers of German normally use their main verbs at the end of a sentence, while in English, action words are almost always near the beginning.

HOW DO WE LEARN LANGUAGE?

Learning language is an issue that has been rife with controversy in psychology. The behavioral approach posits that we learn language the same way we learn anything else: We are **exposed to things in the environment, and if they are reinforced, we repeat the behavior**. Nativists, however, would argue that we are "**hardwired**" to learn language and that humans are unique in this respect. Both sides have their ardent supporters, and the evidence has not yet clearly settled the debate.

LANGUAGE ACQUISITION

According to linguist **Noam Chomsky**, language is learned by exposure to language, but the ability to speak is hardwired. That is, humans are born with the innate ability to speak, and the environment helps that skill emerge. Chomsky argues that the behavioral approaches do not take into account the fact that we learn language differently than we learn other things.

According to Chomsky, there is a **critical period** of language acquisition, and if we do not learn language during that time, we will not learn language well. There is overwhelming evidence to support this, yet Chomsky's argument about the speed with which we learn language may be overstated.

It is true that only humans learn language and that only humans learn to speak without being specifically taught language. However, human learning is more complex than simply learning connections between behavior and consequences. Often, reinforcement can be more subtle.

Suppose that, during a course of babbling, a child utters a sound that approximates a word. The parent will provide reinforcement for the utterance by praising the child. The word then becomes self-reinforcing. In such a way, words will continuously be added to the child's vocabulary.

Regardless of how a child actually learns language, the pattern of language acquisition is remarkably predictable.

Age	Milestone
Birth to 2 months	Cooing
2 months to 12 months	Babbling
Approximately 12 months	First word (typically a simple sound such as "da")
Approximately 16 months	Two-word utterances
2–6 years of age	Add 6–10 new words per day; learn grammar Overextension ("doggie" for every four-legged animal)
Age 5	Over-regularization: "I goed to the store."
From age 5 on	Add words to vocabulary; learn subtleties of language

This pattern is not predictable only in English. Other languages show the same pattern of language acquisition. In addition, children seem to follow the rules of language at about the same time. If children are told that they are looking at a "wug" and are then asked what one would say if there were two of these critters, they will say "wugs." Further, if they are told that a person will "wik," they will generate the forms "wiked" and "wiking." Thus, they seem to learn the rules that they can apply where appropriate.

LANGUAGE AND THOUGHT

A frequent debate arises in psychology over the relationship between language and thought: do our words shape the way we think, or do we have ideas first and then look for ways to articulate them? Linguist Benjamin Whorf believed it was the former; his theory of **linguistic determinism** said that our words shape and restrict our thinking. Many psychologists today have done research to show that while our language may not determine how we think, it may influence us. For example, the use of the word "he" when one means "he or she" makes one's reader far more likely to assume that the author is referring to a male.

LINGUISTIC UNIVERSALS

Children learn language in predictable ways, and, taken further, all languages across cultures have characteristics in common. There are, in fact, over a dozen linguistic universals. A few are presented here to illustrate the unique properties of human language.

ARBITRARINESS

Language is arbitrary. In other words, words are not inherently imbued with meaning. They are selected to stand for objects in the world in an arbitrary manner. *Dog* in English is *chien* in French.

Neither word is better than the other, but as speakers of English and French, we have agreed to call canines *dogs* and *chiens*, respectively.

DISPLACEMENT

Language allows us to talk about events that have already happened, events that will happen, and events that may not happen at all. No other form of communication allows for this.

VOCAL-AUDITORY CHANNEL

All languages in all cultures rely on the vocal-auditory channel as the primary form of communication using language. Other forms are possible, such as sign language, but these are used only in situations when the vocal-auditory channel is somehow compromised.

There are many more linguistic universals. However, this list represents some of the most important for distinguishing between human language and other forms of communication.

REVIEW QUESTIONS

1. When studying memory, we are often concerned with the process of getting information into the system. The process of getting information into short-term memory is called

   (A) retrieval.
   (B) storage.
   (C) encoding.
   (D) sensation.
   (E) perception.

2. According to memory research, the most important factor in memory performance is

   (A) retrieval cues.
   (B) storage capacity.
   (C) encoding context.
   (D) sensation of information.
   (E) perception of reality.

3. The capacity of short-term memory is

   (A) 2±3.
   (B) 5±1.
   (C) 3±2.
   (D) 9±2.
   (E) 7±2.

4. The stage that information first enters when it comes into the information processing system is called

   (A) short-term memory.
   (B) long-term memory.
   (C) encoding stage.
   (D) sensory memory.
   (E) working memory.

5. A student closes his eyes and listens to his teacher read a poem. He is struck by the rhythm of each line and the clever way the poet uses rhyme. This student is primarily using what kind of memory?

   (A) Explicit memory
   (B) Implicit memory
   (C) Visual encoding
   (D) Acoustic encoding
   (E) Semantic encoding

6. An example of explicit memory would be

   (A) learning how to type.
   (B) remembering your locker combination.
   (C) practicing a secret handshake with a friend.
   (D) jumping rope.
   (E) learning how to dance the rumba.

7. Ernie has to be able to list all of the presidents of the United States in chronological order for a history quiz. Using what he learned in AP Psychology, he broke the presidents down into groups of four, so that instead of remembering 44 names, he just learned 11 groups. This method of grouping items together to make them easier to remember is

   (A) chunking.
   (B) encoding.
   (C) storing.
   (D) retrieving.
   (E) cramming.

8. We recall information better when we try to remember it in the same situation as when we learned it. This concept is called

    (A) memory cue.
    (B) encoding specificity.
    (C) retrieval context.
    (D) spreading activation.
    (E) learning context.

9. Suppose you want to remember all the states. You decide that you are going to make up a song to help you. When you do this, you are using what psychologists call a(n)

    (A) mnemonic.
    (B) learning strategy.
    (C) encoding strategy.
    (D) retrieval strategy.
    (E) context cue.

10. What evidence suggests that memory is organized the way it is?

    (A) We say the word *nurse* faster after we see the word *desk*.
    (B) We say the word *doctor* faster after we see the word *nurse*.
    (C) We say *bread* slower after we see the word *butter*.
    (D) We say *pillow* slower after we see the word *couch*.
    (E) We say *computer* faster after we see the word *couch*.

11. Mnemonics help us to remember things more efficiently because they

    (A) provide a catchy tune.
    (B) provide us with instant, photographic memory of information.
    (C) provide us with organization for recall.
    (D) provide us with context.
    (E) provide us with a bigger short-term memory.

12. Dina is frustrated because her teacher just called on her and she couldn't think of the answer. She isn't frustrated because she didn't know the answer, but because she had been studying for several days and had practiced that answer several times—it just wouldn't come to her mind in class. This is most likely an error in what memory system?

    (A) Retrieval
    (B) Encoding
    (C) Storage
    (D) The primacy effect
    (E) The recency effect

13. An example of a task that might lead to poor memory would be

    (A) trying to fit a word into a sentence.
    (B) learning all the names of the children in a class.
    (C) associating words with images that they represent.
    (D) saying the number of letters in a word.
    (E) trying to rhyme a word with a nonword.

14. Short-term memory has a capacity that is

    (A) small.
    (B) large.
    (C) unlimited.
    (D) 6±2 digits.
    (E) variable by individual.

15. Which level is considered to represent the smallest unit of sound in a language?

    (A) Semantic
    (B) Lexical
    (C) Morphemic
    (D) Phonemic
    (E) Syntactic

16. "Curious blue ideas sleep furiously" is a famous statement by a linguist to argue that sentences can be proper but still not make sense. At what level is this sentence ambiguous?

    (A) Semantic
    (B) Lexical
    (C) Syntactic
    (D) Phonemic
    (E) Morphemic

17. The final stage of the information processing model is

    (A) sensory memory.
    (B) attention.
    (C) long-term memory.
    (D) short-term memory.
    (E) working memory.

18. Someone is currently paying attention to something. In what stage of information processing is this person?

    (A) Sensory memory
    (B) Attention
    (C) Long-term memory
    (D) Short-term memory
    (E) Explicit memory

19. The idea that information is better recalled when the encoding context matches the retrieval context is called the

    (A) encoding specificity.
    (B) mnemonics.
    (C) retrieval cue.
    (D) cognitive cue.
    (E) spreading activation.

20. The difference between the cognitive and behavioral perspective on language acquisition is

    (A) the timing of the onset of language.
    (B) the idea that there are differences between boys and girls.
    (C) the time course of language acquisition.
    (D) the source: the environment versus being hardwired.
    (E) none; both are talking about the same process, using different words.

ANSWERS AND EXPLANATIONS

1. C

Encoding is the process of getting information into short-term memory. Retrieval, (A), is extracting information from long-term memory, storage, (B), is saving information for later, and sensation, (D), and perception, (E), refer to the process of taking in information and translating it into a code that we can understand.

2. C

According to memory researchers, encoding is the most important process in memory. Retrieval cues, (A), can help, but not without good encoding. Sensation of information, (D), simply means information entering the system. Perception of reality, (E), refers to how we see the world, but it is a concept more closely associated with the study of personality.

3. E

The capacity of short-term memory is 7±2. The other choices do not represent the capacity as has been demonstrated by several studies, most notably by Miller in 1956.

4. D

Information first enters sensory memory when it is processed. The encoding stage, (C), is a term not used in cognitive psychology, and working memory, (E), is another term for short-term memory.

5. D

When the focus is on sound, the answer has to be that the information is being acoustically encoded. Many of us can recall the sounds of laughter, songs, and the voices of loved ones. These are examples of acoustically encoded memories. There is no image, so visual encoding, (C), cannot be correct. Semantic encoding, (E), is also incorrect because he is listening just to the sounds, not to their meanings. Implicit and explicit memories are part of long-term memory.

6. B

Remembering your locker combination is an example of explicit memory. The other tasks are all implicit memory tasks—they require a memory for how to do something, not a memory for some specific fact.

7. A

Chunking allows anyone with a terrific memory—or anyone who wants to have one—to make the memorizing process easier because, as Ernie discovered, you will have fewer things to remember if you group them together. This is a reason why many of the numbers that we need to remember in our lives (like telephone and Social Security numbers) are conveniently issued to us with numbers already chunked together in groups. Encoding, (B), storing, (C), and retrieving, (D), are the three basic processes of memory, whereas cramming, (E), involves attempting to remember a vast amount of information in a short period of time (and is often ineffective).

8. B

The concept is called encoding specificity. A memory cue, (A), might help, but the concept is not specific enough. Neither is retrieval context, (C). Spreading activation, (D), refers to the process of searching memory. Learning context, (E), is not an appropriate term in cognitive psychology.

9. A

A mnemonic is a learning tool for memorization. Learning strategy, (B), is a general term, but mnemonic is more specific. The same goes for encoding, (C), and retrieval strategy, (D). Context cue, (E), is not an appropriate term in cognitive psychology.

10. B

Saying the word *doctor* faster after we see the word *nurse* explains how memory is organized.

11. C

Mnemonics provide us with organization for recall. They do not rely completely on appropriate context, (D), or on creating a larger short-term memory, (E).

12. A

The problem here is not that Dina never learned the information, but that she just could not get it out at the right time. This is clearly an error of retrieval. Psychologists often refer to this as the "tip of the tongue" problem, where the memory feels so close yet you still cannot retrieve it. This could not have been an error of encoding, (B), because she had been exposed to the answer. It is also not a problem of storage, (C), since she had been studying for several days to remember it. The primacy and recency effects, (D and E), would come into play only if she were trying to remember a list of words, and there is no information in the question about a list.

13. D

Saying the number of letters in a word could lead to poor memory. Learning the names of the children in a class, (B), leads to a deeper level of processing than just trying to say the number of letters. Association, (C), and rhyming, (E), both lead to deeper levels as

well; to complete these tasks, work needs to be done on the words. Trying to fit a word into a sentence, (A), is a deep level of processing.

14. A

Short-term memory is a small-capacity system (7±2) consistently across participants.

15. D

The phonemic level of language represents the smallest units of sound in a language. We often combine these sounds in ways to produce longer, more complex sounds that represent words.

16. A

According to any analysis of language, this sentence is a good one. It is syntactically correct (words in the right order), lexically correct (the words mean something), phonemically correct (the sounds are appropriate), and morphemically correct (the words are put together correctly). The problem is with the interpretation of the sentence. It does not make sense as it is written. The sentence doesn't make sense at the semantic level.

17. C

Long-term memory is the final stage in information processing. Working memory, (E), is another term for short-term memory.

18. D

For something that is currently being focused on, short-term memory is at work. Sensory memory, (A), is the first stage in the system, attention, (B), helps focus information into short-term memory, and both long-term, (C), and explicit memory, (E), are long-term storage systems.

19. A

Encoding specificity describes the idea that information is recalled better when the encoding and retrieval context match. Retrieval cues, (C), help with memory, but encoding specificity is more specific. Cognitive cue, (D), is a very generic term used in cognitive psychology, and spreading activation, (E), is the process of searching long-term memory.

20. D

The main difference between cognitive and behavioral perspectives boils down to the source—behavioral psychologists argue that language is very similar to other behaviors, whereas cognitive psychologists argue that language may be "hardwired" and that we apply the rules we have learned to the input we receive during a critical period.

CHAPTER 10: MOTIVATION AND EMOTION

IF YOU LEARN ONLY FOUR THINGS IN THIS CHAPTER . . .

1. Human motivation is complex, and while there are a number of theories, none by itself sufficiently explains our behavior.

2. Biological motivation includes the role of the hypothalamus, which maintains a state called homeostasis.

3. Theories of social motivation, including the need for achievement and the hierarchy of needs, show the importance of understanding motivation in the context of our environments.

4. Emotions can be explained through a variety of theoretical perspectives, each arguing that emotion emerges in conjunction with physiological response to stimuli.

INTRODUCTION

Everyone knows what motivation is: It is the drive to begin or maintain behavior. Students are keenly aware that being motivated to do something can have great significance. Preparing for the AP Psychology exam, for instance, is something that is better done early in the year and with great frequency.

For most of us, however, it is not easy to become motivated when the consequences of our behavior are distal rather than proximal. If we think we have time to do something, we will use up as much time as possible before we start doing it.

Humans have long been interested in trying to determine ways to improve motivation. But since we don't completely understand the process, it is difficult to manipulate.

First we will review theories of motivation, and then look at the biological and social aspects of motivation.

THEORIES OF MOTIVATION

One of the oldest theories of motivation is that of **instincts**, which comes from the field that we know today as **evolutionary psychology**. Following the ideas of Charles Darwin, this theory suggests that human behavior is driven by innate instinctual drives like those of other animals, such as the nest-building and spawning behaviors that are inherited tendencies for some birds and fish. However, this theory soon revealed its limitations in that it could only describe the behavior of humans but not provide an explanation.

Another theory, which comes from the work of Clark Hull in the 1940s, suggested that human behavior could be explained by what he called **drive-reduction theory**. Hull stated that humans have innate biological needs (for example, thirst) and social needs (for example, love), and that drives compel us to satisfy our needs. A person who realizes she is thirsty (a need) then feels an internal motivation (the drive) to find water to satisfy that need.

Incentive theory offers a counter to drive-reduction theory, in that we are not pushed internally by needs but are pulled from the outside by external **incentives**. For example, if we walk by a bakery, the aroma of bread or the sight of freshly baked loaves may entice us inside whether or not we are hungry.

Finally, we may also be driven by intrinsic and extrinsic motivation. A boy who plays the violin for four hours a day simply to excel is driven by **intrinsic motivation**, but if those practice sessions are motivated by external rewards such as winning a competition or gaining admiration from his parents, then this is **extrinsic motivation**.

BIOLOGICAL MOTIVATION

The **hypothalamus** is the region of the brain most often associated with motivation. It plays an important role in the motivation for **feeding, fighting, fleeing**, and **sexual reproduction**. Research has shown, for instance, that if we lesion the **lateral hypothalamus** in a rat, the rat will lose its appetite. The rat will experience a form of anorexia in which it will not be hungry and, therefore, will not eat. Thus, we believe that the lateral hypothalamus provides motivation for hunger or feeding.

We also know that the **ventromedial hypothalamus** is important in eating behavior. The ventromedial hypothalamus seems to be the satiety center (the part of the brain that tells you that you're full). If we lesion the ventromedial hypothalamus, the rat will not feel full and will continue to eat well beyond what is normally expected. Thus, we can clearly see the motivation in the biological structure of the brain for this behavior.

One of the most important concepts in biological motivation is that of **homeostasis**, the tendency of all organisms to maintain a balanced state. When we are too cold, the hypothalamus releases hormones that cause us to shiver and seek out warmth or put on clothing. When we have not had enough sleep, we are likewise pushed to slow down as we yawn and struggle to keep our eyes open. Homeostasis helps us to return to this balance when we deviate from our normal state.

SOCIAL MOTIVATION

In the 1950s, psychologist David McClelland explored what motivated humans to challenge themselves, particularly in relation to others. He developed a theory called **need for achievement** in which he used experimental data based on participants' descriptions of ambiguous pictures to support his claims. In longitudinal studies, McClelland found that subjects who scored high on tests of achievement were more likely to be entrepreneurs. Other theories of social motivation claim that fear can be a very powerful motivator, with some humans being driven by a fear of failure while others are more afraid of success.

One way that we can provide motivation for ourselves is to delay gratification by holding off on a reward until after we perform some less desirable activity. This is called the Premack principle, and it can be applied in many social situations. It is a form of social reinforcement that has been shown to be very effective.

MASLOW'S HIERARCHY OF NEEDS

Abraham Maslow argued that humans were driven not by a need for achievement but by a need to become **self-actualized**, which means to reach one's own unique potential. Maslow's **hierarchy of needs** theory suggests, however, that before individuals can concern themselves with self-actualization they must first take care of more basic fundamental needs (such as hunger and thirst) and psychological needs (such as love and self-esteem).

EMOTIONS

A concept related to motivation is that of emotions. Psychologists have long asked what causes emotions and even what are emotions. We know that there is consistency among cultures in terms of how we express emotions facially. For example, research has shown that fear is identifiable in faces regardless of culture. What we do not know, however, is how emotions are generated. There are several debated theories about emotion. They are summarized as follows:

James–Lange theory	We have a physiological response and we label it as an emotion: "I see a bear, my muscles tense, I feel afraid."
Cannon–Bard theory	We have an emotional response and we feel the physiological response: "I see a bear, I feel afraid, my muscles tense."
Schacter–Singer theory	We experience feelings and then label them: "I feel bad. I must be scared."
Cognitive appraisal	When there is no physiological arousal, we experience something, we think about it, we label it as an emotion.

As you can see, emotions are difficult to understand. We assume they are physiological at some level, but there is often a cognitive component. However, unlike other cognitions, emotions are not directly under our control (jealousy, for example). So we are left with an experience that is very common but difficult to explain—just like much of psychology.

REVIEW QUESTIONS

1. Assume you hate your job yet you continue to work there. When someone asks why you stay at your job, you say it is because of the money. What might explain this?

   (A) Intrinsic motivation
   (B) Positive punishment
   (C) Groupthink
   (D) Extrinsic motivation
   (E) Negative punishment

2. An animal experiences an injury to its head. it then starts to eat uncontrollably. What part of the brain is probably injured?

   (A) Lateral hypothalamus
   (B) Lateral geniculate nucleus
   (C) Thalamus
   (D) Ventromedial hypothalamus
   (E) Temporal lobe

3. Which part of the brain is responsible for biologically driven motivational processes?

   (A) Thalamus
   (B) Hippocampus
   (C) Limbic system
   (D) Temporal lobe
   (E) Hypothalamus

4. Which part of the brain is responsible for an animal who will not eat at all?

   (A) Lateral hypothalamus
   (B) Lateral geniculate nucleus
   (C) Thalamus
   (D) Ventromedial hypothalamus
   (E) Temporal lobe

5. "I love my job for the sake of doing the work itself." The person making this statement is motivated by

   (A) intrinsic motivation.
   (B) positive punishment.
   (C) groupthink.
   (D) extrinsic motivation.
   (E) negative punishment.

6. An example of intrinsic motivation is

   (A) I exercise because I get a dollar for each pound I lose.
   (B) I exercise because it makes me feel good.
   (C) I exercise because people say I look good.
   (D) I exercise because my clothes look better on me.
   (E) I exercise because others do it and I want to fit in.

7. Assume you want to study more. What could you do to improve your motivation?

   (A) Set small goals.
   (B) Set large goals.
   (C) Work until you believe you have completed what you need to.
   (D) Tell yourself how important it is to study.
   (E) Forget about goals; motivation is simply mind over matter.

8. "Motivation can be described as positive reinforcement." This statement might have been said by

   (A) Carl Rogers.
   (B) B. F. Skinner.
   (C) Sigmund Freud.
   (D) Wilhelm Wundt.
   (E) William James.

9. If we were interested in controlling motivation from the perspective of a behavioral psychologist, we would provide

    (A) positive punishment.
    (B) shaping procedures.
    (C) positive reinforcement.
    (D) extinction procedures.
    (E) negative reinforcement only.

10. A psychologist who wanted to explore the role of motivation by examining how individuals compete with others in their environment would be following the _____ perspective.

    (A) behavioral
    (B) biological
    (C) psychoanalytic
    (D) sociocultural
    (E) cognitive

11. According to Maslow's hierarchy of needs, only after people have taken care of their physiological and psychological needs can they aspire to fulfill their _____ needs.

    (A) hunger
    (B) thirst
    (C) self-esteem
    (D) self-actualization
    (E) belongingness

12. David McClelland studied the need for achievement by asking the participants in his experiments to

    (A) make up a story about an ambiguous picture.
    (B) solve a series of complicated logic puzzles.
    (C) compete against others in physical challenges.
    (D) invent new ways to use a common object such as a hammer.
    (E) play a strategy game against a computerized opponent.

13. What concept is often illustrated using the example of a room thermostat, because its function is to maintain a "steady state" in areas such as body temperature and hunger?

    (A) Instinct
    (B) Homeostasis
    (C) Need
    (D) Incentive
    (E) Extrinsic motivation

14. To motivate ourselves, we sometimes set a goal. Suppose we think, "For every 50 minutes that I study, I'll talk to my friends for 10 minutes." What theory does this describe?

    (A) Gestalt principles
    (B) Cocktail party effect
    (C) Premack principle
    (D) Freudian psychology
    (E) Jungian symbology

15. "I read because I enjoy learning about new things." This is an example of

    (A) intrinsic motivation.
    (B) positive punishment.
    (C) groupthink.
    (D) extrinsic motivation.
    (E) negative punishment.

16. Suppose you are walking through a food court in the mall and you see a new cafe offering an Indian food buffet. At first glance the food looks delicious, and as you get closer you can smell the wonderful aromas of the food. The sight and smell of the food is referred to as a(n)

    (A) need.
    (B) drive.
    (C) instinct.
    (D) incentive.
    (E) intrinsic motivation.

17. Kayla really wants her son to become an excellent golfer, so she has created a system of rewards for him in which he earns money for each round he plays. Which form of motivation is Kayla using?

    (A) Classical conditioning
    (B) Drive
    (C) Homeostasis
    (D) Intrinsic motivation
    (E) Extrinsic motivation

18. Suppose you would be given pizza if you read a certain number of books. Such a motivation would be described by a behavioral psychologist as

    (A) negative reinforcement.
    (B) shaping.
    (C) positive reinforcement.
    (D) negative punishment.
    (E) positive punishment.

19. How could you increase your motivation to study for the AP Psychology exam?

    (A) Give yourself a reward for each chapter you read.
    (B) Give yourself a reward for studying when you take the test.
    (C) Give yourself a reward for studying before you start studying for the test.
    (D) Take away chores when you are done studying.
    (E) Take away chores when you study for one month.

20. Abby wants to motivate Sammi to pick up her clothing every night. In order to do this, she provides positive reinforcement in the form of praise. Which of the following is this an example of?

    (A) Classical conditioning
    (B) Operant conditioning
    (C) Drive reduction
    (D) Intrinsic motivation
    (E) Homeostasis

ANSWERS AND EXPLANATIONS

1. D

If you were unhappy at work but continued to stay for the financial reward, that would be extrinsic motivation at work. Something is extrinsically motivating if it causes you to do an activity because of an external reward. In this situation, the money you earn is the external motivator that propels you to stay at the job, regardless of how you feel about it.

2. D

If an animal were injured and then began to eat a lot, the ventromedial hypothalamus would likely have been affected. Injury to this region damages the satiety center (the part of the brain that tells us that we are full). So an animal who has this type of damage does not have the signals to tell it that it's full. It will continue to eat until it can't eat any longer.

3. E

The hypothalamus is responsible for motivation in biologically driven behavior, such as feeding, fleeing, and so on. The other structures in the brain are important and do play a role in some aspects of motivation (the limbic system, for example, plays a role in sexual reproduction), but the hypothalamus alone is essential for biological motivation.

4. A

Damage to the lateral hypothalamus will result in a sharp downturn in the animal's motivation to eat. The animal will not feel hungry or motivated to eat and will not behave for a food reinforcer.

5. A

A person who loves her job for the sake of the work has intrinsic motivation—a drive from within. Some would argue that it is a subtle form of reinforcement, but essentially, intrinsic motivation is important because it is much less susceptible to extinction than extrinsic motivation. With extrinsic motivation, when the reinforcer is dropped, the behavior will often slow down or stop.

6. B

Intrinsic motivation occurs when we are motivated to behave because of internal processes. Feeling good about oneself is an intrinsic process.

7. A

If you wanted to study more, you could set small, achievable goals. This is the way to use goal setting appropriately. If the goals are too large or if they are not clearly specified, it is far more difficult to know when they have been achieved. Thus, motivation will drop off.

8. B

Skinner argued that motivation is nothing more than appropriately constructed positive and negative reinforcements. To be motivated, according to Skinner, is to develop a behavior that is clearly under stimulus control.

9. C

To create a situation in which we have strong motivation, we can use positive or negative reinforcement to increase the relationship between behavior and consequence.

10. D

While motivation can be seen from the other perspectives, only the sociocultural perspective, (D), would examine motivation in the context of others. Studies have shown that the influence of other people may at times influence us to work harder or even work less, depending on the circumstances. Behavioral, (A), might involve other people, but would focus on how behaviors are reinforced or punished. The other choices are all perspectives but are not involved in viewing individuals in the context of their environments.

11. D

Maslow's hierarchy is an important concept because it suggests that it is difficult to expect people to reach their potential when they are struggling to take care of their minimal physiological (hunger and thirst) and psychological (self-esteem and belongingness) needs. It would be hard to believe that someone who has to worry on a regular basis about having enough food to eat and a safe place to sleep, for example, would be able to focus on becoming self-actualized.

12. D

While all of the other choices are ways that motivation could be studied, only the use of ambiguous pictures, (D), was utilized by McClelland. Participants were asked to tell stories about what was happening in the pictures, and McClelland and his colleagues rated them as to how often themes of achievement were present. One criticism of this approach is the reliability of this scoring system, because raters would not always agree on the score for a response.

13. B

Homeostasis is the internal process that the hypothalamus uses to bring us back in balance when we drift too far from the norm, just as a thermostat in a room might signal the heating system to send out warmer air when the temperature plunges. The other terms are all important in understanding motivation, but none is involved in the homeostatic process. An instinct, (A), is a fixed action pattern, a need, (C), is required for survival or growth, an incentive, (D), entices an organism, and extrinsic motivation, (E), refers to external rewards for actions.

14. C

The Premack principle is a form of self-reinforcement. It states that we should develop goals that are achievable, and by setting a reinforcer that will be given once the goal is met. So you can tell a child, "If you complete your homework, you can play outside." This desired reinforcer helps motivate the child to engage in the appropriate behavior.

15. A

Reading because one enjoys learning new things is an intrinsic motivator. There is no external reinforcer causing the behavior to occur. The pleasure of reading comes from within the person.

16. D

Incentives are those external "pulls" used by restaurants and many other businesses to tempt you and motivate you to buy their products. While needs, drives, and instincts would all be involved in important life processes, an incentive might motivate you to do something unnecessary, such as eating when you might not be hungry. Intrinsic motivation, (E), refers to internal and personal reasons that motivate you, as opposed to external rewards. Each of the other choices is part of motivation but does not involve the enticement that is evoked by an incentive.

17. E

Extrinsic motivation is providing outside or external rewards to motivate behavior. Note that both extrinsic and external begin with "ext," so that pattern should help you keep intrinsic and extrinsic straight. Studies have shown that while extrinsic motivation may be effective under certain circumstances, in the long run it may fail to motivate behavior, particularly if the external motivation is not present. If Kayla decides to stop paying her son, he may stop playing if the money is his only motivation.

18. C

Giving a reward, such as pizza, for reading books is a common technique used by educators to increase reading. They provide the reader with positive reinforcement for the behavior of reading.

19. A

Finishing a chapter is a good goal to set because it is reasonable, achievable, and clearly defined.

20. B

This is a clear example of positive reinforcement being used as a means of providing motivation for Sammi. There is no other answer that involves using a consequence to control behavior.

CHAPTER 11: DEVELOPMENTAL PSYCHOLOGY

IF YOU LEARN ONLY FIVE THINGS IN THIS CHAPTER . . .

1. Cognitive development refers to the ways in which our ability to think and reason change over our life spans.

2. Two theorists important in the area of cognitive development are Jean Piaget and Lev Vygotsky.

3. Social development refers to the changes in our ability to interact with others as we age.

4. Our primary caregiver provides us with our earliest social cues.

5. The stages of prenatal development

INTRODUCTION

Development is the study of how people change over their life span. Typically, psychologists are concerned with three forms of development: physical, social, and cognitive.

Naturally, development occurs throughout the life span, though most psychology texts focus mostly on child development. In this chapter, we will adopt a similar strategy and deal mostly with child development.

PHYSICAL DEVELOPMENT

Children develop according to a fairly well-understood pattern of development. Here is a table that describes a typical pathway of prenatal development.

Major Events of Prenatal Development

Weeks 1 and 2

Fertilization and formation of zygote (30 hours)

Formation of blastocyst (day 4)

Attachment of blastocyst (5–8 days)

Appearance of amniotic cavity (day 8)

Week 3

Development of neural tube (day 18)

Beginning of blood circulation (day 24)

Possible abnormal events:

  Twins

  Teratogens (foreign substances that influence the developing fetus) are very damaging from week 3 to week 8

Weeks 4–8

Formation of head, tail, and lateral folds

Formation of primitive gut

Heart moves to normal position

Appearances of brain, limbs, ears, eyes, and nose

Development of humanlike appearance

Weeks 9–12

Fetal head makes up 1/2 of fetal body

Eyelids fused

Upper limbs develop to normal proportions

Male and female genitalia recognizable by 12 weeks

Weeks 13–16

Rapid fetal growth

Fetus doubles in size

Kidneys secrete urine

Fetus appears human

Placenta is fully formed

Weeks 17–23

Fetal growth slows

Lower limbs fully formed

Fetal movement starts at 20 weeks

Fetal heartbeat begins

Weeks 24–27

Skin growth is rapid

Eyes open

Fetus is viable at 27 weeks

Weeks 28–31

Weight gain is steady

Fetus has a good chance of survival

Weeks 32–36

Weight gain is steady

Fetus has a good chance of survival

Weeks 37–40

Fingernails and toenails grow

Skull is fully developed

Fetus is ready for birth

Brain development occurs during the entire process. The brain starts to develop early (around four weeks) and continues to develop both neurons and connections for the entire gestation period. However, once birth occurs, neural development slows down (some argue that it stops), and **pruning** occurs. During pruning, connections are made among cells, and connections that are redundant are "trimmed."

After birth, other major **maturation** milestones include sitting up (by seven months), walking (one year), running (18 months to two years), and fine motor control (2–4 years). There is a great deal of variability in when children reach these milestones, but these are general guidelines.

Physical development continues throughout the life span, but little attention has been paid to development after puberty in the research literature.

SOCIAL DEVELOPMENT

During the formative years, children are learning much about how to navigate the world. How to get along in a social environment is one of the many important issues that children learn. **Attachment theory** has been proposed as one way to understand social development.

According to **Bowlby and Ainsworth**, children develop an attachment style to their primary caregiver early in development. Attachment leads to an internal working model for relationships later on. Attachment is an emotional and cognitive set of behaviors that are tested through the strange situation.

In the **strange situation**, a child around age 1 is brought into the laboratory with the primary caregiver. The child is provided with toys and other distractions. After a short time, the experiment starts. The child is left in the room under a variety of conditions. First, the child is alone. Then, the researcher comes in. Finally, the primary caregiver is brought back in. The key to understanding attachment is to examine the **reunion** between the parent and the child.

If the child is upset but can be calmed, the child is said to be securely attached. This suggests that the child uses the parent as a safe base to explore the environment. The child can return if there is trouble or if he is upset. If a child is unable to be comforted or is violent or distant upon return, he may be insecurely attached.

These styles have been shown to be related to later relationships. Children who are insecurely attached have more difficulty trusting others later in life. Securely attached people tend to be more comfortable in relationships.

COGNITIVE DEVELOPMENT

One of the pioneers in developmental psychology is **Jean Piaget**. Piaget noticed that his children were able to handle logical problems differently at different ages. Further, he noticed that as children age, their ability to handle logical problems changes. Piaget then spent years studying how cognitive development occurred on average. From this intensive study, Piaget developed a theory of cognitive development that described how people are able to deal with logical problems differently at different points in their lives.

According to Piaget, the most important issue that children are concerned with is adapting to their environment (a process he calls **adaptation**). To adapt, children use different strategies at different ages. This accommodation process relies on the notion that we develop a series of **schemas** (or schemes or schemata) to ease the adaptation process.

A schema is an organized body of knowledge. It can be knowledge based or action based. Most people have organized schemas for going to a restaurant, for instance. They understand that we enter a restaurant, get seated, order drinks, and so on. This schema allows people to know what to do when they enter that situation.

Schemas are not part of the inborn knowledge structures of children. Schemas need to be developed through experience. The process of developing a new schema is called **accommodation**. Early in life, children spend a great deal of time developing schemas, or accommodating. It is essential that the developmental process of accommodation happen early so that children have appropriate schemas to know appropriate actions.

Once we develop schemas, we spend a lot of time fitting new experiences into existing schemas. That process is called **assimilation**. If we have a schema for going to a restaurant and we enter a new restaurant, we typically know the correct set of behavior or actions. Piaget argues that we both accommodate and assimilate throughout life.

STAGE THEORY

According to Piaget, we go through a variety of stages on our way to cognitive development. All human beings pass the stages in a fixed and invariant way. That is, we all go through the stages in the same order, and we all go through *all* the stages during our life span.

STAGE 1: SENSORIMOTOR

The sensorimotor stage is the first stage in development. Children are typically in this stage from birth to around 18 months (the age can vary, but the order does not). During this stage, a child's responses are entirely sensory and motor. That is, the child will receive information from her senses, and the responses to those stimuli are purely motor. Children seem to operate in the here-and-now and do not seem to plan or think about the consequences of behavior. On average, children

do not seem to engage in internal representation until the end of this stage. In fact, children don't even recognize that an object is still present when the object is no longer in their visual field. Piaget referred to this as a lack of **object permanence**, a concept that would be acquired in Stage 2. This lack, though, is why peekaboo is such a fun game for babies, but is no longer interesting for toddlers.

STAGE 2: PREOPERATIONAL

The preoperational stage lasts from around age 2 to 6. A child goes through a period of rapid intellectual growth. Language is learned, and through that process, many intellectual skills needed later in life are learned as well—internal representation, for instance, is learned, as evidenced by children's ability to engage in creative or imaginative play.

One of the main skills that children in the preoperational stage still lack is a term Piaget called **conservation**, the principle that things stay the same no matter if the form changes. For example, when adults pour liquid from a short, wide glass to a tall, narrow glass, they notice that the height of the liquid is greater in the tall glass, but they also understand that the amount of liquid remained constant, so the volume in each glass is the same. Children in Stage 2 are quite confident in their answer that there is now "more" in the taller glass. This lack of conservation also can be seen in length, mass, and number, as well as volume.

STAGE 3: CONCRETE OPERATIONAL

Concrete operational children, aged 6 to 12, develop quite comprehensive logical skills. They are in school, learning many of the building blocks for higher-level intellectual functioning. Children acquire logical skills, learn how to engage in organized problem solving, and so on.

During this stage, children develop a great number of schemas, and they spend much of the time assimilating into those existing schemas. Children do not have complete, higher-level cognitive structures, but they are far beyond the first two stages.

STAGE 4: FORMAL OPERATIONAL

The formal operational stage of cognitive development is the highest level of cognitive development. According to Piaget, children enter this stage around age 12, and it is at this time that they develop high-level logical skills. They become able to solve problems in a systematic way, use reversibility, etc. This stage is the pinnacle of cognitive development.

Piaget's theory is one of the most well-known theories of cognitive development, but there are critics. For one, some believe that Piaget greatly underestimated children's skills on one end and greatly overestimated their skills at the other end. Several researchers rephrased Piagetian tasks and found that younger children were able to understand the questions and respond appropriately. In addition, the children seemed to have internal representation prior to preoperational ages.

And on the other end, another researcher gave a variety of Piagetian tasks to college freshmen and found that only 40 percent of them displayed characteristics of formal operations. Of course, 100 percent should have been in formal operations, according to Piaget. So perhaps children enter formal operations later in life.

Lev Vygotsky

An alternative approach to cognitive development was espoused by Lev Vygotsky. Vygotsky did not agree with Piaget that children moved through stages of cognitive development in an orderly fashion. Rather, he believed that **children learn according to their own schedule**.

Children seem to have a range of abilities under which they are able to operate. By following an adult's example, they eventually develop the ability to do certain tasks alone. The **zone of proximal development (ZPD)** defines the gap (difference) between what a child can do without help and what he can do only with support. We can use a process called **scaffolding** to help children move their ZPD. If children are moving forward in cognitive development, the ZPD needs to change. Scaffolding helps children build higher-level cognitive functioning by isolating the ZPD and providing the assistance to allow children to solve more complex problems.

Although Vygotsky's theory is not as structured as Piaget's, it provides an alternative explanation for cognitive development. Many have argued that Vygotsky's theory provides a better fit for the educational environment because of its focus on individual differences.

REVIEW QUESTIONS

1. Child development occurs quickly from the fetal stage into the development of a fully formed human. Which of the following developmental milestones occurs first?

   (A) Fingernails grow

   (B) Skull fully forms

   (C) Twins occur

   (D) A blastocyst forms

   (E) Implantation happens

2. Sandy complained there were more meatballs on his brother's plate than on his, but his mother explained that they each had the same number, it was just that Sandy's were closer together. According to Piaget, Sandy would be in which stage of cognitive development?

   (A) Sensorimotor

   (B) Preoperational

   (C) Concrete operational

   (D) Formal operational

   (E) Conventional

3. The process of culling neuronal connections to improve the efficiency of brain activity is called

   (A) trimming.

   (B) pruning.

   (C) filling.

   (D) scoring.

   (E) firing.

4. According to Piaget, the most important process of development is

   (A) learning to solve logical problems.

   (B) learning to speak.

   (C) adapting to the environment.

   (D) learning new words.

   (E) cultivating relationships with one's parents.

5. What task might be beyond the reach of a child in the preoperational stage?

   (A) Speaking

   (B) Eating by oneself

   (C) Walking

   (D) Conservation

   (E) Remembering

6. At roughly what age would a child reach the stage of formal operations?

   (A) 5

   (B) 2

   (C) 7

   (D) Birth

   (E) 12

7. A child has a dog and refers to this dog as "doggie." She then sees a kitten for the first time and calls out "doggie!" This process is called

   (A) evolution.

   (B) formalization.

   (C) spreading activation.

   (D) accommodation.

   (E) assimilation.

8. The child in question 7 eventually learns that dogs and cats are different creatures, and she can determine the difference between the two. This process is referred to as

(A) evolution.

(B) formalization.

(C) spreading activation.

(D) accommodation.

(E) assimilation.

9. Which of the following skills makes formal operations different from other stages?

(A) Abstract logic

(B) Ability to conserve

(C) More accommodation than assimilation

(D) Adaptation to the environment

(E) Learning to speak

10. The process of conservation refers to a child's ability to

(A) remember his name.

(B) recognize his mother.

(C) understand a basic law of physics.

(D) know the structure of language.

(E) recognize absurdities in language.

11. The difference between assimilation and accommodation is that

(A) assimilation refers to our ability to adapt.

(B) accommodation refers to our ability to adapt.

(C) assimilation is the process of developing new schemas.

(D) accommodation is the process of developing new schemas.

(E) assimilation happens more when you are younger.

12. According to Piaget, basic knowledge structures are called

(A) accommodation.

(B) assimilation.

(C) equilibration.

(D) schemas.

(E) nodes.

13. Piaget focused mainly on _____, while Vygotsky focused mostly on _____.

(A) culture; stages of development

(B) assimilation; accommodation

(C) accommodation; assimilation

(D) stages of development; culture

(E) logic; language

14. The gap between the skills that children have the ability to do alone versus that which they can do with support is called

(A) adaptation.

(B) zone of proximal development.

(C) scaffolding.

(D) equilibration.

(E) accommodation.

15. According to Keating, many college students do not actually reach formal operations, even though Piaget's theory suggests that they should. Keating makes this claim because college students couldn't

(A) answer abstract logical problems.

(B) conserve.

(C) equilibrate.

(D) answer simple math problems.

(E) respond to riddles.

16. The sensorimotor stage of cognitive development is one during which children do NOT have the ability to

    (A) respond to the environment.
    (B) use simple motor skills.
    (C) engage in imaginative play.
    (D) smile.
    (E) respond to mother's voice.

17. Which of the following is a correct application of Vygotsky's principle of scaffolding?

    (A) Mr. Wrenn gave his math class problems that were so complex they gave up.
    (B) Ms. Sweeney's students finished their work quickly and were bored because the questions were too easy.
    (C) Mr. Geddie planned to assign his students work that was challenging, but not so hard that it would be overwhelming for them.
    (D) Mr. Yarrow alternated throughout the year by giving work that was very challenging, then very easy, so that his students would not get too comfortable in their learning.
    (E) Mrs. Appleton was most concerned with keeping her students' self-esteem very high, so if a student complained that the work was too hard, then he or she was allowed to stop.

18. The process of fitting into the environment is called, according to Piaget,

    (A) equilibration.
    (B) schema.
    (C) accommodation.
    (D) assimilation.
    (E) adaptation.

19. A significant criticism of Piaget's stage theory of cognitive development is that

    (A) children seem to acquire cognitive abilities earlier than Piaget predicted.
    (B) children in some cultures never experience the sensorimotor stage.
    (C) the formal operational stage may come before preoperational in some children.
    (D) parents who do not understand his theory may not adequately develop their children's cognitive talents.
    (E) he places too much emphasis on the psychosexual development of children.

20. According to Piaget's theory, we develop schemas

    (A) during gestation.
    (B) through experience.
    (C) via instinct.
    (D) during adulthood.
    (E) during adolescence.

ANSWERS AND EXPLANATIONS

1. D

The formation of a blastocyst takes place first. Fingernails, (A), develop at the end of gestation, the skull, (B), doesn't fully form until after birth, twins, (C), occur during the first trimester, and implantation, (E), occurs after fertilization.

2. B

Sandy is unable to grasp the concept of conservation, so even though his mother assures him both have the same number, the meatballs are more spaced out on the other plate and so they appear to take up more space (and therefore be more numerous). A child in the sensorimotor stage, (A), also does not understand conservation, but would be too young to articulate that. Children in the concrete, (C), and formal, (D), operational stages have already mastered conservation. Choice (E) is from Kohlberg's theory of moral development.

3. B

Pruning is the process of culling neuronal connections to improve the efficiency of brain activity. The other answer choices are not terms used by developmental psychologists.

4. C

Learning to adapt to one's environment is the most important process of development, according to Piaget. Learning to solve logical problems, (A), is part of the adaptation process. Learning to speak, (B), occurs early, but people who already speak are still developing. Learning new words, (D), is not necessary for development. Cultivating relationships with one's parents, (E), is important for social development but not for cognitive development.

5. D

Conservation might be beyond the reach of a child in the preoperational stage. All of the other activities occur during the preoperational stage.

6. E

At around age 12, a child would reach the stage of formal operations. Prior to that, he would be unable to perform many of the processes involved in that stage, such as solving logical problems.

7. E

The process is called assimilation. Assimilation is the process of fitting experiences into existing schemas. Spreading activation, (C), is a process in cognitive psychology and memory, and accommodation, (D), refers to developing new schemas. Formalization, (B), is not a term used by developmental psychologists.

8. D

Accommodation would explain why the child is able to determine the difference between a dog and a cat.

9. A

Abstract logic makes formal operations different from the other stages. The ability to conserve, (B), occurs during concrete operations, we accommodate, (C), earlier when we have fewer schemas, and adaptation, (D), occurs throughout the developmental process.

10. C

One of the laws of physics says that the amount of material does not change when its shape changes. This is called the law of conservation. Remembering one's name, (A), and recognizing one's mother, (B), occur before conservation. Understanding aspects of language, (D and E), have nothing to do with conservation.

11. D

Assimilation is the fitting of new experiences into existing schemas. Accommodation is the development of new schemas or adapting one's current schemas to incorporate new information.

12. D

Basic knowledge structures are called schemas. Equilibration, (C), is the restructuring of schemas, and nodes, (E), is a term used in cognitive psychology to refer to ideas in memory.

13. D

Piaget was most concerned with describing the stages of cognitive development, while Vygotsky focused on the role of culture and language in individual development.

14. B

The gap is called the zone of proximal development (ZPD). Adaptation, (A), equilibration, (D), and accommodation, (E), are Piagetian concepts. Scaffolding, (C), refers to the assistance needed to bridge the gap of the ZPD; it is the teaching strategy used when one knows a child's ZPD.

15. A

The students in Keating's study could not solve abstract logical problems. Therefore, they seemed not to have reached formal operations as expected.

16. C

In the sensorimotor stage, children do not engage in imaginative play. Children do not form mental representation until the beginning of the preoperational stage. According to Piaget, the other skills mentioned are more reflexive.

17. C

Vygotsky's theory is that there is a zone of proximal development (ZPD) between what the child can do easily and what the child can do only with help, and the job of any teacher, parent, or coach is to use scaffolding to keep the student in this ZPD for optimal learning. If the tasks are too easy, there is no cognitive challenge, and students may give up if the tasks are too hard. Only Mr. Geddie, (C), has the right combination for his students.

18. E

Adaptation is the process of fitting into the environment.

19. A

Piaget's theories have long been considered absolute principles, and only in the past few decades have researchers discovered that children appear to understand concepts such as symbolism and object permanence much earlier than Piaget stated. But in research in many cultures the stages seem to be present and in that order, so choices (B) and (C) are incorrect. (D) is also incorrect in that this process unfolds largely irrespective of parents. Choice (E) is a criticism of Freud's theories, not Piaget's.

20. B

Piaget argued that schemas are developed and added to throughout life through experience.

CHAPTER 12: PERSONALITY

IF YOU LEARN ONLY SIX THINGS IN THIS CHAPTER . . .

1. Personality refers to patterns of behavior that remain constant across situations.

2. There are different approaches to personality, including psychoanalytic, trait, humanistic, and learning theories.

3. Sigmund Freud is responsible for the psychoanalytic approach, which states that we are controlled by unconscious conflicts.

4. Trait theorists argue that our personality is simply a collection of traits.

5. Humanistic theorists argue that humans are basically good and strive for perfection.

6. Learning theorists argue that personality is nothing more than a shorthand description for clusters of behavior.

INTRODUCTION

The study of personality is always interesting to students of psychology. People want to know what "makes us tick." Interestingly, though we use the term *personality* quite a bit and speak about liking someone because he has a "good personality," we don't have a good definition of the term. For the purposes of this chapter, we will define **personality** as a pattern of behavior that remains somewhat consistent across situations.

Psychologists have defined the concept of personality in different ways. In this chapter, we will concern ourselves with the following theories: psychodynamic theory, trait theories, humanist theories, and learning theories. Each approach attempts to explain the individual differences we see in humans. Further, each has its own set of unique explanations for the diversity of behavior that exists.

The study of personality is not easy. We cannot see personality, so measuring the consruct is a challenge. With careful research, however, we can draw certain conclusions that might help us understand human behavior.

PSYCHOANALYTIC THEORY

No discussion of personality would be complete without describing the psychoanalytic approach to understanding human behavior. And no discussion of the psychoanalytic approach would be complete without a description of the work of **Sigmund Freud**.

Freud was not a psychologist. In 1881, he was awarded a medical degree. While he was never interested in pursuing medicine as a career, he believed that his training as a neurologist would help him investigate the causes of human behavior.

Freud spent much of his early career working with other psychologists, as he developed different aspects of his theory—those learning how to treat "hysterical" women, for example. The belief was that some women could not control their emotions because of some unnamed conflict.

Freud first learned how to do hypnotism as a treatment strategy but then decided that this avenue was a dead end. Dream analysis came next, with the help of Breuer. Eventually, the two psychologists had a falling out and parted ways (a common occurrence with Freud), though dream analysis did become part of Freud's theory.

Freud soon developed more than just a description of human behavior—his became one of the most complete theories of the causes of human behavior. The main idea was that many of the **causes of human behavior are outside of consciousness**. We do what we do for reasons that we don't completely understand. Moreover, many of our desires are either sexual or aggressive in nature.

According to Freud, we have **three levels of consciousness:**

Conscious	What we are currently aware of
Preconscious	What we are not aware of but could be if we wanted to recall the information
Unconscious	Information that is potentially dangerous to think about, so it is buried; we are not able to access this information, but it does come out under some circumstances

These three levels of consciousness contain the **three components of personality:**

Id	The pleasure principle—This is the part of our personality that wants what it wants, immediately. According to Freud, the id demands immediate satisfaction. The desires are typically sexual or aggressive in nature.
Superego	Our conscience—This is the part of our personality that is the moral principle. The superego wants to do what is right at all times.
Ego	The mediator—The ego tries to satisfy the demands of the id within the context of the superego. That is, the ego mediates between the id and the superego.

To protect the ego, we often engage in what Freud and his daughter (**Anna Freud**) called **defense mechanisms**. A defense mechanism protects the ego by diverting the anxiety that might occur and deflecting that energy toward something else.

Some of the more important defense mechanisms are listed below:

Repression	Anxiety is so strong that we push the cause of the anxiety deep into the unconscious. At times, the anxiety may rise to the surface via dreams or "Freudian slips."
Projection	We see anxiety-causing behavior in others rather than in ourselves.
Reaction Formation	We engage in the opposite of an anxiety-producing behavior. Suppose one is interested in pornography. This is a socially unacceptable behavior, so to protect his ego, he might engage in a protest against pornography.
Sublimation	We replace a socially unacceptable desire or urge with something socially acceptable. We would replace our desire to hit someone with exercise, for instance.
Displacement	We take out our anxiety on someone other than the person who caused the anxiety.
Regression	When confronted by anxiety, we retreat to an earlier stage of development. We may curl up on the sofa life a baby, or we may ask our parents to bail us out of a dilemma.

Denial	We push the existence of some problem right out of our heads as if it did not exist, or we refuse to acknowledge and confront it.
Rationalization	We legitimize our failures by coming up with logical-sounding excuses for what happened. For example, we might say, "The college that did not accept me has a poor perception in the academic community."

Freud's theory also argued that we go through several stages of **psychosexual development**. We must successfully navigate the issues of each stage to develop without issues that will influence behavior later.

But what happens if the stage is not successfully navigated?

Oral stage Pleasure gained by feeding	If not successfully weaned, child will become orally fixed. Thus, as an adult, one may drink too much, smoke too much, etc.
Anal stage Pleasure gained by controlling one's bowels	If potty training is tough, child will become anal retentive. Thus, as an adult, one will become obsessed with organization and control of environment.
Phallic stage Pleasure gained by exploring one's body	Stifling this stage may result in poor body image or in inappropriate body image.
Latency stage Focus moves away from one area	
Genital stage Mature sexuality	

During the phallic stage, children go through a period where they unconsciously desire their opposite-sex parent (the Oedipus complex in males). During this time, children form a bond with the parent that they are jealous of because of their unconscious fear of what might happen.

Freud's theory is well known, and many people associate it with mainstream psychology. In modern psychology, however, very few completely embrace this theory. The most common complaint is that it does not have any real empirical support.

Neo-Freudians are those psychoanalysts who followed Freud but often veered off in other directions to develop their own ideas. The most well-known is **Carl Jung**, whose theories include the **collective unconscious**, which was similar to Freud's idea of the unconscious, except this was one that would be shared by all humanity. Jung used stories and myths in various cultures to show that the same ideals (called **archetypes**) evolved in all cultures.

Other neo-Freudians include Alfred Adler, who developed the concept called the inferiority complex, and Karen Horney, who stressed the importance of childhood anxiety and countered Freud's view of women as the weaker sex.

TRAIT THEORIES

Other theories of personality focus on different aspects of behavior. Trait theorists, for example, argue that **personality consists of a collection of traits or personality characteristics**. People vary on traits such as introversion/extraversion, aggression, talkativeness, etc. Each person is born or learns behavior patterns that represent these traits. Take the test for introversion or extraversion developed by Hans Eysenck, for example. One could ask questions that would allow the development of a score. The score represented the degree to which one might possess this trait.

HUMANISTIC THEORIES

According to humanistic theories, **humans are born inherently good**. What drives them is the **goal of self-actualization**. Self-actualization is the achievement of one's personal best. To achieve self-actualization, we strive toward becoming better people. So the goal becomes being the best person one can be. Noted humanistic psychologists are **Carl Rogers** and **Abraham Maslow**.

LEARNING THEORIES

Learning theories argue that **personality is an explanatory fiction**. Rather, what is called "personality" is really a **collection of behaviors**. We learn patterns of behaviors through the traditional strategies of reinforcement and punishment, just like we learn everything else. Personality is just a description of behaviors under certain environmental circumstances.

AP EXPERT TIP

Trait theorists argue that traits such as introversion/ extraversion are stable across a lifetime. Learning theorists argue that introverts could become extraverts if properly reinforced.

REVIEW QUESTIONS

1. Which of the following statements best captures Freud's point of view about personality?

   (A) Personality is the result of our reinforcement history.

   (B) Personality is learned from our parents by being around them.

   (C) Personality is the result of a group of clustered traits.

   (D) Personality is the result of our shared evolutionary history with all those that came before us.

   (E) Personality is the result of unconscious drives or conflicts that we need to resolve.

2. "Our personality is nothing more than acquired habits that we learned though our experience." What theory would support this statement?

   (A) Trait

   (B) Psychoanalytic

   (C) Learning

   (D) Cognitive

   (E) Humanistic

3. The approach of personality championed by Carl Rogers is called

   (A) learning.

   (B) trait.

   (C) psychoanalytic.

   (D) humanistic.

   (E) neo-Freudian.

4. The personality theory that is most likely to use an objective test to determine someone's personality is

   (A) psychoanalytic.

   (B) cognitive.

   (C) humanistic.

   (D) trait.

   (E) learning.

5. During the _____ stage of Freud's theory, the focus is on controlling one's environment.

   (A) oral

   (B) anal

   (C) phallic

   (D) latency

   (E) genital

6. You have three friends: the first is bossy and always tells you what to do, the second is always telling you what is right or wrong, and the third tries to help mediate between the two. If you were giving Freudian nicknames to your friends, they would be, in order,

   (A) Id, Superego, Ego.

   (B) Id, Ego, Superego.

   (C) Ego, Superego, Id.

   (D) Superego, Id, Ego.

   (E) Superego, Ego, Id.

7. According to Freud, your memory of your own birth would be at what level of consciousness?

   (A) Unconscious

   (B) Subconscious

   (C) Conscious

   (D) Preconscious

   (E) REM

8. Proponents of which theory might suggest that traits such as introversion and extraversion could be changed over time if properly reinforced?

    (A) Cognitive
    (B) Psychoanalytic
    (C) Learning
    (D) Humanistic
    (E) Sociocultural

9. The humanistic approach to personality makes which of the following claims?

    (A) We are all inherently good.
    (B) We are all inherently bad.
    (C) We are born a blank slate.
    (D) We are born with genes that determine who we become.
    (E) We are born with genes that give us potential, but our experience really determines who we become.

10. Phil has anxiety because he has very strong anger toward his parents. He knows this isn't right, so he decides to work hard to do all his chores and homework. According to the psychoanalytic approach, Phil is engaging in which defense mechanism?

    (A) Projection
    (B) Sublimation
    (C) Reaction formation
    (D) Transference
    (E) Denial

11. The most common complaint about Freud's psychoanalytic theory is that it

    (A) does not discuss the role of sexuality.
    (B) ignores unconscious forces that drive behavior.
    (C) overemphasizes the role of reinforcement and punishment.
    (D) is too optimistic about the ability of humans to change their behavior.
    (E) lacks real empirical support.

12. Information that is not available to conscious awareness because it would be too damaging is in the _____ level of consciousness.

    (A) subconscious
    (B) unconscious
    (C) conscious
    (D) presubconscious
    (E) preconscious

13. José applied for a full scholarship to a local university and made it to the semifinals, but then it was announced that another student at his school won. José was later heard by several friends criticizing the school, saying that the people there were rude and the professors he met didn't seem very smart. Freud would day that José is using the defense mechanism of

    (A) denial.
    (B) projection.
    (C) reaction formation.
    (D) regression.
    (E) rationalization.

14. In Freud's theory of personality, the _____ is the seat of impulses.

    (A) ego
    (B) superego
    (C) mask
    (D) anima
    (E) id

15. Humanistic psychologists see people as inherently good. They believe that people are trying to reach their potential at all times. This process is called

    (A) perfecting.
    (B) self-actualization.
    (C) performance enhancement.
    (D) levels of processing.
    (E) general adaptation syndrome.

16. According to a learning perspective, the most important determinant of how we behave in any given situation is

    (A) our previous learning history.
    (B) our unconscious.
    (C) the traits we have.
    (D) our need for achievement.
    (E) our socialization needs.

17. A proponent of learning theory might be

    (A) Freud.
    (B) Jung.
    (C) Rogers.
    (D) Maslow.
    (E) Skinner.

18. Which of the following defense mechanisms involves pushing painful information deep into our memory so that we don't have access to it?

    (A) Regression
    (B) Reaction formation
    (C) Sublimation
    (D) Denial
    (E) Repression

19. According to Freud, a defense mechanism is used when a person encounters anxiety, and it acts to protect the person's

    (A) ego.
    (B) id.
    (C) superego.
    (D) death instinct.
    (E) life instinct.

20. Archetypes and the collective unconscious are mostly associated with which neo-Freudian?

    (A) Abraham Maslow
    (B) Carl Jung
    (C) Carl Rogers
    (D) Alfred Adler
    (E) Karen Horney

ANSWERS AND EXPLANATIONS

1. E

Freud believed that personality is formed from unconscious drives or conflicts that we need to resolve. Someone who subscribed to learning theory would say that it is formed from our reinforcement history, (A), and someone who subscribed to trait theories would say it is formed by being around our parents, (B).

2. C

A learning theorist would believe this statement. He would believe that we are born as a blank slate and that experience is the key to personality. Trait theorists, (A), believe we are born with traits from our parents, psychodynamic theorists, (B), believe we carry trauma from birth in our unconscious, cognitive theorists, (D), are also called trait theorists, and humanistic psychologists, (E), believe we are all born inherently good.

3. D

Rogers championed the humanistic approach of personality. Learning perspective, (A), is similar to the theory of Skinner, trait theory, (B), is associated with Kelley, and neo-Freudians, (E), are psychologists like Carl Jung.

4. D

An objective personality test is one in which a subject is given a multiple-choice test and asked to select which of the following items most describes his or her personality. A widely known trait test that uses this format is the Myers-Briggs test. Psychoanalytic proponents, (A), would use some form of projective tests, like the Rorschach inkblot test, while the other options do not have specific tests associated with them.

5. B

During the anal stage, children learn that much of their behavior is out of their control. However, potty training helps them to realize that there are some behaviors that they can control. A child who becomes anal retentive will eventually become a very controlling adult.

6. A

The order would be id, superego, and ego. The id is the part of the personality that is always demanding immediate gratification, the superego is your conscience, and the ego is the mediator between the two structures.

7. A

Any memory you have of your birth would be buried in the unconscious. Subconscious, (B), is a term that is often confused in psychology, but Freud used *unconscious*. The conscious, (C), and preconscious, (D), are both areas that we have access to, and REM, (E), refers to paradoxical sleep.

8. C

Remember, whenever you see the word "reinforced," immediately look for choices that involve learning or behaviorism. Those who believe in the learning theory of personality argue that our personality forms as a reaction to the events in our lives, and as our behaviors are reinforced or punished, our personality will follow.

9. A

The humanistic theory claims that we are all inherently good. That we are inherently bad, (B), is not a perspective held by psychologists. That we are born with genes that give us potential only, (E), is a belief held by many developmental psychologists who subscribe to the theory of behavior genetics.

10. B

In sublimation, we suffer anxiety about particularly troubling thought. To avoid the anxiety, we throw ourselves into a socially acceptable activity.

11. E

While Freud's work is known widely around the world and can frequently be found in popular culture, most modern psychologists criticize it for relying on theories that were based on case studies of his patients. Tests of his theories using modern scientific techniques like experiments and correlational studies have yielded little support for these ideas. Choices (A) and (B) are core components of psychoanalytic theory, while option (C) is a criticism of learning theory and option (D) is a criticism of humanistic theory.

12. B

Our unconscious contains information that would be too damaging at the conscious level. Subconscious, (A), sounds correct, but Freud used the term *unconscious*.

13. E

José was very much in favor of the school as he was getting closer to winning the scholarship, but according to Freudian theory, when he lost the scholarship it created an enormous amount of anxiety for him. To deal with this anxiety and protect his ego, he offered a logical, rational explanation for why he didn't like the school in the first place. Denial, (A), is the refusal to acknowledge something that causes anxiety, projection, (B), is the attributing of one's own problems to others, reaction formation, (C), is acting in an opposite way from what you feel, and regression, (D), involves retreating to an earlier stage of development in the face of anxiety.

14. E

The id is the seat of impulses, according to Freud. The ego, (A), is the mediator, and the superego, (B), is the conscience. The mask, (C), and anima, (D), are both Jungian concepts, not Freudian.

15. B

The term used by Rogers and others is *self-actualization*. This is the idea that we are striving toward perfection. The other terms are not used in personality psychology.

16. A

According to learning theory, we are products of our environment. We act the way we do because in the past, we were reinforced for certain behaviors and punished (or not reinforced) for competing behaviors.

17. E

Skinner could be considered a proponent of learning theory. Freud, (A), supported psychodynamic theory, as did Jung, (B). Rogers, (C), and Maslow, (D), were both proponents of humanistic/phenomenological theories of personality.

18. E

Repression is when we push painful information deep into our memory so we do not have to deal with it. Don't confuse that with regression, (A), which is reverting back to a previous developmental stage to deal with anxiety. Reaction formation, (B), is engaging in a competing behavior to avoid having to engage in an inappropriate behavior, and sublimation, (C), is substituting a socially acceptable urge for an unacceptable one.

19. A

The ego, according to Freud, emerges from the conflict between the internal id and the externally imposed superego. The ego is fragile, though, and defense mechanisms serve the purpose of diverting anxiety away from the ego to protect it. The life and death instincts are also parts of Freud's theories, but do not fit here.

20. B

Carl Jung believed that a collective unconscious connects all cultures, and he supported this theory by showing that the same types of figures and ideas appear in the stories and legends of many different cultures. He called these archetypes; some examples are The Great Mother, The Wise Old Man, The Mentor, and The Trickster. Adler and Horney are neo-Freudians, but neither is associated with archetypes or the collective unconscious. Maslow and Rogers are humanistic psychologists and not neo-Freudians.

CHAPTER 13: TESTING AND INDIVIDUAL DIFFERENCES

IF YOU LEARN ONLY FIVE THINGS IN THIS CHAPTER . . .

1. Binet created the first intelligence test and developed the concept of mental age, but Terman's revision, the Stanford-Binet, created a way to compute an IQ score.

2. Aptitude tests predict future success and achievement tests assess what individuals already know.

3. When designing tests, psychometricians focus on standardization, reliability, validity, and culture fairness.

4. Normal distributions are bell-shaped curves in which most scores fall near the average and the percentage of scores between standard deviations is fixed by a formula.

5. Reliability refers to a test being repeatable and validity refers to a test being accurate.

INTRODUCTION

Debate continues in psychology over the meaning of **intelligence**, but a generally accepted definition is the mental capacity to solve problems and adapt to the environment. **Francis Galton**, who originally coined the phrase *nature versus nurture*, researched the hereditary basis of intelligence by studying twins. He developed the field of psychometrics by applying key statistical concepts including correlation and percentile rank to studies on human intelligence and other factors.

The first intelligence measure, the **Binet-Simon scale** created by **Alfred Binet**, was designed for French schools to identify students who would benefit from additional support. Binet also developed the concept of **mental age**, which indicated an individual was capable of reasoning at the level of a typical person at that chronological age. **Lewis Terman** revised and expanded Binet's test for use in the United States and renamed it the **Stanford-Binet Intelligence Scale**. The new test included a formula for determining intelligence quotient (IQ), developed by William Stern, and allowed for testing of adults. IQ was determined by dividing mental age by chronological age and multiplying the result by 100, providing a method for comparing individuals. **David Wechsler** suggested IQ tests were limited because they measured intelligence only verbally; he devised a test that included both **verbal** and **performance** components to compute a total IQ score. Wechsler developed separate intelligence tests for adults (WAIS) and children (WISC) and used a scoring system based on normal distribution.

THEORIES OF INTELLIGENCE

Charles Spearman presented a two-factor theory of intelligence separating general and specific mental abilities. Utilizing the statistical method of **factor analysis**, which identifies groups of associated ideas by combining like items, Spearman discovered that most cognitive skills are related to a single essential trait he called general mental ability or g factor intelligence. The **g factor** or **general intelligence** is the ability of individuals to solve complex problems, and the **s factor** or **specific mental abilities** is what he called the ability of an individual to utilize math or verbal skills.

Robert Sternberg proposed the **triarchic theory of intelligence,** in which intelligence was divided into three aspects: **practical**, the ability to adapt to changes in the environment; **analytical**, the reasoning and problem solving that is evaluated by most intelligence tests; and **creative**, the capacity to create new ideas and unique solutions to problems.

Howard Gardner's multiple intelligences theory states that intelligence is not fixed and that all individuals possess at least eight different types of intelligences. The eight intelligences are linguistic, logical-mathematical, visual-spatial, musical, bodily-kinesthetic, intrapersonal, interpersonal, and naturalistic.

DESIGNING INTELLIGENCE TESTS— PSYCHOMETRICS

The field of **psychometrics** is engaged in the design and analysis of quantitative tests for measuring psychological variables such as intelligence and personality traits.

AP EXPERT TIP

To remember the three parts of Sternberg's intelligence and love theories, utilize the acronyms P.A.C. (practical, analytical, and creative intelligence) and P.I.C. (passion, intimacy, and commitment in love).

Aptitude tests are used to predict future success and assess the ability to acquire new skills.
Achievement tests evaluate how well a person has mastered a subject.

Three major aspects of psychometrics in terms of test construction are standardization, reliability, and validity. **Standardization** involves utilizing scores from a representative sample to determine how well an individual did on the test relative to other test takers, and creating similar testing conditions for all individuals taking the exam to prevent any potentially confounding variables. Intelligence tests originally indicated a ratio between a person's mental age and chronological age, but modern tests are based on a normal distribution created through standardization. **Normal distributions** of scores form symmetrical bell-shaped curves in which the **mean**, **median**, and **mode** are equal and located in the center of the distribution and the percentages of scores falling between **standard deviations** are fixed by a formula. In a normal distribution, 68 percent of scores fall within one standard deviation, 95 percent within two standard deviations, and 98 percent within three standard deviations of the mean in either direction. Because percentages in normal distribution are fixed, it is possible to compute the **percentile rank**, or the percentage of scores in a distribution below the score you are considering. For example, an individual with a score of 68, which is greater than 90 percent of scores of all people taking the test, is in the 90th percentile.

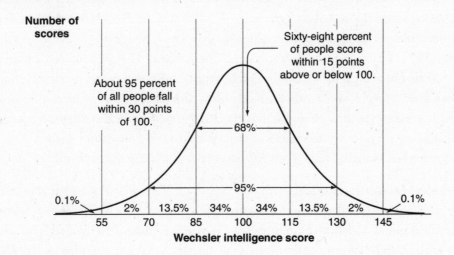

Reliability is the degree to which a psychological test such as an IQ test is consistent or dependable. To determine if a test is reliable, psychologists utilize three main methods. **Test-retest** reliability is computed by having the same individuals take the same test at two different times. **Alternate form** reliability involves testing the same individuals twice but giving a different version on the retake date. **Split-half** reliability involves checking for consistency between the scores on two halves of the same test, which can mean comparing the first half to the second half of the test or even questions to odd.

Validity is the degree to which a particular psychological test is accurate and inferences drawn from the results are correct. **Content validity** evaluates how well a test measures the total meaning of the concept and if it is reasonably representative of the material it is evaluating. **Construct validity** refers to whether a test is really evaluating an abstract psychological or theoretical idea. Constructs are difficult to measure and define operationally and include ideas such as extraversion or intelligence. **Criterion** or **predictive validity** refers to how well test results relate to another measure of what you are evaluating or how well they predict success in the future.

EXTREMES IN INTELLIGENCE

The average IQ score is 100 and scores below 70 signify **mental retardation**. The term *mental retardation* has received much criticism and will likely be replaced with the term *cognitively disabled*. Generally, anyone with an IQ below 70 can be considered mentally retarded; however, psychologists do not use IQ exclusively to determine mental retardation and now utilize additional social factors when making a diagnosis. IQ scores between 50 and 70 are considered mild mental retardation, which makes up the largest percentage of individuals with cognitive deficits. These individuals are capable of achieving grade 6 education levels and living independently. IQ scores between 35 and 49 are considered moderate, scores between 20 and 34 are considered severe, and scores below 20 are classified as profoundly mentally retarded. Known causes of mental retardation include **Down syndrome**, in which individuals are born with all or part of an extra chromosome, or other genetic problems such as **phenylketonuria (PKU)** and **fragile X syndrome**. Mental retardation can also have external causes related to problems during pregnancy such as malnutrition, exposure to toxins, fetal alcohol syndrome, and injuries during birth.

Psychologists also investigate individuals with extremely high IQ scores who are often referred to as **gifted**. One of the most well-known studies of gifted individuals was **Lewis Terman**'s longitudinal study of a group of gifted students whom he called "Terman's Termites." Individuals from the study scored higher than average in terms of family income, physical and mental health, and reported happiness. Terman's research disproved a popular misconception that gifted individuals were not well adjusted or successful socially.

IMPACT OF SOCIOCULTURAL FACTORS ON INTELLIGENCE

Although intelligence tests are widely used in the United States and other Western cultures, they are not utilized worldwide. In addition, tests standardized on Western samples do not accurately measure intelligence in other parts of the world. When creating intelligence tests for other cultures, it is important that the tests are designed with the values and experiences of the people in that culture in mind. Differences related to ethnicity, culture, and gender that exist within Western societies can affect performance on intelligence tests, and critics argue that **culture-fair tests** must include examples relevant to the experiences of the individuals taking the test. The reason for the disparities in scores among groups is a subject of debate in which most psychologists believe that both genetics and environment influence an individual's IQ. A **heritable** or genetic component to intelligence has been established with twin and adoption studies, but research also indicates that socioeconomic status has an impact on IQ.

The **Flynn effect** is the finding that IQ scores have been steadily improving across generations. The reason for the Flynn effect has not been identified, but it is generally considered to have an environmental basis such as better education and nutrition, because 100 years is not long enough to create an evolutionary change. Another potential cause for the gap in intelligence scores among groups may be stereotype threat. **Stereotype threat** results when individuals are reminded of a negative stereotype about a group they belong to prior to a test, which results in their scoring lower. Psychologists today work to create culture-fair tests that eliminate racial, ethnic, socioeconomic, and gender biases.

REVIEW QUESTIONS

1. The person who revised the first IQ test to include test items for adults and the use of an IQ formula was

    (A) Sir Francis Galton.

    (B) Alfred Binet.

    (C) Theodore Simon.

    (D) Charles Spearman.

    (E) Lewis Terman.

2. The statistical process that reveals common aspects among large groups of variables is known as

    (A) the Flynn effect.

    (B) factor analysis.

    (C) stereotype threat.

    (D) construct validity.

    (E) content validity.

3. The SAT is designed to predict success in college, which makes the SAT a(n)

    (A) emotional intelligence test.

    (B) culture-biased test.

    (C) achievement test.

    (D) aptitude test.

    (E) interpersonal test.

4. Psychologists creating an assessment tool to determine if individuals would be well suited to a career in air traffic control first administer the exam to a representative sample to serve as a source of comparison and make certain that all individuals take the test under the same testing conditions. The psychologists are focused on establishing

    (A) standardization.

    (B) content validity.

    (C) construct validity.

    (D) test-retest reliability.

    (E) inter-rater reliability.

5. Charles Spearman referred to the ability of individuals to solve complex problems as

    (A) performance scales.

    (B) creative intelligence.

    (C) practical intelligence.

    (D) g factor intelligence.

    (E) s factor intelligence.

6. Principal Scott created a math readiness test to give to eighth graders prior to entering high school. He chose a representative group of students to give the test to and compared each student's scores on odd versus even questions. He found a strong positive correlation between the odd and even scores, which gave him evidence that the test he made had

    (A) content validity.

    (B) construct validity.

    (C) inter-rater reliability.

    (D) test-retest reliability.

    (E) split-half reliability.

7. Which intelligence test includes separate verbal and performance sections and also provides an overall intelligence score?

   (A) WAIS

   (B) Simon-Binet

   (C) Stanford-Binet

   (D) Sternberg-Binet

   (E) Gardner

8. Because IQ tests are based on a normal distribution in which 100 is the average and the standard deviation is 15, about _____ percent of IQ scores fall between 70 and 115.

   (A) 13

   (B) 34

   (C) 68

   (D) 81.5

   (E) 85

9. Comparing average IQ scores from the original Stanford-Binet test to the scores of individuals taking the current version provides support for

   (A) multiple intelligences.

   (B) standardization.

   (C) the stereotype threat.

   (D) the Flynn effect.

   (E) factor analysis.

10. All of the following are aspects of Howard Gardner's multiple intelligences theory EXCEPT

    (A) practical intelligence.

    (B) visual-spatial intelligence.

    (C) logical-mathematical intelligence.

    (D) interpersonal intelligence.

    (E) bodily-kinesthetic intelligence.

11. The psychologist famous for a landmark longitudinal study of gifted individuals was

    (A) Howard Gardner.

    (B) Lewis Terman.

    (C) David Wechsler.

    (D) Charles Spearman.

    (E) Robert Sternberg.

12. Ms. Dorsey asks other psychology teachers at her school to look over the final exam that she created for her psychology class to ensure that the test fairly represents the material covered during the semester. Ms. Dorsey is having others assist her in evaluating her exam for

    (A) split-half reliability.

    (B) alternate form reliability.

    (C) test-retest reliability.

    (D) content validity.

    (E) criterion validity.

13. The original formula for determining IQ scores utilized by Terman was

    (A) chronological age divided by mental age × percentile rank.

    (B) mental age divided by chronological age × z score × 100.

    (C) chronological age divided by mental age × z score × 100.

    (D) chronological age divided by mental age × 100.

    (E) mental age divided by chronological age × 100.

14. Women in studies have been found to score lower on math tests when they are tested in the same location as men if they are reminded of the belief that males typically outscore females in math. This highlights the concept of

    (A) stereotype threat.
    (B) standardization.
    (C) practical intelligence.
    (D) the Flynn effect.
    (E) creative intelligence.

15. All of the following are environmental causes of mental retardation EXCEPT

    (A) fetal alcohol syndrome.
    (B) phenylketonuria.
    (C) malnutrition.
    (D) exposure to lead.
    (E) physical injuries during birth.

16. Alfred Binet worked for the French government to create an intelligence test that would

    (A) avoid all cultural biases while measuring intelligence.
    (B) evaluate analytical and creative intelligence in separate subtests.
    (C) determine intelligence without reliance on verbal measures.
    (D) evaluate abilities of public school teachers.
    (E) determine which students would benefit the most from extra services.

17. After taking the ACT and receiving a 29, Mario decides to retake it the following month. Although he is given a different version of the test, he ends up with a score of 30. One reason his two scores are so close is that the ACT has strong

    (A) test-retest reliability.
    (B) alternate form reliability.
    (C) split-half reliability.
    (D) construct validity.
    (E) face validity.

18. Individuals who are considered to be mildly mentally retarded are capable of reaching the level of a grade 6 education and can often live independently. The IQ range of an individual with mild mental retardation is

    (A) 5 to 20.
    (B) 20 to 35.
    (C) 35 to 50.
    (D) 50 to 70.
    (E) 75 to 90.

19. The aspect of Sternberg's triarchic theory of intelligence that is typically measured by traditional IQ tests is

    (A) verbal-linguistic intelligence.
    (B) creative intelligence.
    (C) emotional intelligence.
    (D) practical intelligence.
    (E) analytical intelligence.

20. The psychologist who pioneered psychometrics by creating concepts like percentile rank and correlation was

    (A) William Stern.
    (B) Charles Spearman.
    (C) Alfred Binet.
    (D) Sir Francis Galton.
    (E) David Wechsler.

ANSWERS AND EXPLANATIONS

1. E

Lewis Terman developed the first IQ test, which utilized the IQ formula and allowed for testing on adults. Galton, (A), founded psychometrics and the concept of nature versus nurture. Binet, (B), created the first method for measuring intelligence and created the concept of mental age, but his test did not use the IQ formula or norms. Simon, (C), collaborated with Binet to create the Simon-Binet test. Spearman, (D), developed a theory of intelligence based on g and s factors.

2. B

Factor analysis reduces a large amount of potential variables by combining like items. The Flynn effect, (A), refers to the increase in average IQ scores with each successive generation. Stereotype threat, (C), refers to a self-fulfilling prophecy that results if before taking the assessment, test takers are reminded of a negative stereotype about the performance of a group they belong to. Construct validity, (D), refers to a test's ability to measure an abstract idea. Content validity, (E), refers to how well a test measures the complete meaning of a concept.

3. D

The SAT is considered an aptitude test because it is intended to predict how successful a person will be in college. Emotional intelligence tests, (A), are designed to evaluate people's capacity to understand emotions in themselves and others. Culture-biased tests, (B), are flawed assessments because they provide an advantage to members of one group over another. Achievement tests, (C), evaluate how well an individual has mastered a particular subject.

Interpersonal, (E), refers to one of the multiple intelligences articulated in Gardner's theory.

4. A

Standardization involves creating a comparison group for the creation of norms and maintaining consistent testing conditions for all participants. Validity, (B) and (C), refers to accuracy in a test. Reliability, (D) and (E), refers to methods to determine whether a test gives the same results over multiple trials.

5. D

The description in the question is of Charles Spearman's g factor of intelligence. Performance scales, (A), refers to intelligence tests that evaluate without the use of verbal measures. Creative intelligence, (B), is part of Sternberg's triarchic theory. Practical intelligence, (C), is part of Sternberg's triarchic theory. The s factor, (E), is Spearman's term for the specific mental abilities of an individual, which are dependent upon g factor.

6. E

This is an example of evaluating a test for split-half reliability or checking for consistency within the same test. Content validity, (A), refers to how well a test measures the total meaning of the concept and whether it includes a reasonable representation of the material it is evaluating. Construct validity, (B), refers to a test's ability to measure an abstract idea. Inter-rater reliability, (C), involves evaluating a test by having two or more individuals give the same score. Test-retest reliability, (D), involves having the same individuals retake the same test and then comparing the scores.

7. A

The Wechsler Adult Intelligence Scale (WAIS) includes both verbal and performance measurements and creates an overall intelligence score. The Simon-Binet scale, (B), was the original intelligence test created by Theodore Simon and Alfred Binet, which included measurements for only verbal intelligence and was used to measure whether children were scoring the same as other students their age. The Stanford-Binet test, (C), was created by Louis Terman and included a method for determining an IQ score and testing adults, but did not include performance scales. The Sternberg-Binet, (D), and Gardner, (E), are not existing tests.

8. D

The mean for IQ scores is 100 and the standard deviation is 15. This makes a score of 115 one standard deviation to the right of the mean for 34 percent of the scores. A score of 70 lies two standard deviations to the left of the mean, which accounts for 47.5 percent of the scores. When added together, these quantities equal 81.5 percent.

9. D

The average scores on the original Wechsler Intelligence test would be lower than on the current version, providing evidence for the Flynn effect, which shows that IQ scores have been rising with each successive generation. Multiple intelligences, (A), is a theory by Howard Gardner that states that there are actually eight different ways in which to be intelligent. Standardization, (B), is a test development tool that involves comparing scores to a representative sample group and ensuring that all test takers have the same testing conditions. Stereotype threat, (C), is the idea that reminding individuals about a negative stereotype relating to a group they belong to prior to taking a test results in lower scores. Factor analysis, (E), is a statistical procedure used in psychometrics that identifies groups of related items and combines them to create fewer overall categories.

10. A

All of the choices are aspects of Gardner's multiple intelligences theory except practical intelligence, (A), which is part of Sternberg's triarchic theory. In Gardner's theory, visual-spatial intelligence, (B), refers to an individual's capacity to visualize and generate accurate mental pictures. Logical-mathematical intelligence, (C), is Gardner's measure of a person's capacity to discern logical or mathematical patterns and is one of the aspects of intelligence that is traditionally evaluated by intelligence tests. Interpersonal intelligence, (D), is Gardner's description of a person's ability to accurately estimate the emotions, needs, and motives of others, which allows for effective teamwork and leadership. Bodily-kinesthetic intelligence, (E), is Gardner's term for having skill at controlling physical bodily actions and includes balance, coordination, and fine motor control.

11. B

Lewis Terman studied gifted individuals nicknamed "Terman's Termites" in a major longitudinal study, which is an in-depth research method that retests the original participants periodically over a long period of time, resulting in exceptionally detailed results across the lifespan. Terman's subjects were retested every five to ten years and data from his research has been used in many subsequent studies. Howard Gardner, (A), created the theory of multiple intelligences, which states that all individuals possess eight different types of intelligences to varying degrees. David Wechsler, (C), created intelligence tests that contain both verbal and performance scales to more accurately assess intelligence in individuals that have received less formal education. Charles Spearman, (D), proposed a two-factor theory of intelligence that included general intelligence (g factor) and specific abilities or s factors. Robert Sternberg, (E), is known for his triarchic theory of intelligence, which involves practical, analytical, and creative intelligences.

12. D

The test was being evaluated to determine if it included items that were reasonably representative of the content of the course, which is content validity. Split-half reliability, (A), is a tool for determining if the test is consistent by comparing scores on two halves of the same test for a high positive correlation. Alternate form reliability, (B), involves evaluating tests for consistency by comparing the results of the same individuals who are tested twice using two different versions. Test-retest reliability, (C), is used to check consistency in a test by having the same individuals take the same assessment on two different occasions and looking for a high positive correlation between the two scores. Criterion validity, (E), involves evaluating a test for accuracy in terms of how well the results match up to another measure or how well they predict future success.

13. E

Mental age divided by chronological age × 100 was the initial method used to determine an IQ score. For example, an eight-year-old child who scores as well as a typical 10-year-old would have an IQ score of 125. Currently, if you take an IQ test, your total score is compared with those of others your same age to determine where you fall in the normal distribution.

14. A

Choice (A) is an example of how stereotype threat can negatively impact scores for a group. Standardization, (B), refers to a psychometric method that involves comparing scores to a representative sample group and ensuring that all test takers have the same testing conditions. Practical intelligence, (C), is one of the three aspects of Sternberg's triarchic theory of intelligence; it refers to a person's ability to succeed in a variety of environments and is sometimes referred to as "street smarts." The Flynn effect, (D), is a recent finding that IQ scores have been steadily improving across generations. Creative intelligence, (E), is another of the three aspects of Sternberg's triarchic theory of intelligence; it refers to a person's skill at generating unique solutions and ideas.

15. B

Phenylketonuria is a genetically inherited problem that if untreated causes mental retardation. Fetal alcohol syndrome, (A), is the number-one cause of mental retardation in the United States, and is due to the teratogen alcohol, which is an environmental cause. Issues related to poor prenatal care, such as malnutrition, (C), and exposure to lead, (D), are also known environmental teratogens that can cause mental retardation. Physical injuries during birth, (E), can result in mental retardation with no connection to genetics.

16. E

Alfred Binet worked on an intelligence test that would help identify students that could benefit from supplemental services to improve their performance in school. Binet's test did not address issues related to cultural bias, (A), or evaluate Sternberg's concepts of analytical and creative intelligences, (B). Binet's test relied solely on verbal measures and did not include performance sections, (C). It was not designed to determine teacher effectiveness, (D).

17. B

Mario is given a different version or test form and his score remains basically the same, which indicates that the two versions have alternate form reliability. Test-retest reliability, (A), would involve having Mario take the exact same test two different times to determine if his scores were similar. Split-half reliability, (C), would evaluate the test for consistency by comparing Mario's scores on the first and second halves of the test or by comparing his scores on odd and even sections. Construct validity, (D), would involve evaluating the exam to determine if it predicted future success such as college performance. Face validity, (E), would involve having a nonexpert evaluate whether or not the test fairly covered the material it was designed to test.

18. D

Mildly mentally retarded individuals generally fall within the IQ range of 50 and 70. Individuals with IQ scores in the range of 5–20, (A), would be considered profoundly mentally retarded and would be in need of full-time care. IQs in the range of 20–35, (B), are categorized as severely mentally retarded, and scores ranging from 35–50, (C), are moderately mentally retarded. IQ scores from 75–90, (E), do not represent mental retardation, although they would be considered below the average IQ score, which is 100.

19. E

Analytical intelligence, the ability to solve problems and reason, is typically measured on traditional IQ tests. Verbal-linguistic intelligence, (A), is part of Howard Gardner's multiple intelligences theory. Creative intelligence, (B), is Sternberg's idea that intelligence involves the capacity to generate novel solutions and new ideas. Emotional intelligence tests, (C), evaluate the capacity to understand emotions. Practical intelligence, (D), is Sternberg's concept that intelligence includes the ability to adapt to change.

20. D

Sir Francis Galton pioneered the field of psychometrics. William Stern, (A), created the IQ formula, which would be used by Lewis Terman for the Stanford-Binet intelligence test. Charles Spearman, (B), developed a two-factor theory of intelligence. Alfred Binet, (C), created the first intelligence measure, which was created to identify students in French schools who needed additional support. David Wechsler, (E), developed an intelligence test that utilized both verbal and performance measures.

CHAPTER 14: ABNORMAL BEHAVIOR

IF YOU LEARN ONLY FOUR THINGS IN THIS CHAPTER . . .

1. The *Diagnostic and Statistical Manual of Psychiatric Disorders* is the handbook used by mental health professionals to diagnose psychiatric disorders.

2. There are many types of disorders, but they all involve debilitation that makes routine life situations difficult.

3. Schizophrenia is *not* dissociative identity disorder. It is a disorder that involves a break with reality and auditory hallucinations.

4. Personality disorders are the most difficult disorders to diagnose and treat.

INTRODUCTION

When students first enroll in psychology, they often believe that they'll be learning about "crazy" behavior. They soon learn, however, that there is a great deal more to the study of psychology.

Some areas of this discipline, of course, do deal extensively with psychological disorders. This chapter will present an overview of the major disorders and will describe the strategies that have been developed to understand and potentially treat these problems. Our knowledge of this area is very tenuous, however, as we continue to explore all aspects of human behavior.

SOME STATISTICS

According to Myers, the prevalence of psychological disorders is higher than one might think:

1. Roughly 2 million people in the United States are in-patients in psychiatric units. These people are essentially under lock and key because they have the most serious disturbances.

2. Over 2.4 million people in the United States are residents in group homes. Group homes are shared living spaces that provide patients with assistance potentially to transition back into the community. Residents of group homes typically are able to come and go, but they are under the supervision of a staff that provides support.

3. Roughly 15 percent of Americans utilize services for treatment of a psychological disorder. This number represents people who either use medication to treat a disorder (such as Xanax for anxiety) or are under the treatment of a psychotherapist. This number is probably a low estimate, as some have speculated that many homeless people should—but do not—receive some psychological assistance.

4. Over 400 million people worldwide are in need of some form of psychological assistance.

These statistics suggest that psychological disorders are not rare. In fact, the disorders are becoming more prevalent, if only because less stigma is attached now than in the past.

WHAT MAKES SOMETHING A PSYCHOLOGICAL DISORDER?

A psychological disorder has the following characteristics:

- **Atypical**
  The behavior displayed by someone who has a psychological disorder is not what might be considered normal. The behavior is not just quirky, however; it is considered extremely odd.

- **Maladaptive**
  A psychological disorder makes everyday life difficult for an individual. It typically interferes with the ability to lead a normal life.

AP EXPERT TIP

Keep in mind that a common problem in classifying and diagnosing disorders is that what is "atypical," "maladaptive," or "unjustifiable" in one country or culture may not be so in another.

- **Unjustifiable**

    A psychological disorder is not easy to explain to most people. For example, it might lead a person to engage in behavior that calls a great deal of attention to her. This kind of behavior may not make sense to the outsider, but the person with the disorder does not know how to act otherwise.

CATEGORIES OF PSYCHOLOGICAL DISORDERS

Psychological disorders are categorized according to the ***Diagnostic and Statistical Manual of Psychiatric Disorders*** (DSM-IV). The major categories follow.

ANXIETY DISORDERS

Anxiety in general is a combination of physical, cognitive, and psychological symptoms in which a person's sympathetic nervous system has initiated a fight-or-flight response. Anxiety is very common among people in the United States. In general, however, it is situational—we can usually point to the cause of the anxiety. When we cannot identify the cause, it is more problematic.

GENERALIZED ANXIETY DISORDER (GAD)

The most common form of anxiety, GAD occurs when someone suffers from general anxiety with no specific cause for longer than two weeks. Symptoms include an unfocused feeling of being out of control, being jittery, and having problems sleeping.

PHOBIC DISORDER

A phobic disorder occurs when a phobia (an irrational fear of an object or situation) becomes so disruptive that it interferes with normal functioning. Most people have some form of a phobia, but it does not interfere with their lives to a large degree.

POST-TRAUMATIC STRESS DISORDER (PTSD)

PTSD occurs when someone has gone through a traumatic event. That event, or the memory of that event, causes the person to continuously re-experience the stress associated with that event. The re-experiencing of the event can take the form of a panic attack.

PANIC DISORDER

A panic disorder occurs when someone has uncontrollable panic attacks for an extended period of time (longer than two weeks). The typical panic attack involves shortness of breath, racing heart, and an unfocused feeling of being out of control. The attacks come on rapidly and are debilitating.

Obsessive-Compulsive Disorder (OCD)

OCD involves having obsessive stress or anxiety over a particular event or issue and performing ritualistic or compulsive behavior to ameliorate the stress. Obsessive behavior is fairly common: It becomes a disorder when the compulsive behavior impairs everyday functioning.

Dissociative Disorders

A dissociative disorder is one in which there is a break in the connection between reality and perception of reality. In most cases, this gives rise to an inability to deal with reality; what is real and what seems real are not the same.

Psychogenic Fugue

A psychogenic fugue state occurs when a person forgets his past and essentially creates a new history. In fact, the person isn't aware that he has had another past. Rather, the invented past is the only reality that he knows. Fugue also involves "fleeing"—going to a new location.

Psychogenic Amnesia

Psychogenic amnesia occurs when one forgets her past but realizes she has forgotten it. To be diagnosed as psychogenic amnesia, there must be no form of biological insult to the brain; the amnesia must stem from a psychological cause.

Dissociative Identity Disorder (DID)

Previously called multiple personality disorder, DID occurs as a result of trauma (as per case studies). During that trauma, the personality is split into distinct personalities. Those personalities are called forth under different circumstances, and often, one personality does not know about the others. There is a great deal of controversy over this disorder, as psychologists try to determine the causes as well as the prevalence.

Somatoform Disorders

A somatoform disorder is one in which an individual suffers from some form of physical ailment, when there is, in fact, no real cause for that ailment to occur.

Conversion Disorder

A conversion disorder is one in which a person will suffer from a great deal of stress concerning an upcoming event. As a strategy for dealing with the stress, the person will "convert" the stress into some physical ailment. For example, if a person is anxious because she has to give an oral presentation to her class, she might suddenly develop a case of laryngitis the day before. In such a situation, the stress was "converted" into the problem of not being able to talk.

HYPOCHONDRIA

Someone who suffers from hypochondria believes he has a major medical malady, yet doctors can find nothing physically wrong. The patient seeks treatment for an "ailment" that he believes exists.

MOOD DISORDERS

A mood disorder results in an inability to control or stabilize mood. In a disorder of this type, a patient will have trouble emerging from a depressed state or will lack the ability to maintain mood at a constant level.

MAJOR CLINICAL DEPRESSION

Clinical depression occurs when a person becomes so depressed that he is unable to engage in the basic behaviors required for normal functioning. This is not just "being down" about something; it is being *so* depressed that even the thought of getting out of bed is too overwhelming. In addition, the depression must last for longer than two weeks. Depression is more common in women than men.

One explanation for depression is that people suffer from **learned helplessness** (a term originally used by **Martin Seligman**). No matter what a person does, he cannot avoid the pain or bad consequences, so he "learns to give up."

BIPOLAR DISORDER

A person suffering from bipolar disorder vacillates between periods of extreme hyperactivity (called **mania**) and periods of deep depression. The person is unable to maintain an appropriate level of stabilized mood.

SCHIZOPHRENIA

Schizophrenia is not, as many people think, the same thing as dissociative identity disorder (or multiple personality disorder). Schizophrenia is marked by two major symptoms: (1) **auditory hallucinations** (the person hears voices) and (2) **a break between reality and perception of reality**.

A person suffering from schizophrenia has a difficult time dealing with reality and often suffers because he cannot articulate the issue. There are several types of schizophrenia marked by various symptoms, yet all share this basic feature.

PARANOID SCHIZOPHRENIA

Paranoid schizophrenia is a disorder marked by many of the same characteristics of schizophrenia in general. What differentiates it is the **paranoia**. A person suffering from paranoid schizophrenia will have both delusions of grandeur (belief that she is someone very important) and extreme suspiciousness of others' actions. The typical person (if there is such a thing) afflicted with this disorder believes that because she is someone important, many people are out to "get her." She will likely have trouble communicating this, but it has a big impact on her behavior.

DISORGANIZED SCHIZOPHRENIA

A person with disorganized schizophrenia has difficulty communicating and has auditory hallucinations, but without a significant degree of paranoia. He will often neglect his appearance and has difficulty fitting in, but he does not believe that people are plotting against him. He displays a flat affect, showing very little emotion at all, or an inappropriate affect, where he shows an affect that conflicts with what would be expected (laughing uproariously at a funeral, for example).

CATATONIC SCHIZOPHRENIA

Catatonic schizophrenia looks very much like disorganized schizophrenia but, in addition, is marked by periods of complete immobility called **waxy flexibility**. The person with catatonic schizophrenia will stop moving and remain in that position for several minutes. During that period of immobility, the person's arms can be moved, and they will remain in that position until the catatonic phase passes. Some have attributed this immobility to mild epileptic seizures, but we are not certain why the disorder occurs.

PERSONALITY DISORDERS

A personality disorder is a pervasive pattern of behavior involving difficulty interacting with others. Personality disorders are some of the most misunderstood disorders in psychology, and to date, we have neither a complete grasp of the causes nor an adequate strategy for treatment.

BORDERLINE PERSONALITY DISORDER

A borderline personality disorder results in a repeated pattern of difficulty in maintaining relationships. This is the result of the manner in which a person with borderline personality disorder views other people—she sees people as either good or bad. If a friend violated some perceived trust boundary, the person with this disorder would perceive that friend as being bad.

ANTISOCIAL PERSONALITY DISORDER (APD)

Perhaps one of the most severe of the personality disorders, the antisocial personality disorder patient repeatedly violates the rights of others with no remorse. Typically, patterns of behavior will emerge early (in the teen years) but will become more evident as the person reaches the 20s and 30s. Some APD people are violent and engage in horrific behavior, though the majority are not. They do, however, commonly violate the rights of others and have very little concern for the consequences of their behavior.

REVIEW QUESTIONS

1. In the DSM-IV, multiple personality disorder is categorized as a(n)

    (A) schizophrenic disorder.

    (B) dissociative disorder.

    (C) anxiety disorder.

    (D) somatoform disorder.

    (E) personality disorder.

2. Franco hears voices and believes he is wanted by the CIA. He would most likely be diagnosed with

    (A) schizophrenic disorder.

    (B) dissociative disorder.

    (C) anxiety disorder.

    (D) somatoform disorder.

    (E) personality disorder.

3. Suzanne reports persistent irrational thoughts that produce tension and repetitive impulses to perform certain acts that cause significant impairment. She would most likely be diagnosed with

    (A) schizophrenia.

    (B) obsessive-compulsive disorder.

    (C) Tourette's syndrome.

    (D) schizoid personality disorder.

    (E) post-traumatic stress disorder (PTSD).

4. Psychological disorders are said to be atypical, unjustifiable, and maladaptive. In this sense, maladaptive means

    (A) interfering with a person's daily life.

    (B) dangerously violent and a menace to society.

    (C) out of the ordinary or unusual.

    (D) violating the rights of others without remorse.

    (E) not getting along well with others in social situations.

5. The DSM-IV is used to

    (A) establish best practices for treating disorders.

    (B) provide patients with information about support groups for their disorders.

    (C) document case studies of people with severe disorders.

    (D) establish guidelines for diagnosing disorders.

    (E) establish the legal rights of people who are mentally ill and commit crimes.

6. Which of the following is NOT a common symptom of schizophrenia?

    (A) Delusions

    (B) Auditory hallucinations

    (C) Inappropriate affect

    (D) Panic attacks

    (E) Disorganized thought

7. A person who alternates between periods of depression and periods of mania is probably suffering from

   (A) depression.
   (B) schizophrenia.
   (C) bipolar disorder.
   (D) amnesia.
   (E) post-traumatic stress disorder.

8. The disorder that is marked by auditory hallucinations and a fear of persecution is

   (A) catatonic schizophrenia.
   (B) clinical depression.
   (C) hypochondriasis.
   (D) antisocial personality disorder.
   (E) paranoid schizophrenia.

9. With what disorder is learned helplessness most commonly associated?

   (A) Depression
   (B) PTSD
   (C) Generalized anxiety disorder
   (D) Dissociative fugue
   (E) Paranoid schizophrenia

10. A person with which of the following disorders would be MOST likely to get into an altercation with law enforcement because she frequently violates the rights of others?

    (A) Antisocial personality disorder
    (B) Hypochondriasis
    (C) Disorganized schizophrenia
    (D) Obsessive-compulsive disorder
    (E) Conversion disorder

11. Richie is having problems with his hip, but doctors can find nothing wrong with it. As an athlete, Richie is preparing for the biggest race of the year. This hip problem is likely going to keep him from competing. Richie most likely suffers from

    (A) schizophrenia.
    (B) a conversion disorder.
    (C) depression.
    (D) hypochondriasis.
    (E) an anxiety disorder.

12. Fred has no regard for the rights or privileges of others and consistently violates those rights with no remorse. He probably suffers from

    (A) schizophrenia.
    (B) antisocial personality disorder.
    (C) obsessive-compulsive disorder.
    (D) bipolar disorder.
    (E) somatoform disorder.

13. Which of the following disorders is more likely to be found in women than in men?

    (A) Depression
    (B) Post-traumatic stress disorder
    (C) Obsessive-compulsive disorder
    (D) Bipolar disorder
    (E) Hypochondriasis

14. Jane wakes up one morning and can't remember where she is from. She struggles with even simple chores because she doesn't know where anything is in her own house. Eventually, she realizes that she can't remember who she is and simply leaves and wanders around for several days. She eventually starts a new identity. Jane is the victim of

    (A) psychogenic amnesia.

    (B) schizoid personality disorder.

    (C) psychogenic fugue.

    (D) multiple personality disorder.

    (E) hypochondriasis.

15. Which of the following disorders is most associated with Freudian psychology?

    (A) Anxiety disorders

    (B) Schizophrenia

    (C) Depression

    (D) Bipolar disorder

    (E) Catatonia

16. Someone who suffers from paranoid schizophrenia is NOT likely to experience

    (A) extreme suspicion.

    (B) delusions of grandeur.

    (C) auditory hallucinations.

    (D) difficulty in communication.

    (E) depression.

17. While at school, Joel experiences an acute onset of anxiety. His heart rate increases, his blood pressure increases, and he feels jittery. Joel is probably experiencing a(n)

    (A) heart attack.

    (B) panic attack.

    (C) episode of mania.

    (D) psychotic break.

    (E) catatonic experience.

18. Carla and her best friend Curtis, both aged 25, have been close since third grade, but Curtis said something unkind about Carla's latest haircut. Carla decided he was a mean and evil person, and she didn't want anything to do with him. Curtis complains that this is a pattern with Carla—that she consistently identifies people as being good or bad. Carla is likely to be experiencing symptoms of

    (A) anxiety disorder.

    (B) antisocial personality disorder.

    (C) borderline personality disorder.

    (D) depressive disorder.

    (E) obsessive-compulsive disorder.

19. Waxy flexibility is a symptom most closely associated with

    (A) paranoid schizophrenia.

    (B) catatonic schizophrenia.

    (C) bipolar disorder.

    (D) post-traumatic stress disorder.

    (E) hypochondriasis.

20. Karen is afraid of heights. This fear inhibits her daily life. This is an example of

    (A) phobic disorder.

    (B) panic disorder.

    (C) somatoform disorder.

    (D) schizophrenic disorder.

    (E) anxiety disorder.

ANSWERS AND EXPLANATIONS

1. B

In the DSM-IV, multiple-personality disorder is categorized as a dissociative disorder. Other dissociative disorders include dissociative fugue and amnesia.

2. A

One of the hallmarks of schizophrenia is hearing voices. Other disorders do not have this characteristic. Dissociative disorders, (B), are similar to multiple personality disorders, anxiety disorders, (C), occur when one suffers from anxiety that does not have a specific cause, somatoform disorders, (D), occur when one suffers from an illness or disorder but there is no physical cause, and personality disorders, (E), do not result in hearing voices.

3. B

Suzanne probably has obsessive-compulsive disorder. Her irrational thoughts are obsessions, and the impulsive, repetitive actions are compulsions.

4. A

Maladaptive means anything that interferes with someone's daily life and makes it harder for the person to live every day. Depression, for example, may make one want to stay in bed and avoid social situations, while agoraphobia may make one a prisoner in one's own house. Note that choices (B) and (D) mention violence, but only a small number of people with diagnosed disorders are ever violent.

5. D

The *Diagnostic and Statistical Manual,* fourth edition (DSM-IV), was created by the American Psychiatric Association to be the standard by which all disorders of abnormal behavior can be diagnosed. For one to be diagnosed with depression, for example, the feelings of sadness must last for at least two weeks and significantly interfere with daily activities. The manual is updated periodically to reflect the current view of what constitutes a disorder; these revisions are always controversial because the standards of diagnoses can change, or entire disorders can suddenly be eliminated from the next version of the DSM.

6. D

Panic attacks are not a symptom of schizophrenia, though they are linked to certain phobias and anxiety disorders. Delusions, (A), auditory hallucinations, (B), inappropriate affect, (C), and disorganized thought, (E), are all symptomatic of schizophrenia.

7. C

Bipolar disorder occurs when one vacillates between periods of highs and lows. Depression, (A), occurs when one is suffering from being really down. To be bipolar, one must experience both the highs and the lows of mood. Schizophrenia, (B), is not a mood disorder but rather one of cognitive processing, and amnesia, (D), and post-traumatic stress disorder, (E), deal with dissociation and anxiety.

8. E

Paranoid schizophrenia is marked by auditory hallucinations and a fear of persecution. Catatonic schizophrenia, (A), is marked by periods of immobility but not by fear of persecution. A person with antisocial personality disorder, (D), has impaired social functioning.

9. A

Seligman first coined the concept of learned helplessness after experiments with dogs that gave up trying to escape a shock when they felt that nothing they tried would make a difference. The connection to humans is that there are times when some people look at their past failures and assume that nothing they have tried has been successful, so they choose to just give up. Psychotherapists work with these patients to help them see that despite old problems, they can learn new ways to cope with their current situations. PTSD, (B), and generalized anxiety disorder, (C), both involve anxiety but are not linked to learned helplessness, nor are dissociative fugue, (D), or paranoid schizophrenia, (E).

10. A

A common misconception for students is that people diagnosed with psychological disorders are violent and a danger to themselves and others; this is true in only a minority of cases. Someone with antisocial personality disorder will have a long history of defying authority and may often have conflicts with law enforcement, but ironically, these people may not see themselves as having a problem.

11. B

Richie has a conversion disorder. He is converting his anxiety about the race into a physical symptom.

12. B

The antisocial personality disorder is unique in that it has fairly clear signs and symptoms. The lack of regard for the rights of others is a clear indication of a personality disorder, and the violation of rights is a clear indication of antisocial personality disorder.

13. A

Depression is significantly more likely to be found in women than men. This is true both in adults and in adolescents.

14. C

Jane has psychogenic fugue. She has lost a sense of identity and created a new one. Psychologists are not sure why these cases occur, and they do not occur very often. Note that a person suffering from a fugue state does not show characteristics of personality disorders, anxiety disorders, or schizophrenia. Much has been made about the use of such a disorder to avoid responsibility, but the evidence is not clear as to why this occurs.

15. A

Anxiety disorders can be most associated with Freudian psychology. Freud spent most of his early career studying ways to deal with anxiety and most of his later career helping people in that regard. All of the defense mechanisms he defined helped people with anxiety.

16. E

A person suffering from paranoid schizophrenia will have all the symptoms listed except clinical depression.

17. B

Joel is having a panic attack. Panic attacks are marked by a rapid, acute case of anxiety with no real trigger. The person feels as though he has no control and is unable to cope with the situation.

18. C

Carla has borderline personality disorder. A person with this disorder suffers from lack of social skills and is unable to see shades of gray in personality. A person is either good or bad, a friend or not. The person with borderline personality disorder is unable to utilize social judgment to make decisions about relationships.

19. B

Waxy flexibility is a condition characterized by disordered motor activity and is a component of catatonic schizophrenia. A person in this state may not only appear to be inactive, but if one were to move a patient's arm and then release it, the limb would remain in the same position as if the person was a wax figure. It is believed that the trigger for these catatonic events is a stressful situation, and even people who are not diagnosed with schizophrenia have slipped into catatonic states due to an overwhelming stressor (such as the death of a loved one).

20. A

Karen has a phobic disorder, a fear of a particular object or event that interferes with normal activities. The other disorders also inhibit daily life, but they are not associated with fear of one particular thing.

CHAPTER 15: TREATMENT OF ABNORMAL BEHAVIOR

IF YOU LEARN ONLY FIVE THINGS IN THIS CHAPTER . . .

1. The most common treatment for psychiatric disorders today is the use of medication.

2. Medication is effective as a treatment, but it is often combined with a form of "talk therapy" to provide a more complete therapeutic technique.

3. Most medications have side effects.

4. Behavioral and cognitive therapies are very popular forms of "talk therapy."

5. Freudian therapy, though well known, is not utilized much anymore.

INTRODUCTION

Treating psychological disorders poses one of the biggest problems for psychologists. It is important to have a realistic perspective: we can treat the symptoms, but according to most perspectives, we cannot cure the disorders.

Several treatment methods have been designed, each with a different degree of effectiveness.

DRUG THERAPY

The first course of treatment for many psychological disorders is to provide relief of the symptoms. Drugs are often the most effective strategy for doing this.

The following drugs have been used for the following psychological disorders:

Depression	Antidepressants, including the selective serotonin reuptake inhibitors, such as Prozac, Wellbutrin, Zoloft
Anxiety disorders	Anxiolytics, such as Xanax or Paxil
Schizophrenia	Early antipsychotics included drugs that caused side effects such as tardive dyskinesia. The most well-known of these drugs was chlorpromazine (Thorazine). More recent drugs, such as Zyprexa and Risperdal, reduce the effects on the muscle systems.

Drug therapy is designed to reduce the symptoms of psychological disorders. But typically, it is combined with "**talk therapy**" to alleviate symptoms overall and to help the afflicted person handle the disorder more effectively.

Of the various "talk therapies," the techniques of Sigmund Freud have served as the face of psychology. What is interesting about this is that Freud offered some of the least testable techniques of any of the therapies.

FREUD'S THERAPEUTIC TECHNIQUE

In Freud's therapy, the goal is to help the patient uncover the **unconscious conflicts** that give rise to **anxiety**. Anxiety typically causes a person difficulty in dealing with everyday life. The cause of anxiety is, according to Freud, deep-rooted conflicts set in the unconscious. To get at them, the therapist must use a variety of techniques, including intensive one-on-one therapy. This therapy is called **psychoanalysis**.

Psychoanalysis is a long-term commitment; it typically lasts one hour a day, several days a week—possibly for several years. Various techniques are used to get to the unconscious, but the setup, according to Freud, is important. The therapist should sit behind a client in a chair, and the client should lie in a chaise lounge so she can relax. The therapist asks questions, and the client answers as honestly as possible. Therapy takes so long because the techniques to get to the unconscious cannot be direct. To uncover what is in the unconscious, the therapist must use techniques that require interpretation before the true meaning can be divined.

AP EXPERT TIP

Note: Some therapeutic techniques are designed to treat the *actual cause* of a disorder (Freud), while others treat the *symptoms or behaviors* associated with the disorder (drug therapy, behavioral therapy).

DREAM ANALYSIS

Freud argued that dreams were the "royal road to the unconscious." By using dream analysis, a therapist could take notes on the **manifest content** (the dream itself) and then interpret the **latent content** (the hidden, underlying symbolic meaning of the dream). By using what Freud knew about the symbolism of dreams, a therapist can determine some of the potential causes of anxiety.

TRANSFERENCE

Freud discovered that some of his patients developed strong feelings about him—some of love, some of hate—but after contemplation he realized that these patients were experiencing strong emotions for their loved ones and temporarily transferring those to their therapist. Freud had the great insight that this transference was an unconscious process—and, indeed, a way that he could illuminate this issue and help the patients see the unresolved conflicts with people they were close to.

HYPNOSIS

Freud practiced hypnosis early in his career. He believed that hypnosis would ease the grip that repression had on the unconscious and allow some of those issues to percolate to consciousness. He later argued, however, that it was far less effective than he once believed.

FREE ASSOCIATION

Free association was Freud's preferred method of therapy. With free association, a person says the first thing that comes to mind when a therapist says something. If a person does this fast enough, according to Freud, the first thing he says can be a "glimpse" into the unconscious. By getting such a glimpse, the therapist can determine the causes of the anxiety.

DRUGS

Freud also believed that a variety of drugs (including cocaine) could be used to alleviate anxiety.

It is interesting to note that Freud did not spend much of the therapeutic situation practicing these techniques but, rather, collecting detailed histories of his clients. He believed that small details of one's childhood could be critical in explaining how the anxiety had developed.

After years of intensive therapy and after much of the unconscious has been laid bare through the treatment, the client is presumably "cured."

Other forms of psychoanalysis also focused on determining the cause of anxiety in the unconscious but used different techniques. The underlying assumption is that therapy should uncover the issues in the unconscious that are the root of anxiety.

COGNITIVE THERAPY

Cognitive therapies assume that people suffer from problems when their beliefs about the world are disconnected from reality itself. One feels anxiety because the perspective that one brings to the world is inconsistent and, typically, much worse than reality. People who see a cognitive therapist will describe their perspective on reality, to which the therapist responds by helping them see reality more clearly. In the technique called **cognitive restructuring**, the therapist helps the client restructure his thoughts to make them more consistent with reality.

Cognitive therapies have been used with a variety of disorders, but the most common disorder they help is **depression**. **Aaron Beck** (among others) pioneered the use of cognitive therapy with depression when he learned that depressed people tend to catastrophize issues in their lives. That is, they tend to view their issues as being worse than they are. Cognitive restructuring helps these individuals realize that life situations are not as severe as they perceive. With that understanding, they can deal more effectively with their depression.

HUMANISTIC THERAPY

The most well-known humanistic therapy is the approach championed by **Carl Rogers**. According to Rogers, and humanistic theory in general, people are **inherently good** and **strive to reach their potential**. Therapy is designed to help people understand the essential human characteristics and help them work toward achieving their potential.

Essentially, the philosophy of humanistic therapy is to **provide a sounding board for people to voice opinions and thoughts**. The therapist gives the client **unconditional positive regard**. By doing this, he helps the client understand conditions of worth, which in turn helps her understand how to deal better with situations in life.

Much of this therapeutic approach is reflective toward the person; all that might be required is for a person to hear an objective opinion. Humanistic psychologists do this by parroting back to the client what she says. This technique is known as **active listening** and is an important part of the humanistic approach, because it helps people feel that someone is listening to them and that their concerns are being validated. Humanistic psychologists often view those whom they work with not as patients but as clients, so the term often used for this approach is **client-centered therapy**.

BEHAVIORAL THERAPY

The behavioral approach to therapy assumes that **psychological disorders are really behavior disorders**. To treat the "disorder," we need only treat the behavior. The techniques that modify human behavior are appropriate to dealing with the disorders. Essentially, the goal of behavioral therapy is to create an **environmental context** that is in conflict with the behaviors demonstrated by the person with the disorder. When that occurs, we are able to alter the behavior because the reinforcement is stronger for the alternative behavior choice than it is for the disordered behavior.

The best example for a behavior therapy is called **systematic desensitization**. This technique was developed by Joseph Wolpe and is most effective in dealing with **phobias**. The technique borrows from the **progressive relaxation** literature. First, a client is taught how to relax. This is more than just relaxing the way one might do while watching a baseball game—it is a systematic approach to relaxation.

In progressive relaxation, a person is taught to relax each body part in sequence. The relaxation is made observable to the client by using biofeedback (a technique that allows one to see a measure of heart rate, breathing rate, etc.). Finally, in very small steps, the phobia-causing stimulus is introduced. When the client feels anxiety, she is told to practice relaxation. In such a way, and in small steps, the client can learn to relax in the presence of the phobia-causing stimulus.

Behavioral approaches have been shown to be very effective treatments for a wide variety of disorders.

REVIEW QUESTIONS

1. The concept most associated with Rogerian or client-centered therapy is

   (A) flooding.

   (B) free association.

   (C) unconditional positive regard.

   (D) positive reinforcement.

   (E) punishment.

2. The concept most associated with a form of behavioral therapy is

   (A) dream analysis.

   (B) free association.

   (C) unconditional positive regard.

   (D) positive reinforcement.

   (E) hypnosis.

3. A client goes to see a psychiatrist and is diagnosed with schizophrenia. He is likely to be prescribed

   (A) Haldol.

   (B) Prozac.

   (C) Risperdal.

   (D) lithium.

   (E) Zoloft.

4. Which of the following psychologists developed the concept of systematic desensitization?

   (A) Freud

   (B) Rogers

   (C) Skinner

   (D) Wolpe

   (E) Wundt

5. A patient is given the task of restructuring the way she thinks about the issues in her life. This is an example of _____ therapy.

   (A) cognitive

   (B) psychoanalytic

   (C) humanistic

   (D) behavioral

   (E) biological

6. A patient who suffers from a phobia will most likely be treated with

   (A) psychoanalytic therapy.

   (B) drug therapy.

   (C) systematic desensitization.

   (D) cognitive restructuring.

   (E) Rogerian therapy.

7. Which of the following is NOT a technique utilized by practitioners of Freudian psychoanalysis?

   (A) Progressive relaxation

   (B) Transference

   (C) Free association

   (D) Dream analysis

   (E) Projective tests

8. A client is asked to express his perspective no matter what people think of him. The therapist is going to give him unconditional positive regard and accept the person for who he is. This is a form of

   (A) client-centered therapy.

   (B) Freudian therapy.

   (C) cognitive therapy.

   (D) drug therapy.

   (E) behavioral therapy.

9. If a person was seeking a therapist who would help her get her life back together and offer very direct ways that she could fix her problems, which of the following therapists would she be LEAST successful with?

(A) Cognitive therapist

(B) psychoanalyst

(C) Behavioral therapist

(D) Gestalt therapist

(E) Client-centered therapist

10. A client feels as though he is beginning to develop feelings for the therapist. He previously had the same feelings for someone else. According to Freudian theory, this is a process called

(A) projection.

(B) repression.

(C) regression.

(D) denial.

(E) transference.

11. The goal of cognitive therapy is to

(A) understand the theories of behavior.

(B) treat the symptoms of the client.

(C) help the client see inconsistencies in thoughts and behaviors.

(D) understand the reasons behind behavior.

(E) treat the disorder medically.

12. You have a dream that you go to class but have forgotten an important assignment. You are embarrassed as the teacher points out to everyone that you did not follow instructions. According to Freud, this description of the dream is the

(A) true meaning.

(B) deep structure.

(C) latent content.

(D) manifest content.

(E) surface structure.

13. With that same dream, if Freud said that it was really a response to a threat and you were feeling scared of dealing with that threat, that would be called the _____ of the dream.

(A) true meaning

(B) deep structure

(C) latent content

(D) manifest content

(E) surface structure

14. Jim realizes that his fear of heights is becoming overwhelming and he really needs a therapist who can most effectively "fix" him in the least amount of time. He doesn't want to know where the fear comes from, but just wants it gone. What type of therapy would be best for Jim?

(A) Psychoanalysis

(B) Behavioral therapy

(C) Cognitive therapy

(D) Client-centered therapy

(E) Transference

15. Therapy is a difficult process. One reason stated in the text is that

    (A) it is expensive.

    (B) it is time consuming.

    (C) it is not effective.

    (D) we treat the symptoms, not the disease.

    (E) we don't have enough therapists.

16. According to cognitive therapists, clients who think that their problems are much bigger than they actually are are said to be

    (A) confabulating.

    (B) exaggerating.

    (C) catastrophizing.

    (D) projecting.

    (E) sublimating.

17. Which of the following techniques was NOT used by Sigmund Freud?

    (A) Dream analysis

    (B) Hypnosis

    (C) Free association

    (D) Collecting detailed histories

    (E) Cognitive restructuring

18. "A person suffers from depression because she has been reinforced for acting depressed in the past." Which of the following perspectives might provide this explanation for depression?

    (A) Behavioral

    (B) Cognitive

    (C) Rogerian

    (D) Psychoanalytic

    (E) Medical

19. Client-centered therapy was originally developed by

    (A) Wolpe.

    (B) Rogers.

    (C) Freud.

    (D) Wundt.

    (E) Skinner.

20. Patients who have been on antipsychotic medications for many years may experience a disabling series of side effects such as repetitive movements, rapid eye blinking, and grimacing. This collection of side effects is known as

    (A) tardive dyskinesia.

    (B) systematic desensitization.

    (C) Tourette syndrome.

    (D) post-traumatic stress.

    (E) hypochondriasis.

ANSWERS AND EXPLANATIONS

1. C

Unconditional positive regard is most often associated with Rogerian therapy. This type of therapy works under the assumption that the therapist does not judge the client but, rather, accepts the client as he is and provides primarily respect to him as an individual. Flooding, (A), positive reinforcement, (D), and punishment, (E), might be used by learning therapists. Free association, (B), would be used in psychoanalysis.

2. D

In behavioral therapy, the goal is to provide positive reinforcement for behaviors that are inconsistent with the aberrant behaviors. The other mentioned techniques are associated with either psychoanalysis or client-centered, Rogerian therapy.

3. C

Risperdal is not the only drug for schizophrenia, but it is a popular choice among psychiatrists. Haldol, (A), is used for anxiety, Prozac, (B), and Zoloft, (E), for depression, and lithium, (D), for bipolar disorder.

4. D

Wolpe developed the idea of systematic desensitization. Skinner and Wundt were not clinicians but rather experimentalists who were determined to develop theories to explain human behavior.

5. A

This would be cognitive therapy. In cognitive therapy, the goal is to help a client understand inconsistencies in the ways he perceives the world.

The therapist and client work together to develop a more coherent and appropriate view of the world.

6. C

A patient with a phobia would likely receive systematic desensitization. Though the other mentioned forms of therapy are appropriate to one degree or another, systematic desensitization is the form of therapy most often utilized with success for treating phobic disorders.

7. A

Psychoanalysis does not use progressive relaxation. Freud used transference, (B), free association, (C), dream analysis, (D), and projective tests, (E), as a way to get at the unconscious of a person during therapy.

8. A

Client-centered therapy puts the emphasis on the client rather than the therapist. In this form of therapy, the client directs the course of the therapy and helps himself, really, by providing most of the fodder for the needed work. The therapist is there to guide but not to provide a great deal of structure, as is the case with the other forms of therapy mentioned.

9. E

All of these therapists have the ultimate goal of helping their patients, but they approach this goal in very different ways. Client-centered therapy offers the most supportive and nurturing environment, giving the client unconditional positive regard and allowing any thoughts and feelings to be expressed. However, these therapists are also strong proponents of being nondirective in their statements, so if a client asks for a solution to his or her problems, the client-centered therapist is most likely to decline and turn the question back to the client. For some clients this is helpful, because it leads to further introspection, but for others this can be frustrating.

10. E

This is a case of transference. Freud actually encouraged this in some cases when he believed the feelings were directed at inappropriate sources. By transferring the feelings to the therapist, a client could work on the feelings more efficiently during the analysis.

11. C

Cognitive therapy is designed to help clients see the faulty reasoning they engage in, as they try to deal with the stress of life. In many cases, clients will exaggerate or catastrophize the issues in their lives. In cognitive therapy, the client will be guided to see the error in those ways. By doing that, he is better equipped to deal with stress.

12. D

Manifest content is the description of the dream itself. True meaning, (A), is not a term used in psychology. Deep, (B), and surface structure, (E), are terms used in the study of language. Latent content, (C), is the true meaning of the dream.

13. C

The latent content is the meaning of the dream as decided by the therapist and the client after the dream is fully described.

14. B

The most "solution-oriented" therapy is behavioral therapy. Practitioners of the talk therapies of psychoanalysis, (A), cognitive therapy, (C), and client-centered therapy, (D), tend to build relationships with their patients that may take months or years to establish, and all help their patients explore the root causes of their behaviors. Behavioral therapy, which is a branch of operant conditioning, seeks only to help patients learn to deal with their problems more effectively without searching for the initial reasons that triggered the phobias.

15. D

Because we don't have a strong handle on what causes psychological disorders, it is difficult to treat the disorder at its roots. We spend more time dealing with and treating the symptoms. Clients are not really "cured," though they are able to manage the symptoms better.

16. C

These individuals are catastrophizing. This is the term used by practitioners of cognitive therapy.

17. E

Freud did not use cognitive restructuring.

18. A

A behavioral approach would state that a person suffers from depression because she was reinforced for acting depressed in the past. The cognitive perspective, (B), suggests depression results from inappropriate views of the world; the Rogerian perspective, (C), that people don't recognize their self-worth. The medical perspective, (E), states we suffer depression because of a chemical imbalance in the brain.

19. B

Rogers first developed client-centered therapy.

20. A

Tardive dyskinesia was first discovered after antipsychotic medications were introduced around 1960. This was a devastating blow for those who suffered from it, because the antipsychotic medications were effectively dealing with their schizophrenia, and now these side effects made them even more vulnerable to the outside world. Some patients were so upset and humiliated by these symptoms that it led them to discontinue their medications altogether. Tourette syndrome, (C), may involve repetitive behaviors, but these are not side effects from drugs.

CHAPTER 16: SOCIAL PSYCHOLOGY

IF YOU LEARN ONLY FIVE THINGS IN THIS CHAPTER . . .

1. Social psychology refers to how groups influence the behavior of an individual.

2. Attribution theory refers to how we make judgments about others.

3. Obedience and conformity both refer to the influence of others on our behavior.

4. Milgram did studies in social psychology that seem to be on the ethical edge.

5. Behavior can be influenced by the presence of a group.

INTRODUCTION

The study of social psychology is one of the older branches of psychology and is an enormous area of research. This area is most concerned with how the social environment impacts an individual's behavior. As more research is performed, we develop a better sense of what social psychology is really all about. Typically, it looks at a variety of processes, including impression formation, making attributions, and interpersonal relations such as attraction, prosocial behaviors and aggression, and social influence.

Much has been made in the media about many of the findings of social research; however, the area is still filled with much uncertainty.

IMPRESSION FORMATION

The notion of **impression formation** begins with the premise that, to form an impression, we need to have a target and a perceiver. In such a situation, we often fall back on a preconceived notion of a person or a thing. This is, of course, called a **stereotype**, and it is something we use all the time to determine how we should behave or what course of action we should take.

We form stereotypes in a variety of ways, and they can be positive or negative. The problem with stereotypes is not that we form them (it is probably impossible given the enormity of the human experience not to form them) but that their consequences sometimes lead us to make choices or perform behaviors that are not appropriate.

The **cognitive-confirmation bias**, for example, has demonstrated that participants are more likely to search for information that confirms a previously learned bias than to seek information that contradicts the bias. Suppose you want to buy a particular car. You will actively seek out information that supports the good aspects of that car and will overlook information that doesn't support that choice.

Likewise, the **self-fulfilling prophecy** suggests that if you hear something good or bad about a person, you will perceive that skill in the person more than if you hadn't previously heard that information.

ATTRIBUTION THEORY

One of the things that we do when we are interacting with others is to make guesses, or "**attributions**," about the causes of their behavior. We are not perfect in this process, but it doesn't stop us from doing it. We often make mistakes because of biases we have.

The **fundamental attribution error (FAE)** suggests that we tend to make attributions about causes of behavior being internal and not external. In other words, we often believe that someone does something because of who he is, not because of the situation.

The **actor-perceiver bias** is another attribution error we make. If we are doing something, we believe our behavior is due to external causes; if we are watching someone else, we believe behavior is internally motivated.

AP EXPERT TIP

Many sports announcers and reporters are guilty of the FAE when they make guesses about the causes of athletic performance.

Finally, the **self-serving bias** occurs as well, where we attribute causes of behavior to external causes if we fail and internal causes if we succeed. So if we have done well on an exam, we are smart, but if we have not done well, then the teacher made a very tough test.

INTERPERSONAL RELATIONS

What causes **attraction**? Research has shown that proximity, affect (emotions), similarity, and reinforcement all contribute to attraction. What is interesting about this is that we are not certain which is the most important factor and which is the least. All seem to play a role in attraction, and with more research, we might better be able to tease these variables apart.

Prosocial behavior is when we engage in behavior that leads to some good outcome. **Altruism**, for example, is helping behavior that is motivated by helping others for the sake of helping. Psychologists became interested in this topic because a great deal of research done in the 1960s and 1970s suggested that people are not likely to help others unless they are alone with that person. If someone needs help and there are many people around, **diffusion of responsibility** occurs (called the **bystander effect**): the probability of someone helping another in distress decreases as the number of people available to help increases. (Interestingly, people today are slightly more likely to help because of the well-publicized research on the bystander effect.)

AGGRESSION

Aggression is behavior that is intended to inflict harm on others. We are aggressive because of frustration or anger. Typically, aggression takes place when the aggressive act does not have an immediate negative consequence. That is, we are aggressive when it appears that we can get away with it. Sometimes, that is due to what psychologists call deindividuation. **Deindividuation** is the tendency for people to lose individuality, often because one is a member of a group or because the situation warrants it.

Aggression is common in all animals. Interestingly, only mammals kill out of anger or in an organized fashion, such as war.

SOCIAL INFLUENCE

One of the biggest areas of social psychology has to do with social influence. That is, how does the situation we are in influence our behavior? **Persuasion** is one area that has attracted a great deal of attention. How are we persuaded to alter our behavior?

Several variables can persuade us to alter our behavior:

- The **source** of the information or persuasion (Is it an authority? Is it a person attractive to me?)
- **How** we are persuaded (in person or via some communication channel)
- **What** we are hearing
- Our **background**

We can be persuaded to alter our behavior in a variety of ways (through newspapers, television ads) depending on how the persuasive situation is set up. Think of the commercials on TV that are designed to persuade. The makers of these commercials are well trained in persuasion. They target these messages to a particular audience and use the techniques that work best with that audience. On channels that cater to children, for instance, the commercials are shorter (children have a short attention span) and are filled with appealing images (sweets, toys). The commercials on other channels are likewise designed.

One of the more well-studied forms of social influence is obedience. **Obedience** is performing a behavior because one is told to do so. In **Milgram**'s famous study, participants "shocked" other participants because they were told to do so. Milgram argued that anyone can be obedient and that obedience is not limited to the lab. He pointed to Nazi Germany as evidence that this is so. We obey because the person telling us to do something is an authority and we assume he takes responsibility. This is not always the case, but it is part of human behavior.

Compliance and conformity are two other types of social influence. **Compliance** occurs when behavior changes because of a request, not a command or order. For instance, we may allow a salesperson to give us details about a vacuum cleaner after we have inquired about a carpet cleaning. We are more willing to listen to those details because we had initiated a request for other information. This is called **reciprocity**. Another form of compliance is the **foot-in-the-door technique**. If you comply with a small request, you may then comply with a larger request. These techniques have been known for years and have led to a large number of sales for people in the business.

Conformity is slightly different. In **conformity** situations (such as the famous study by **Asch**), participants often change behavior (and opinion) when faced with others who make a different choice. Of the numerous studies on conformity, many show that if enough people are engaging in a certain behavior or attitude, it is very difficult for others to resist that and engage in their own—unique (different)—behaviors. **Private conformity** occurs when we change our behaviors and our attitudes. **Public conformity** occurs when we just change our behavior.

GROUP PROCESSES

Much has been made of the issue of **how groups influence behavior**: Does group size matter, for instance? In fact, it does matter. People are more likely to conform in larger groups. One dissenter decreases the probability that people will conform, but group size matters. If the group is small, **social facilitation** might occur. That is, our performance can be enhanced by competing (this is why in the Olympics, people run against each other, even though they are really running against the clock).

In groups, we sometimes see social loafing. **Social loafing** occurs as one member of the group does not "carry his weight." **Groupthink** can occur as well, where people have a desire to maintain good relations within the group. The views of the group leader are known early on, and no one is designated to voice a dissenting opinion. Thus, the group reaches a consensus it might not otherwise have reached because of a strong leader at the beginning. This will sometimes happen in juries.

REVIEW QUESTIONS

1. Which of the following is an example of the "foot-in-the-door" technique?

    (A) You buy a car because your brother does.

    (B) You wear a shirt because your friend bought it for you.

    (C) You face the front of the elevator because everyone else is facing front.

    (D) You buy expensive perfume because the salesperson gives you a small gift.

    (E) You stand while everyone else is saying the "Pledge of Allegiance."

2. The fact that people are not likely to help someone if they are in a large group is called the

    (A) foot-in-the-door.

    (B) bystander effect.

    (C) obedience effect.

    (D) conformity.

    (E) compliance effect.

3. Social loafing typically occurs when

    (A) one is alone.

    (B) one is in a very small group.

    (C) one is in a very large group.

    (D) a project is past deadline.

    (E) someone forgets about social responsibility.

4. When someone assumes that a person behaved the way he did because of internal causes, this is called the

    (A) fundamental attribution error.

    (B) bystander effect.

    (C) actor-perceiver bias.

    (D) stereotyping bias.

    (E) self-fulfilling prophecy.

5. In the research on attraction, proximity, affect, similarity, and reinforcement have all been shown to contribute to attraction. Which is the MOST important?

    (A) Proximity

    (B) Similarity

    (C) Affect

    (D) Reinforcement

    (E) Psychologists are still uncertain.

6. In his famous study on obedience, Milgram argued that people

    (A) were obedient because they were men.

    (B) were obedient because of the situation.

    (C) were not obedient because the requests were unreasonable.

    (D) in general do what they think is right.

    (E) today typically do not listen to authorities.

7. Which of the following is an example of conformity?

    (A) Your friend says, "Let's go to the mall," and you do.

    (B) You stop at a red light.

    (C) You sing the national anthem because everyone else is singing.

    (D) You arrive home when you are told to do so by your parents.

    (E) You wait in line for a ride at an amusement park.

8. In speed skating, two people skate together, but they are not competing so much with each other as they are with the clock. This is done because psychologists have discovered _____, which suggests that we do better when in the presence of others.

    (A) Social loafing
    (B) Groupthink
    (C) Conformity
    (D) Obedience
    (E) Social facilitation

9. The idea that someone is willing to commit aggressive acts when he is in a group because there is no immediate consequence for his behavior is called

    (A) groupthink.
    (B) social loafing.
    (C) deindividuation.
    (D) obedience.
    (E) social facilitation.

10. We are sometimes persuaded to do something that we wouldn't normally do. Which of the following is considered to be important as a persuasive tool?

    (A) Source of the information
    (B) Accuracy of the information
    (C) Direct orders
    (D) Subliminal messages
    (E) Backward masking

11. If we help someone simply for the sake of helping, this is called

    (A) bystander effect.
    (B) altruism.
    (C) social loafing.
    (D) deindividuation.
    (E) obedience.

12. People in groups will modify their own behavior to that of the larger group without ever being asked to. This tendency to change behavior to fit that of a peer group is known as

    (A) reciprocity.
    (B) obedience.
    (C) the bystander effect.
    (D) conformity.
    (E) altruism.

13. The fact that people sometimes do things they don't want to do because they are told to do so is called

    (A) private conformity.
    (B) obedience.
    (C) social facilitation.
    (D) public conformity.
    (E) persuasion.

14. The fundamental attribution error occurs when someone attributes causes

    (A) to the environment.
    (B) to the person.
    (C) to the group process.
    (D) to groupthink.
    (E) to sociocultural variables.

15. The fact that we attribute our success to internal causes and failure to external causes is called

(A) fundamental attribution error.

(B) actor-perceiver bias.

(C) self-serving bias.

(D) groupthink.

(E) self-fulfilling prophecy.

16. In a classic study, it was demonstrated that children who were labeled as potential high achievers outdistanced those labeled as low achievers, even though there was no difference between the groups prior to the study. This is an example of

(A) fundamental attribution error.

(B) actor-perceiver bias.

(C) self-serving bias.

(D) groupthink.

(E) self-fulfilling prophecy.

17. The fact that we attribute our errors to the environment and other people's errors to internal causes is called

(A) fundamental attribution error.

(B) actor-perceiver bias.

(C) self-serving bias.

(D) groupthink.

(E) self-fulfilling prophecy.

18. If you are doing a group project and one member of the group is not pulling his own weight, social psychologists might call that behavior

(A) bystander effect.

(B) altruism.

(C) social loafing.

(D) deindividuation.

(E) obedience.

19. Suppose you need help with a homework assignment. You ask your friend, and she agrees. You end up doing very well on the assignment. Later, your friend needs a ride to the airport. Even though you are very busy, you agree. This is an example of

(A) social loafing.

(B) deindividuation.

(C) obedience.

(D) conformity.

(E) reciprocity.

20. If you are on a jury, you might find that you have an opinion upon entering the jury room. However, after a while, and after several persuasive arguments, you find yourself agreeing with everyone else. In fact, everyone is very certain about the outcome. This is an example of

(A) bystander effect.

(B) altruism.

(C) social loafing.

(D) groupthink.

(E) obedience.

ANSWERS AND EXPLANATIONS

1. D

According to the foot-in-the-door technique, you will comply with a larger request when you have already complied with a smaller request. In this example, by accepting the small gift, you now feel like you should buy the perfume.

2. B

According to the bystander effect, a person will be less likely to help when in a large group. In a small group, it is harder to not help because of the responsibility one might feel.

3. C

Social loafing occurs when one is in a large group. A person is likely to coast when there is less of a chance of being forced to take responsibility.

4. A

The bystander effect, (B), occurs when someone doesn't help because there is a large crowd, the actor-perceiver bias, (C), occurs when we attribute our behavior to external causes and others' behavior to internal causes, stereotyping bias, (D), occurs when we stereotype based on group, and the self-fulfilling prophecy, (E), occurs when people's behavior changes as a result of expectations.

5. E

We do not know which of those important variables is the most important predictor of attraction.

6. B

According to Milgram, people in general will do what they are told when the situation is right. That is, if there is an authority and the situation seems as though responsibility does not entirely rest with the individual, then people will often perform behavior they did not think they would.

7. C

The other responses are examples of either rules or direct orders. Conformity is more subtle than that. That is, with conformity, we tend to do what others are doing without actually being told to do it.

8. E

Social facilitation was demonstrated by Norman Triplett in 1897 when he demonstrated that people ride bicycles faster when they are competing against another.

9. C

Deindividuation is the process of giving up responsibility because there is a large group. In such a situation, it is difficult to assign responsibility for one person's actions because so many people could be culpable.

10. A

The source of the information is often very persuasive. We often listen to authorities even if they are not accurate. Subliminal messages, (D), and backward masking, (E), are old techniques used for "persuasion," but the research suggests that these two techniques are not effective.

11. B

The bystander effect, (A), refers to the tendency of one not to help in a group, social loafing, (C), occurs when a member of a group "coasts," deindividuation, (D), occurs when a group commits behavior that members do not feel responsible for, and obedience, (E), is our response to "authority figures."

12. D

Remember that obedience, (B), is viewed as following the orders or requests of someone who is somehow above you in status; this could be a parent, a teacher, or other figure of authority. You may fear the repercussions of failing to obey this figure. Conformity, (D), is much more subtle, in that a person changes behavior to fit in with others often without being explicitly asked. This may be because the person does not know how to behave properly—watching when others clap at the theater, for example—or it may just be that it is easier to "go along with the crowd."

13. B

As described earlier, people often do what they are told because an "authority" tells them to.

14. B

The fundamental attribution error occurs when we attribute causes to internal events.

15. C

The self-serving bias occurs when we assume that our good behavior is the result of internal causes and bad behavior is the result of external causes. The fundamental attribution error, (A), occurs when we attribute causes to internal events, the actor-perceiver bias, (B), occurs when we attribute our behavior to external causes and others' behavior to internal causes, groupthink, (D), occurs when consensus is reached because of a strong leader, and the self-fulfilling prophecy, (E), occurs when expectations lead to behavior.

16. E

In this study, it was found that students labeled as bloomers were more likely to achieve than those labeled as slower. However, the key to this study is that students were assigned to conditions randomly. Although there were no differences before the labeling, the label seemed to influence the way people achieved or were perceived to achieve.

17. B

The fundamental attribution error, (A), occurs when we attribute other people's actions to internal factors, the self-serving bias, (C), occurs when we attribute our behavior to external causes when we fail and to internal causes when we succeed, groupthink, (D), occurs when groups come to a consensus, and the self-fulfilling prophecy, (E), occurs when expectations lead to behavior.

18. C

The bystander effect, (A), occurs when we don't help because we are in a group, altruism, (B), is helping behavior, deindividuation, (D), occurs when we are in a group and we believe responsibility can be shifted from us, and obedience, (E), is the response of performing a behavior because of an order from an authority.

19. E

Reciprocity occurs when someone else complies with our request or does a favor for us. We then feel we must pay back that individual by complying with her request, no matter how unreasonable it might be.

20. D

Groupthink occurs during times of stress when an idea is floated and people tend to come to agreement after a while. People come to believe that the opinion they hold is one that they held the entire time.

| Part Four |

PRACTICE TESTS

HOW TO TAKE THE PRACTICE TESTS

This section of this book contains two full-length Practice Tests. Taking a practice test gives you an idea of what it's like to sit through a full AP Psychology exam. You'll find out in which areas you're strong and where additional review may be required. Any mistakes you make now are ones you won't make on the actual exam, as long as you take the time to learn where you went wrong.

The two tests here each include 100 multiple-choice questions and two free-response (essay) questions. You will have 70 minutes for the multiple-choice questions and 50 minutes to answer the free-response questions.

Before taking a test, find a quiet place where you can work uninterrupted for three hours. Time yourself according to the time limit at the beginning of each section. It's okay to take a short break between sections, but for the most accurate results, you should approximate real test conditions as much as possible.

Remember to pace yourself. Train yourself to be aware of the time you are spending on each problem. Take note of the general types of questions you encounter, as well as what strategies work best for them.

When you are done, read the detailed answer explanations that follow. These will help you identify areas that could use additional review. But don't focus only on the questions you got wrong. For those you got right, too, you can benefit from reading the answer explanations. You might learn something you didn't already know.

For the **free-response questions**, this is your opportunity to express what you know in essay form. A few points to consider:

1. Use your time carefully. Read both questions and answer the one you know better first.

2. Answer the parts of the question in the order they are asked. Each part is worth points, and real people are scoring these. Give them the opportunity to see the points clearly.

3. Provide examples to help explain your points but don't get lost in examples.

4. Answer in full sentences. Don't get caught up trying to answer the questions with bullets. AP does not allow incomplete sentences to score points.

5. Finally, and most obviously, *answer all parts of the question*!

The sample free-response answers that follow the exam are intended to help you understand how a reader will look for the correct information.

Good luck!

HOW TO COMPUTE YOUR SCORE

SCORING THE MULTIPLE-CHOICE QUESTIONS

To compute your score on the multiple-choice portion of each test, count the number of questions you got wrong, then deduct that number from 100. If you got 7 questions wrong, your score would be a 93 for the multiple-choice portion of the exam.

SCORING THE FREE-RESPONSE QUESTIONS

The readers will have specific points that they will be looking for in each essay (called a rubric). Readers use the rubric as the guide for assigning points. Each free-response question is worth a certain number of points, and each point is awarded based on the answers that you provide. Each piece of information that the readers check off in your essay is a point toward a better score.

To figure out your approximate score for the free-response questions, look at the key points found in the sample response for each question. For each key point you include, add a point. Figure out the number of key points there are in each question, then add up the number of key points you included out of the total number. Set up a proportion equal to 100 to obtain your approximate numerical score.

Suppose, for example, you earn a 6 out of 9 on essay 1 and a 5 out of 8 on essay 2. You would take 11/17 (total points divided by total points possible). That would give you 65 percent.

CALCULATING YOUR COMPOSITE SCORE

Your score on the AP Psychology exam is a combination of the multiple-choice and the free-response scores. The free-response section is worth 1/3 of the exam score, and the multiple-choice is worth 2/3.

To determine your score, obtain the percentage of points you earned in your free-response and multiple-choice sections. Multiply the percentages by 0.33 for free-response and 0.66 for the multiple-choice. Continuing with our example, you would multiply $(0.93 \times 0.66 = 0.61)$ for the multiple-choice section and $(0.65 \times 0.33 = 0.22)$ for the free-response section. Add those together, and you get a final score of 0.83 (or 83), which would yield an AP score of approximately 5.

Remember, however, that much of this depends on how well all of those taking the AP test do. If you do better than average, your score would be higher. The numbers here are just approximations.

The approximate score range is as follows:

5 = 75–100 (extremely well qualified)
4 = 60–74 (well qualified)
3 = 50–59 (qualified)
2 = 40–49 (possibly qualified)
1 = 0–39 (no recommendation)

If your score falls between 60 and 100, you're doing great. Keep up the good work! If your score is lower than 59, there's still hope—keep studying, and you will be able to obtain a much better score on the exam before you know it.

Practice Test One Answer Grid

1. Ⓐ Ⓑ Ⓒ Ⓓ Ⓔ
2. Ⓐ Ⓑ Ⓒ Ⓓ Ⓔ
3. Ⓐ Ⓑ Ⓒ Ⓓ Ⓔ
4. Ⓐ Ⓑ Ⓒ Ⓓ Ⓔ
5. Ⓐ Ⓑ Ⓒ Ⓓ Ⓔ
6. Ⓐ Ⓑ Ⓒ Ⓓ Ⓔ
7. Ⓐ Ⓑ Ⓒ Ⓓ Ⓔ
8. Ⓐ Ⓑ Ⓒ Ⓓ Ⓔ
9. Ⓐ Ⓑ Ⓒ Ⓓ Ⓔ
10. Ⓐ Ⓑ Ⓒ Ⓓ Ⓔ
11. Ⓐ Ⓑ Ⓒ Ⓓ Ⓔ
12. Ⓐ Ⓑ Ⓒ Ⓓ Ⓔ
13. Ⓐ Ⓑ Ⓒ Ⓓ Ⓔ
14. Ⓐ Ⓑ Ⓒ Ⓓ Ⓔ
15. Ⓐ Ⓑ Ⓒ Ⓓ Ⓔ
16. Ⓐ Ⓑ Ⓒ Ⓓ Ⓔ
17. Ⓐ Ⓑ Ⓒ Ⓓ Ⓔ
18. Ⓐ Ⓑ Ⓒ Ⓓ Ⓔ
19. Ⓐ Ⓑ Ⓒ Ⓓ Ⓔ
20. Ⓐ Ⓑ Ⓒ Ⓓ Ⓔ
21. Ⓐ Ⓑ Ⓒ Ⓓ Ⓔ
22. Ⓐ Ⓑ Ⓒ Ⓓ Ⓔ
23. Ⓐ Ⓑ Ⓒ Ⓓ Ⓔ
24. Ⓐ Ⓑ Ⓒ Ⓓ Ⓔ
25. Ⓐ Ⓑ Ⓒ Ⓓ Ⓔ

26. Ⓐ Ⓑ Ⓒ Ⓓ Ⓔ
27. Ⓐ Ⓑ Ⓒ Ⓓ Ⓔ
28. Ⓐ Ⓑ Ⓒ Ⓓ Ⓔ
29. Ⓐ Ⓑ Ⓒ Ⓓ Ⓔ
30. Ⓐ Ⓑ Ⓒ Ⓓ Ⓔ
31. Ⓐ Ⓑ Ⓒ Ⓓ Ⓔ
32. Ⓐ Ⓑ Ⓒ Ⓓ Ⓔ
33. Ⓐ Ⓑ Ⓒ Ⓓ Ⓔ
34. Ⓐ Ⓑ Ⓒ Ⓓ Ⓔ
35. Ⓐ Ⓑ Ⓒ Ⓓ Ⓔ
36. Ⓐ Ⓑ Ⓒ Ⓓ Ⓔ
37. Ⓐ Ⓑ Ⓒ Ⓓ Ⓔ
38. Ⓐ Ⓑ Ⓒ Ⓓ Ⓔ
39. Ⓐ Ⓑ Ⓒ Ⓓ Ⓔ
40. Ⓐ Ⓑ Ⓒ Ⓓ Ⓔ
41. Ⓐ Ⓑ Ⓒ Ⓓ Ⓔ
42. Ⓐ Ⓑ Ⓒ Ⓓ Ⓔ
43. Ⓐ Ⓑ Ⓒ Ⓓ Ⓔ
44. Ⓐ Ⓑ Ⓒ Ⓓ Ⓔ
45. Ⓐ Ⓑ Ⓒ Ⓓ Ⓔ
46. Ⓐ Ⓑ Ⓒ Ⓓ Ⓔ
47. Ⓐ Ⓑ Ⓒ Ⓓ Ⓔ
48. Ⓐ Ⓑ Ⓒ Ⓓ Ⓔ
49. Ⓐ Ⓑ Ⓒ Ⓓ Ⓔ
50. Ⓐ Ⓑ Ⓒ Ⓓ Ⓔ

51. Ⓐ Ⓑ Ⓒ Ⓓ Ⓔ
52. Ⓐ Ⓑ Ⓒ Ⓓ Ⓔ
53. Ⓐ Ⓑ Ⓒ Ⓓ Ⓔ
54. Ⓐ Ⓑ Ⓒ Ⓓ Ⓔ
55. Ⓐ Ⓑ Ⓒ Ⓓ Ⓔ
56. Ⓐ Ⓑ Ⓒ Ⓓ Ⓔ
57. Ⓐ Ⓑ Ⓒ Ⓓ Ⓔ
58. Ⓐ Ⓑ Ⓒ Ⓓ Ⓔ
59. Ⓐ Ⓑ Ⓒ Ⓓ Ⓔ
60. Ⓐ Ⓑ Ⓒ Ⓓ Ⓔ
61. Ⓐ Ⓑ Ⓒ Ⓓ Ⓔ
62. Ⓐ Ⓑ Ⓒ Ⓓ Ⓔ
63. Ⓐ Ⓑ Ⓒ Ⓓ Ⓔ
64. Ⓐ Ⓑ Ⓒ Ⓓ Ⓔ
65. Ⓐ Ⓑ Ⓒ Ⓓ Ⓔ
66. Ⓐ Ⓑ Ⓒ Ⓓ Ⓔ
67. Ⓐ Ⓑ Ⓒ Ⓓ Ⓔ
68. Ⓐ Ⓑ Ⓒ Ⓓ Ⓔ
69. Ⓐ Ⓑ Ⓒ Ⓓ Ⓔ
70. Ⓐ Ⓑ Ⓒ Ⓓ Ⓔ
71. Ⓐ Ⓑ Ⓒ Ⓓ Ⓔ
72. Ⓐ Ⓑ Ⓒ Ⓓ Ⓔ
73. Ⓐ Ⓑ Ⓒ Ⓓ Ⓔ
74. Ⓐ Ⓑ Ⓒ Ⓓ Ⓔ
75. Ⓐ Ⓑ Ⓒ Ⓓ Ⓔ

76. Ⓐ Ⓑ Ⓒ Ⓓ Ⓔ
77. Ⓐ Ⓑ Ⓒ Ⓓ Ⓔ
78. Ⓐ Ⓑ Ⓒ Ⓓ Ⓔ
79. Ⓐ Ⓑ Ⓒ Ⓓ Ⓔ
80. Ⓐ Ⓑ Ⓒ Ⓓ Ⓔ
81. Ⓐ Ⓑ Ⓒ Ⓓ Ⓔ
82. Ⓐ Ⓑ Ⓒ Ⓓ Ⓔ
83. Ⓐ Ⓑ Ⓒ Ⓓ Ⓔ
84. Ⓐ Ⓑ Ⓒ Ⓓ Ⓔ
85. Ⓐ Ⓑ Ⓒ Ⓓ Ⓔ
86. Ⓐ Ⓑ Ⓒ Ⓓ Ⓔ
87. Ⓐ Ⓑ Ⓒ Ⓓ Ⓔ
88. Ⓐ Ⓑ Ⓒ Ⓓ Ⓔ
89. Ⓐ Ⓑ Ⓒ Ⓓ Ⓔ
90. Ⓐ Ⓑ Ⓒ Ⓓ Ⓔ
91. Ⓐ Ⓑ Ⓒ Ⓓ Ⓔ
92. Ⓐ Ⓑ Ⓒ Ⓓ Ⓔ
93. Ⓐ Ⓑ Ⓒ Ⓓ Ⓔ
94. Ⓐ Ⓑ Ⓒ Ⓓ Ⓔ
95. Ⓐ Ⓑ Ⓒ Ⓓ Ⓔ
96. Ⓐ Ⓑ Ⓒ Ⓓ Ⓔ
97. Ⓐ Ⓑ Ⓒ Ⓓ Ⓔ
98. Ⓐ Ⓑ Ⓒ Ⓓ Ⓔ
99. Ⓐ Ⓑ Ⓒ Ⓓ Ⓔ
100. Ⓐ Ⓑ Ⓒ Ⓓ Ⓔ

PRACTICE TEST ONE

> **Directions:** You will have 1 hour and 10 minutes to answer 100 multiple-choice questions.

1. If a psychologist investigates the effects of a high-fat diet on weight loss, the high-fat diet would be the

   (A) placebo.
   (B) operational definition.
   (C) dependent variable.
   (D) independent variable.
   (E) control condition.

2. Jean Piaget would argue that a child who cannot conserve liquid volume, but who can engage in very simple problem solving, is in the _____ stage.

   (A) sensorimotor
   (B) preoperational
   (C) latency stage
   (D) concrete operational
   (E) formal operational

3. The study of emotions has been of interest to psychologists for many years, taking the form of different theories. Which of the following controversies is most important in this area?

   (A) Whether people really have emotions
   (B) Whether emotions happen before or after thought
   (C) Whether emotions happen before or after physiological response
   (D) Whether people "make up" their own emotions
   (E) Whether people are unaware of their own emotions

4. If a person's score on the WAIS is the mean, his IQ score would be about what percentile?

   (A) 2
   (B) 10
   (C) 16
   (D) 50
   (E) 84

5. When we see a circle that is partially completed with only broken lines around the perimeter, our minds fill in the spaces and we perceive an intact circle. Gestalt psychologists refer to this principle as

   (A) continuity.
   (B) figure-ground.
   (C) similarity.
   (D) proximity.
   (E) closure.

6. Jean Piaget's major contribution to theories of child development stem from his studies on

   (A) social development.
   (B) cognitive development.
   (C) recessive gene inheritance.
   (D) physical development.
   (E) IQ scores and heredity.

GO ON TO THE NEXT PAGE ⟶

7. In some pioneering work on development, Harry Harlow examined how food was delivered to infant monkeys. His work with monkeys and surrogate mothers suggests that

  (A) bottle-fed infants are less attached to their mothers than breast-fed infants.

  (B) infants prefer to be around their mother.

  (C) contact comfort is more important than provision of food.

  (D) infant monkeys generally refuse all milk but that of their mother.

  (E) infants will cling to any object that provides food.

8. A professor wants to investigate the behavior of shoppers in a mall clothing store, so with permission he sets up a hidden video camera to record the behavior of the shoppers. This is an example of what type of research?

  (A) Experiment

  (B) Longitudinal study

  (C) Survey

  (D) Case study

  (E) Naturalistic observation

9. In an experiment, over a series of trials, food is paired with a loud noise. Later, the loud noise continues to occur but is no longer paired with food. This experiment is probably studying

  (A) extinction.

  (B) learned helplessness.

  (C) learned taste aversion.

  (D) reinforcement.

  (E) encoding specificity.

10. People typically believe that flying in an airplane is more dangerous than driving a car. However, research has shown that more people die in car crashes every year than in airplane disasters. Which of the following could best explain this misconception?

  (A) Actor-observer bias

  (B) The availability heuristic

  (C) Groupthink

  (D) The representativeness heuristic

  (E) Social loafing

11. Most likely to criticize Skinner's theory on language acquisition would be

  (A) Raymond Cattell.

  (B) Noam Chomsky.

  (C) Lev Vygotsky.

  (D) Walter Mischel.

  (E) Jean Piaget.

12. The importance of vicarious learning was most clearly demonstrated by

  (A) Carl Jung.

  (B) B. F. Skinner.

  (C) Raymond Cattell.

  (D) Albert Bandura.

  (E) John Watson.

13. An Olympic speed skater has never been able to beat a time of 4:50 in a race. During the Olympics, however, he is paired with a very strong skater and ends up beating his best time. This exemplifies the theory of

  (A) social influence.

  (B) self-fulfilling prophecy.

  (C) social facilitation.

  (D) foot-in-the-door.

  (E) groupthink.

GO ON TO THE NEXT PAGE

14. Which of the following statements characterizes a child in the preoperational stage of cognitive development, as described by Jean Piaget?

    (A) The child can solve high-level logical problems.

    (B) Given long division, the child can solve a problem using a variety of strategies.

    (C) The child cannot speak yet.

    (D) The child can understand and produce language but can solve only simple logical problems.

    (E) The child can perform conservation tasks.

15. Which of the following is the best example of a correlational study?

    (A) A psychologist gives one group of rats a drug and another group a placebo to see the effect of the drug on learning.

    (B) A psychologist examines a client's background to help provide therapy.

    (C) A psychologist analyzes case studies to determine what traits people vary on.

    (D) A psychologist attempts to determine if there is a relationship between income and IQ.

    (E) A psychologist gives students two forms of exams, before and after taking a course, to determine if the course improved learning.

16. In the nervous system, we have several mechanisms that allow us to act "instinctually." One of those systems is the fight-or-flight response to a threat. Which of the following systems is responsible for this response?

    (A) Somatic nervous system

    (B) Parasympathetic nervous system

    (C) Sympathetic nervous system

    (D) Peripheral nervous system

    (E) Central nervous system

17. Dr. Fredrick notices that the subjects who take his test of mechanical reasoning several times over a one-year period have virtually identical scores. This suggests that this test has

    (A) high content validity.

    (B) high reliability.

    (C) high predictive validity.

    (D) a large standard deviation.

    (E) been standardized.

18. In a normal distribution, approximately what percentage of cases will fall within one standard deviation of the mean?

    (A) 34%

    (B) 48%

    (C) 68%

    (D) 96%

    (E) 100%

GO ON TO THE NEXT PAGE

19. George Kelly was a personality psychologist. Which of the following best describes Kelly's basic description of what causes personality?

    (A) Behavior is determined by unconscious forces.

    (B) Behavior is determined by the family structure.

    (C) Behavior is controlled by the environment.

    (D) Behavior is controlled by a hierarchy of needs.

    (E) Behavior is determined by a person's trait structure.

20. Each time a puff of air is administered to the eye of a rabbit, the rabbit blinks its eye. Before the puff of air, the experimenter rings a bell. Eventually, the bell elicits the eyeblink. The bell would be labeled the

    (A) unconditioned response.

    (B) conditioned response.

    (C) unconditioned stimulus.

    (D) conditioned stimulus.

    (E) learned stimulus.

21. An example of a mood disorder is

    (A) schizophrenia.

    (B) post-traumatic stress disorder.

    (C) bipolar disorder.

    (D) obsessive-compulsive disorder.

    (E) conversion disorder.

22. Most measures of personality are created by comparing a group of clinical patients with "normals." This concept is an example of

    (A) predictive validity.

    (B) face validity.

    (C) concurrent validity.

    (D) construct validity.

    (E) content validity.

23. If a diagnostic test for depression is given to people who have been diagnosed with depression and people who have no signs of depression, and both groups receive very similar scores, then this suggests that the test

    (A) has not been standardized.

    (B) has not been factor-analyzed.

    (C) is not reliable.

    (D) is not valid.

    (E) does not produce scores that form a normal distribution.

24. Which psychologist developed the first modern test of intelligence?

    (A) Henry Murray

    (B) Alfred Binet

    (C) David Wechsler

    (D) Sigmund Freud

    (E) B. F. Skinner

GO ON TO THE NEXT PAGE ⇒

25. A teacher notices that one of her students is having trouble listening to directions, staying on task, and so on. This child is exhibiting symptoms of

    (A) schizophrenia.

    (B) depression.

    (C) attention deficit disorder.

    (D) autism.

    (E) bipolar disorder.

26. Neurotransmitters can be inhibitory or excitatory. Which of the following neurotransmitters is considered excitatory?

    (A) Dopamine

    (B) GABA

    (C) Serotonin

    (D) Acetylcholine

    (E) Epinephrine

27. If we suffer a lesion of the ventromedial hypothalamus, we will most likely experience

    (A) hyperphagia.

    (B) aphasia.

    (C) aphagia.

    (D) polydipsia.

    (E) amnesia.

28. The idea of "majority rules" is most closely analogous to

    (A) the process that determines the resting potential of a membrane.

    (B) the process that determines the postsynaptic potential.

    (C) the all-or-nothing law governing the action potential.

    (D) the process of memory.

    (E) the fact that our brain waves correspond to stages of consciousness.

29. The brain structure implicated in motivation for the "4 Fs" is the

    (A) thalamus.

    (B) medulla.

    (C) hypothalamus.

    (D) frontal lobe.

    (E) temporal lobe.

30. The process of repeating a previously published scientific experiment by using different participants but following the original experiment's specifications is called

    (A) random sampling.

    (B) correlational research.

    (C) replication.

    (D) naturalistic observation.

    (E) the double-blind procedure.

31. Phil sees that Tony flunks a test in math. Because of this, Phil thinks that Tony isn't very bright. Later, Phil flunks a math test. He now believes that this is because the teacher hates him and made a very hard test. This is an example of

    (A) the halo effect.

    (B) the recency effect.

    (C) social loafing.

    (D) groupthink attribution.

    (E) actor-perceiver attribution.

32. There are several subtypes of schizophrenia, all marked by auditory hallucinations. Which of the following is also marked by delusions of grandeur and persecution?

    (A) Catatonic

    (B) Disorganized

    (C) Undifferentiated

    (D) Paranoid

    (E) Psychotic

GO ON TO THE NEXT PAGE

33. When Ms. Ettson asks her students to solve a problem by generating as many answers as possible, she is asking them to show their

    (A) neural plasticity.
    (B) factor analysis.
    (C) divergent thinking.
    (D) predictive validity.
    (E) convergent thinking.

34. Salespeople paid on commission who maintain high levels of perseverance despite infrequent sales display the effect of

    (A) a fixed-ratio schedule.
    (B) negative reinforcement.
    (C) a fixed-interval schedule.
    (D) positive reinforcement.
    (E) a variable-ratio schedule.

35. In experiments with rats, destroying the ventromedial hypothalamus leads to which of the following?

    (A) An increased desire for thirst
    (B) Increased sweating to compensate for higher internal temperatures
    (C) A total lack of interest in sexual activity
    (D) A refusal to eat food, to the point of near starvation
    (E) Increased eating of food, to the point of dangerous obesity

36. Which test do psychologists use most frequently to assess students' developmental delays?

    (A) Standford-Binet Intelligence Test
    (B) MMPI
    (C) The Wechsler scales
    (D) Thematic Apperception Test
    (E) IRT

37. A person hears a horrifying scream, runs away, and feels afraid. This sequence is predicted by which of the following theories of emotion?

    (A) Social construction theory
    (B) Cannon-Bard theory
    (C) Schachter-Singer theory
    (D) Dual processing theory
    (E) James-Lange theory

38. Who is most well known for studying the influence of misleading information on eyewitness testimony?

    (A) Frederic Bartlett
    (B) Elizabeth Loftus
    (C) Max Weber
    (D) B. F. Skinner
    (E) John Watson

39. Which of the following is the Freudian stage during which you suffer from the Oedipus complex?

    (A) Oral
    (B) Latency
    (C) Genital
    (D) Phallic
    (E) Anal

40. A man has a stroke. Following the stroke, he suffers from impaired language comprehension. This would most probably be diagnosed as

    (A) Broca's aphasia.
    (B) dyslexia.
    (C) aphagia.
    (D) Wernicke's aphasia.
    (E) dyspraxia.

GO ON TO THE NEXT PAGE ▷

41. Zimbardo's prison experiment suggested that both cruel and meek behavior could be elicited from ordinary people because of the power of

    (A) inherited traits.
    (B) genetic predispositions.
    (C) learned helplessness.
    (D) social roles.
    (E) groupthink.

42. To solve a problem in an experiment, participants must use a book to adjust the height of a chair. The book must be used creatively. This experiment is most directly concerned with

    (A) demand characteristics.
    (B) intelligence.
    (C) functional fixedness.
    (D) semantic priming.
    (E) learned helplessness.

43. Trait theory is often criticized because it

    (A) places too great an emphasis on early childhood experiences.
    (B) focuses too heavily on the role of reinforcement and punishment.
    (C) overestimates the consistency of behavior in different situations.
    (D) underestimates the influence of heredity in personality development.
    (E) overemphasizes positive traits.

44. Client-centered therapy differs from psychoanalysis most substantially in that the client-centered therapist

    (A) is more controlling.
    (B) tries to use free association to uncover hidden urges.
    (C) encourages expression of feelings without judgment from the therapist.
    (D) forces regression to earlier years.
    (E) works with the client versus against the client.

45. Visual illusions are used to help us understand perception because they show us ways that our visual system is fooled. The reason we typically see illusions is that

    (A) the size of the retinal image remains constant.
    (B) motion parallax tends to make objects appear larger.
    (C) afterimages distort the true image.
    (D) we use prior knowledge to interpret sensory information.
    (E) the size of the retinal image is increasing.

46. An example of a biological therapy is

    (A) token economies.
    (B) operant conditioning.
    (C) electroconvulsive therapy (ECT).
    (D) classical conditioning.
    (E) insight therapy.

GO ON TO THE NEXT PAGE

47. Albert Bandura studied aggression in several of his studies. In his most famous study, he found that

    (A) frustration is a necessary antecedent condition of aggressive modeling.

    (B) observation of aggressive responses increases the likelihood of aggressive behavior in children if there is reinforcement for the aggression.

    (C) girls have a stronger innate tendency toward aggression than boys.

    (D) direct expression of hostile feelings is not common in children.

    (E) peer models have no impact on aggression in children.

48. Wendy believes that her mother treats everyone badly because she doesn't like people. The truth is, Wendy is the one who doesn't like people. The tendency to attribute one's own feelings and thoughts to an external object is known as

    (A) projection.

    (B) identification.

    (C) catharsis.

    (D) displacement.

    (E) sublimation.

49. Which of the following would a psychologist use if she wanted to be sure that the participants in her experiments were representative of the larger population?

    (A) Random assignment

    (B) Replication

    (C) Correlation

    (D) Naturalistic observation

    (E) Random sampling

50. Which psychologist is correctly linked with his theoretical perspective?

    (A) Jung: collective unconscious

    (B) Skinner: structuralism

    (C) Wundt: operant conditioning

    (D) Freud: classical conditioning

    (E) Piaget: clinical psychology

51. "Motivation comes largely from an attempt to achieve a state of balance or equilibrium among competing drives." Which of the following terms is associated with this theory?

    (A) Homeopathy

    (B) Homeostasis

    (C) Entropy

    (D) Complacency

    (E) Cognitive dissonance

52. A patient goes to a therapist and complains that he does not feel it is safe to leave his house. In fact, he has organized his entire existence in such a way that he won't ever have to leave. This person is likely to be suffering from

    (A) a personality disorder.

    (B) schizophrenia.

    (C) obsessive-compulsive disorder.

    (D) a somatoform disorder.

    (E) agoraphobia.

GO ON TO THE NEXT PAGE ⇒

53. A child calls her pet dog "Doggie." When her parents bring home a cat one day, the child calls out "Doggie!" After a short time, the child learns that dogs and cats are different and then is able to call the cat "Kitty." This is an example of

    (A) accommodation.
    (B) adaptation.
    (C) organization.
    (D) equilibration.
    (E) assimilation.

54. Of the following leadership styles, which tends to produce the most satisfied members?

    (A) Autocratic
    (B) Authoritative
    (C) Authoritarian
    (D) Laissez-faire
    (E) Democratic

55. The goal of attribution theory is to help us

    (A) understand the causes of behaviors.
    (B) know that we are rarely accurate in our perception of others.
    (C) understand breakthroughs in attitude measurement.
    (D) develop good procedures for studying obedience.
    (E) construct a clear understanding of our psychopathology.

56. If someone takes antipsychotic medication for too long, he may suffer from which of the following problems?

    (A) Tardive dyskinesia
    (B) Cravings for nicotine
    (C) Blindness
    (D) Parkinson's disease
    (E) Dysphasia

57. John had a brain injury that caused aphasia; he can no longer comprehend language clearly. What part of his brain is most likely damaged?

    (A) Cerebellum
    (B) Amygdala
    (C) Corpus callosum
    (D) Wernicke's area
    (E) Broca's area

58. Phobias are usually treated most successfully with

    (A) systematic desensitization.
    (B) electroconvulsive therapy.
    (C) psychoanalysis.
    (D) transactional analysis.
    (E) client-centered psychotherapy.

59. If a researcher wants to study which areas of a person's brain were most active when they were solving complicated math problems, he should use a(n)

    (A) X-ray.
    (B) brain lesion.
    (C) MRI.
    (D) PET scan.
    (E) EEG.

GO ON TO THE NEXT PAGE

60. Zajonc's research has demonstrated that if we are with other people, performance of

    (A) dominant responses deteriorates, while performance of nondominant responses improves.
    (B) dominant responses improves, while performance of nondominant responses deteriorates.
    (C) all types of responses improve.
    (D) all types of responses deteriorate.
    (E) correct responses improve.

61. Which of the following theories provides a different perspective than the original theory on color vision?

    (A) Frequency theory
    (B) Localization theory
    (C) Opponent-process theory
    (D) Volley theory
    (E) Trichromatic theory

62. While reciting the alphabet, Freddie says the first 10 letters correctly but then slips up and recites the remaining letters in incorrect order. This is an example of

    (A) selective attention.
    (B) the recency effect.
    (C) short-term memory effect.
    (D) serial position effect.
    (E) the primacy effect.

63. You want to compare people aged 6, 26, 46, and 66 on how many "close friends" they think they have. You match these participants on where they live, their race, and their religion. Such a study would be considered to be a(n)

    (A) study of age differences.
    (B) cross-sectional study.
    (C) longitudinal study.
    (D) experiment.
    (E) group study.

64. Lithium is the drug of choice for

    (A) bipolar disorder.
    (B) schizophrenia.
    (C) depression.
    (D) personality disorders.
    (E) somatoform disorders.

65. Hans Selye argued that we often overreact to stressful situations when we are already stressed. The term he and others gave to describe this process is

    (A) global assessment of functioning.
    (B) general adaptation syndrome.
    (C) opponent process theory.
    (D) the Hawthorne effect.
    (E) systematic desensitization.

66. According to Piaget, a child who knows that clay doesn't change in size when it changes shape is probably

    (A) in the sensorimotor stage of development.
    (B) between one and two years old.
    (C) too young to learn a complex logical skill.
    (D) able to conserve mass.
    (E) in the preoperational stage of cognitive development.

GO ON TO THE NEXT PAGE

67. Baumrind identified three styles of parenting. They were

  (A) autocratic, democratic, laissez-faire.

  (B) securely attached, insecurely attached, loosely attached.

  (C) authoritarian, authoritative, permissive.

  (D) moving against, moving toward, moving away from.

  (E) socially motivated, interpersonally motivated, intrapersonally motivated.

68. The DSM-IV is important because it

  (A) focuses on the etiology of mental disorders.

  (B) provides a biological system of assessment.

  (C) provides psychologists with consistent criteria for diagnosis.

  (D) provides a completely behavioral perspective.

  (E) helps us understand personality.

69. During a group project, several members of the team do not carry their weight and leave most of the work to the others. This is an example of

  (A) social loafing.

  (B) groupthink.

  (C) self-fulfilling prophecy.

  (D) the Hawthorne effect.

  (E) deindividuation.

70. "Paradoxical sleep" is so called because

  (A) its EEG pattern is much slower than would be expected in sleep.

  (B) it is so easy to wake someone in paradoxical sleep.

  (C) its EEG pattern resembles that of the waking state more than that of slow-wave sleep.

  (D) it is apparently unnecessary; organisms deprived of paradoxical sleep do not compensate for the loss when allowed to resume sleeping.

  (E) investigators are unsure what transpires during this sleep stage.

71. To test whether or not a new drug to reduce hyperactivity is effective, a researcher would give a pill with the drug to one group and a pill that appears identical but does not have the drug to the second group. What do we call the second group?

  (A) Control group

  (B) Random sample

  (C) Case study

  (D) Experimental group

  (E) Independent variable

72. Which of the following pairings of psychologist and theory is correct?

  (A) Wundt: attribution theory

  (B) Bandura: social learning theory

  (C) James: cognitive dissonance theory

  (D) Watson: instinctual drift

  (E) Skinner: depth perception

GO ON TO THE NEXT PAGE ⇨

73. Wolfgang Kohler demonstrated evidence of _____ when one of his chimps fastened two sticks together to reach a bunch of bananas.

    (A) operant conditioning
    (B) learned response
    (C) classical conditioning
    (D) heuristics
    (E) insight

74. A patient has a fear of crossing bridges. To help this person, the therapist designs a treatment involving slow introduction into bridge crossing. This is paired with relaxation techniques. This therapeutic technique is called

    (A) flooding.
    (B) systematic desensitization.
    (C) implosion.
    (D) psychoanalysis.
    (E) time out.

75. John Watson is most well known for his work that eventually led to which approach of psychology?

    (A) Biological
    (B) Social
    (C) Behavioral
    (D) Humanistic
    (E) Cognitive

76. "Children can perform at a higher level with support than they can without." The theory that posits this is

    (A) Jean Piaget's theory of conservation.
    (B) Sigmund Freud's theory of psychosexual development.
    (C) B. F. Skinner's theory of learning.
    (D) Lev Vygotsky's theory of the zone of proximal development.
    (E) Wilhelm Wundt's theory of consciousness.

77. Assume that if a person has a particular genetic disease, there's a 50 percent chance that his sibling will also have the disease. If an afflicted person has a fraternal twin, what is the chance that the fraternal twin has the disease?

    (A) 100%
    (B) 75%
    (C) 50%
    (D) 25%
    (E) 0%

78. Typically, people have cycles that their bodies go through during the day. This body "clock" controls many physiological changes that occur in everyone, such as the slight change in heart rate during the day. This is called

    (A) a narcoleptic pattern.
    (B) a circadian rhythm.
    (C) a sleep-wake cycle.
    (D) sleep spindles.
    (E) cataplexy.

GO ON TO THE NEXT PAGE ⇨

79. Which of the following statements is most likely to produce cognitive dissonance?

(A) "I plan to spend my life doing this job, even though I hate it."

(B) "I love to exercise because it makes me feel better."

(C) "I often read because I am stimulated by the material."

(D) "I find myself speeding, but I love the fear of getting caught."

(E) "I will stop working when I feel that I have done all I can."

80. In the eye, the retina is where the photoreceptors are located. On the retina is a structure called the fovea. If we shine different lights in various parts of the eye, which of the following is true?

(A) Object discrimination will be worst in the fovea.

(B) Object discrimination will be best in the fovea.

(C) Color discrimination will be best in the fovea.

(D) Color discrimination will be best at the periphery of the retina.

(E) Visual sensitivity will be the same across the retina.

81. Operant conditioning was first described by

(A) John Watson.

(B) B. F. Skinner.

(C) Wilhelm Wundt.

(D) Jean Piaget.

(E) Ivan Pavlov.

82. Drugs such as morphine are classified as narcotics. Which neurochemicals are these like?

(A) Endogenous endorphins

(B) Epinephrine

(C) GABA

(D) Serotonin

(E) L-dopa

83. Which of the following correlation coefficients reflects the weakest degree of relationship between two variables?

(A) −0.99

(B) +1.00

(C) −0.45

(D) −0.11

(E) +0.34

84. Milgram's experiments on obedience demonstrated that

(A) most participants refused to administer the shocks.

(B) most participants did obey the command to give the shocks.

(C) about half the participants gave the shocks.

(D) participants with poor moral reasoning skills gave the shocks.

(E) female participants shocked more than male participants.

85. A large number of people observe a hit-and-run accident, yet no one reports it to the police. This is an example of

(A) groupthink.

(B) diffusion of responsibility.

(C) altruism.

(D) stereotyping.

(E) reinforcement.

GO ON TO THE NEXT PAGE

86. An example of using a mnemonic would be to associate a list of items to remember with a mental map of specific places. This mnemonic is called

    (A) state-dependent learning.
    (B) the method of loci.
    (C) natural language mnemonics.
    (D) cognitive mapping.
    (E) peg-word method.

87. Psychoanalysis is a form of therapy most closely associated with the work of

    (A) Joseph Wolpe.
    (B) Carl Rogers.
    (C) Wilhelm Wundt.
    (D) Noam Chomsky.
    (E) Sigmund Freud.

88. The visual cliff was created for an experiment to test infants for the development of their

    (A) upper-body muscular development.
    (B) selective attention.
    (C) perceptual adaptation.
    (D) figure-ground perception.
    (E) depth perception.

89. The psychologist credited with developing the technique of introspection is

    (A) George Sperling.
    (B) John Watson.
    (C) Max Wertheimer.
    (D) Wilhelm Wundt.
    (E) B. F. Skinner.

90. When participants have problems learning new information because old information is causing them confusion, psychologists call this

    (A) proactive interference.
    (B) anterograde inhibition.
    (C) interference effect.
    (D) retroactive interference.
    (E) state-dependent learning.

91. According to Carl Jung, which archetype represents the feminine side of men?

    (A) Persona
    (B) Anima
    (C) Animus
    (D) Shadow
    (E) Self

92. Psychologists often talk about the body's ability to deal with pain. Which of the following has been described as a natural painkiller?

    (A) GABA
    (B) Dopamine
    (C) Serotonin
    (D) Endorphins
    (E) Prozac

93. Doing your chores to avoid being grounded is an example of

    (A) positive reinforcement.
    (B) negative reinforcement.
    (C) punishment.
    (D) conditioning.
    (E) unconditioned response.

GO ON TO THE NEXT PAGE

94. Bipolar disorder is

    (A) a severe form of clinical depression.
    (B) characterized by episodes of depression and mania.
    (C) a form of schizophrenia.
    (D) not very common in the United States.
    (E) treated best by using psychoanalysis.

95. When a person is in a room and the lights are turned out, her vision changes. Which of the statements best describes this change?

    (A) Vision gets good for color but bad for black and white.
    (B) Vision gets good after a few minutes.
    (C) Vision gets good for black and white but bad for color.
    (D) Vision does not improve.
    (E) Vision goes away completely.

96. You are playing softball. A ball hits you on the head, and you lose your ability to see. What part of the head have you most likely hit?

    (A) Top
    (B) Front
    (C) Left side
    (D) Right side
    (E) Back

97. A rat presses a bar, and a shock is delivered to its brain. The result is an increase in bar-pressing behavior. In this situation, the shock is serving as

    (A) an unconditioned stimulus.
    (B) an unconditioned response.
    (C) a positive punisher.
    (D) a negative reinforcer.
    (E) a positive reinforcer.

98. Which of the following cues is important in helping us perceive depth?

    (A) Binocular convergence
    (B) Binocular disparity
    (C) Depth convergence
    (D) Visual acuity
    (E) Space location

99. Psychologists Wilhelm Wundt and Edward Titchener developed the process of _____, in which subjects were asked to monitor and report their sensory experiences to differently colored objects.

    (A) structuralism
    (B) spaced practice
    (C) introspection
    (D) rehearsal
    (E) psychoanalysis

100. Which of the following studies is likely to be completed by someone who is interested in developmental psychology?

    (A) A study of memory
    (B) An investigation into age-related changes in social relations
    (C) The study of reinforcement in infant rats
    (D) The impact of dopamine on memory
    (E) Obedience: What are the causes?

IF YOU FINISH BEFORE TIME IS CALLED, YOU MAY CHECK YOUR WORK ON THIS SECTION ONLY. DO NOT TURN TO ANY OTHER SECTION IN THE TEST.   STOP

SECTION II

Time—50 Minutes

Percent of total grade—$33\frac{1}{3}$

Directions: You have 50 minutes to answer BOTH of the following questions. It is not enough to answer a question by merely listing facts. You should present a cogent argument based on your critical analysis of the questions posed, using appropriate psychological terminology.

1. Alana recently attended her first fencing match and enjoyed it so much that she began taking fencing lessons. After the first week she threatened to quit because she was so frustrated, and she yelled at her parents a few times when they picked her up from her lessons. First, define each of the following psychological topics, and then give an example for each, including advice that you could give to Alana based on that concept.

- Procedural memory

- Displacement

- Scaffolding

- Intrinsic motivation

- Social learning

_____

_____

_____

_____

_____

_____

_____

_____

_____

_____

GO ON TO THE NEXT PAGE

2. Dr. Smith is interested in determining the relationship between IQ and success in life. Design a correlational study to examine this issue. Using the following concepts, first define each term and then explain how the term would be used within the context of the study.

- Operational definitions of variables

- Sampling

- Validity

- Ethical principles

_____

_____

_____

_____

_____

_____

_____

_____

_____

_____

_____

_____

_____

_____

_____

_____

_____

_____

Practice Test One: **Answer Key**

1. D	21. C	41. D	61. C	81. B
2. B	22. D	42. C	62. E	82. A
3. C	23. D	43. C	63. B	83. D
4. D	24. B	44. C	64. A	84. B
5. E	25. C	45. D	65. B	85. B
6. B	26. D	46. C	66. D	86. B
7. C	27. A	47. B	67. C	87. E
8. E	28. C	48. A	68. C	88. E
9. A	29. C	49. E	69. A	89. D
10. B	30. C	50. A	70. C	90. A
11. B	31. E	51. B	71. A	91. B
12. D	32. D	52. E	72. B	92. D
13. C	33. C	53. A	73. E	93. B
14. D	34. E	54. E	74. B	94. B
15. D	35. E	55. A	75. C	95. C
16. C	36. C	56. A	76. D	96. E
17. B	37. E	57. D	77. C	97. E
18. C	38. B	58. A	78. B	98. B
19. E	39. D	59. D	79. A	99. C
20. D	40. D	60. C	80. C	100. B

Practice Test One: **Assess Your Strengths**

Use the following tables to determine which topics (chapters) you need to review most.

Chapter and Topic	Question
Chapter 3: History and Approaches	75, 89, 99
Chapter 4: Research Methods	1, 8, 15, 18, 30, 49, 63, 71, 85
Chapter 5: Biological Bases of Behavior	16, 26, 28, 40, 57, 59, 77, 92, 96
Chapter 6: Sensation and Perception	5, 45, 61, 80, 88, 95, 98
Chapter 7: States of Consciousness	70, 78, 82
Chapter 8: Learning	9, 12, 20, 34, 47, 72, 81, 93, 97
Chapter 9: Cognition	10, 11, 38, 42, 62, 73, 83, 86, 90
Chapter 10: Motivation and Emotion	3, 27, 29, 31, 37, 51, 65
Chapter 11: Developmental Psychology	2, 6, 7, 14, 53, 66, 67, 76, 100
Chapter 12: Personality	19, 22, 39, 43, 48, 50, 91
Chapter 13: Testing and Individual Differences	4, 17, 23, 24, 33, 36
Chapter 14: Abnormal Behavior	21, 25, 32, 52, 68, 88, 94
Chapter 15: Treatment of Abnormal Behavior	44, 46, 56, 58, 64, 74, 87
Chapter 16: Social Psychology	13, 31, 41, 54, 55, 60, 69, 79, 84

Chapter and Topic	Number of Questions on Test	Number Correct
Chapter 3: History and Approaches	3	
Chapter 4: Research Methods	9	
Chapter 5: Biological Bases of Behavior	9	
Chapter 6: Sensation and Perception	7	
Chapter 7: States of Consciousness	3	
Chapter 8: Learning	9	
Chapter 9: Cognition	9	
Chapter 10: Motivation and Emotion	7	
Chapter 11: Developmental Psychology	9	
Chapter 12: Personality	7	
Chapter 13: Testing and Individual Differences	6	
Chapter 14: Abnormal Behavior	7	
Chapter 15: Treatment of Abnormal Behavior	7	
Chapter 16: Social Psychology	9	

ANSWERS AND EXPLANATIONS

SECTION I

1. D

The independent variable is what the researcher is trying to investigate, and he is looking for any possible change (effect) this variable might cause—thus the idea of an experiment as a way to study a cause-and-effect relationship. The dependent variable, (C), is what is being measured (weight loss), the control condition, (E), refers to a group who would not have the independent variable, a placebo, (A), might be used by a control group, and the operational definition, (B), is how a researcher specifically defines what is being measured to enable replication.

2. B

Children who cannot conserve struggle with complex issues and problems. Thus, they would be in the preoperational stage. Children who can solve complex problems would be in either the concrete stage or the formal operational stage of cognitive development.

3. C

Most of the research on emotion, especially the early research, focused on when emotions happened, whether before or after physiological response. Psychologists agreed that emotions and physiology went together. They just weren't sure which happened first.

4. D

The Weschsler Adult Intelligence Scale is the same as any other measurement scale. If a score is at the mean on any scale, the percentile of scores that are above or below the score is 50 percent.

5. E

Gestalt psychologists explore how we see a "whole" object from individual parts. In closure, we mentally fill in the gaps and perceive an object as a whole. In continuity, (A), we see one simple object intersecting another. Figure-ground, (B), allows us to see an object in an image as being in either the foreground or background. Similarity, (C), means that we see similar things as together. Proximity, (D), means that we see things that are closer together as connected.

6. B

Piaget spent most of his career trying to understand how children develop the skills to engage in higher-level cognitive skills. The other issues are of interest to many developmental psychologists, but Piaget focused almost exclusively on cognitive development.

7. C

In Harlow's work, it was demonstrated that monkeys will, in fact, cling more to a food supply that provides more than just food. In this work, there were two food sources the monkey could feed from: a wire "mother" or a cloth-covered "mother." Monkeys were much more likely to feed from the cloth mother than the wire mother, suggesting that warmth and support are important to the juvenile monkey, in addition to food.

8. E

In naturalistic observation, the researcher wants to view the participants in their most natural habitat, in this case the clothing store. Remember that the cardinal rule of naturalistic observation is not to disturb the group you are watching, so the professor is careful to use the hidden camera. This kind of research allows for the observation of behavior but does not allow for controls such as in an experiment, (A). Surveys, (C), and case studies, (D), do not involve this kind of direct observation, and a longitudinal study, (B), is normally carried out over several years.

9. A

Extinction is the process of breaking a connection between a conditioned stimulus and a conditioned response. If the connection is not made for several trials, the stimulus will no longer lead to the response. Learned helplessness, learned taste aversion, and reinforcement deal with issues in operant conditioning. Encoding specificity refers to a concept in cognitive psychology.

10. B

The availability heuristic refers to the idea that we rely on information that is available to make judgments about the probability of an event occurring, rather than the true probability of it actually happening. The other concepts listed are important in social psychology but do not explain the situation in the question.

11. B

Chomsky would most likely criticize Skinner's theory on language acquisition. In fact, one of the biggest controversies in language acquisition is the difference between these two psychologists' views. Skinner argued for a nativist approach to language

acquisition, with reinforcement being the primary process involved.

12. D

Jung and Cattell were both personality psychologists interested in what makes people unique. Skinner and Watson were both behavioral psychologists who focused on the role of the environment on the shaping of behavior. Bandura, on the other hand, extended the work of Skinner by demonstrating that reinforcement does not have to be given directly for it to be effective. A person can *watch* someone being reinforced, and that alone could be enough to lead to reinforcement.

13. C

Social facilitation was first noted in 1897. The concept states that if we are in competition with someone, we will perform better than we would if we were not. Thus, if a skater has someone to skate against, he or she will skate faster than if alone.

14. D

A child in the preoperational stage has acquired some basic logical skills and has language abilities, but a child in this stage cannot conserve, solve complex logical skills, or do long division.

15. D

In a correlational study, a psychologist will attempt to determine a relationship between two variables that already exist in the world. Comparing two conditions to see which one is better (an experiment) or doing case studies are not correlational in nature.

16. C

The sympathetic nervous system helps us prepare for a response when a situation calls for one. For example, if we are scared, the sympathetic nervous system prepares us to respond appropriately. The other systems play a different role in maintaining behavior.

17. B

This kind of question appears frequently on the AP exam: can you tell the difference between two very similar kinds of terms that have to do with the same concept? In this case, the answer would come down to how well you understand reliability and validity of any kind. Reliability means that the test will yield a consistent result each time, while either validity choice, (A) or (C), refers to whether the test is measuring what it is supposed to and whether we accurately predict behavior from the results.

18. C

In a normal distribution, 34 percent of the scores fall between the mean and one standard deviation. If we are talking about scores falling within one standard deviation of the mean, we are talking about one standard deviation above *and* below the mean. Thus, we have 34 percent above the mean and 34 percent below the mean.

19. E

Kelly is best known for his work on the trait theory. According to Kelly, our personalities are shaped by the traits that we demonstrate. These traits come from our experience, but not just experience shapes behavior. Rather, it is the structure and organization of those traits that produce our personality.

20. D

In this example, the unconditioned response and the conditioned response are the same: the eyeblink. The unconditioned stimulus is the puff of air. *Learned stimulus* is not a term used in behavioral psychology.

21. C

Schizophrenia is not characterized as a mood disorder, post-traumatic stress disorder and OCD are both anxiety disorders, and a conversion disorder is a category of disorders versus being a diagnostic label.

22. D

To determine that a test is providing a measure of a characteristic, psychologists often compare the measured population with a population that also displays that behavior. This is done to make sure that the construct of interest is actually being measured. The other forms of validity are important, but construct validity makes sure we are measuring the concept that we are really interested in.

23. D

A test that is supposed to be an indicator of depression but that yields similar scores when given to both depressed and non-depressed people must reflect greater depression among the former group. In this case, the answer could not be (C) because we don't know any information about how the test scores change when repeated, but we do know that test doesn't measure what it is supposed to. Choices (A), (B), and (E) are all important test construction principles, but are not involved with questions of validity.

24. B

Binet was hired by the French government to develop a test to determine who would not do well in school. Binet's test diverged from other measures at the time and forged a new way of thinking about intelligence. Eventually, other tests of intelligence were developed along the same lines as Binet's. His pioneering work paved the way for David Wechsler to develop the form of intelligence tests that are used today.

25. C

ADD is a very common diagnosis today. The typical ADD child will exhibit lack of ability to sit still, pay attention, or follow directions.

26. D

All the other listed neurotransmitters have been described as having an inhibitory influence on the postsynaptic membrane. Essentially, they all serve to make a cell *less* likely to fire an action potential. The excitatory neurotransmitter makes a cell *more* likely to fire an action potential.

27. A

Hyperphagia is the disorder that leads to a decrease in the ability to stop eating. Thus, one never feels full. Aphasia is a disorder of language, aphagia is the inability to swallow, polydipsia occurs when we can't stop drinking, and amnesia refers to memory loss.

28. C

During an action potential, the cell membrane is constantly bombarded with messages that are either excitatory or inhibitory. If the excitatory messages have a slight advantage and move the charge inside the cell to the threshold of excitation, the cell will fire. As long as the cell reaches the threshold of excitation, it will fire.

29. C

The "4 Fs" of motivation (feeding, fleeing, fighting, and sexual reproduction) are controlled by the hypothalamus. The thalamus is important in hormone regulation, the medulla helps with autonomic behavior, the frontal lobe helps control higher-order processes, and the temporal lobe helps with language and audition.

30. C

For results of scientific research to be considered significant and meaningful, the results must be true for more than one set of subjects. It is vital that researchers replicate the work of others so that it can be determined if the results seem to be true of a larger population and not just the small sample in the study. Random sampling, (A), and the double-blind procedure, (E), are important to experimental design, but neither one is involved with repeating a study, nor are correlational research, (B), or naturalistic observation, (D).

31. E

According to the actor-perceiver attribution error, we tend to attribute our failures to external factors, while we attribute others' failures to internal processes. The halo effect suggests we see someone in good light no matter what, the recency effect is a cognitive term, social loafing states that we work less hard when we work with others, and groupthink suggests that we become polarized on one side of an argument by persuasion.

32. D

Paranoid schizophrenia is differentiated from other forms of the disorder by delusions of grandeur and threats of persecution. The other forms of schizophrenia have other hallmarks.

33. C

Neural plasticity, (A), refers to the brain's internal ability to change over time, a process that would not happen during a class period. Factor analysis, (B), and predictive validity, (D), are both terms related to intelligence and testing, while convergent thinking, (E), looks for one possible correct solution and is the opposite of divergent thinking. A tip to remember divergent thinking is to recall that when a river or road diverges, it splits off into more than one river or road, just as divergent thinking creates many possible avenues of thought.

34. E

Salespeople paid on commission are unable to predict when reinforcement is going to occur. Thus, the behavior is on a variable-interval schedule of reinforcement, as sporadic reinforcement leads to maintenance of behavior even if the reinforcement comes very infrequently.

35. E

While the hypothalamus had long been believed to be the center of regulation of hunger, it wasn't until the 1960s that experiments revealed the destruction of the ventromedial hypothalamus would lead rats to gorge themselves, while destruction of the lateral hypothalamus would lead to starvation, (D). There is no evidence that destroying this part of the hypothalamus would affect thirst, (A), temperature regulation, (B), or sexual activity, (C).

36. C

The other exams are useful, but the Wechsler scales are the measures of choice today among school psychologists.

37. E

The James-Lange theory suggests that the physiological response takes place first, and then we experience the emotion. The other theories do not explain the response in that order.

38. B

Bartlett studied memory distortions, but not with eyewitnesses. Weber studied sensory processes, and Skinner and Watson were behavioral psychologists. Loftus's work has been groundbreaking, and she has served as an expert witness for many years on this very topic.

39. D

During the phallic stage, a person might suffer from an uncomfortable attraction to the parent of the opposite sex. This is an unconscious attraction but one that causes a great deal of anxiety.

40. D

Damage to Wernicke's area would result in what has been called receptive aphasia. Damage to Broca's area would result in production difficulties, dyslexia is a reading disorder, aphagia is a swallowing disorder, and dyspraxia is another form of a production disorder.

41. D

Zimbardo's experiment lasted only six days, but it turned regular college students into sadistic guards and compliant prisoners. We learned that the power of the situation can have enormous effects on our behavior and mental processes, despite inborn inclinations from traits, (A), or genetics, (B). Learned helplessness, (C), only refers to passive and helpless behavior when one gives up, and not cruel behavior. Groupthink, (E), involves silent conformity to a group, which is not present here.

42. C

In such a problem, a person needs to think creatively and not be bound by the normal uses of an object. Functional fixedness refers to the process of not being able to "think outside the box" and instead find novel uses for objects.

43. C

Trait theorists believe that we are a collection of fixed characteristics (like extraversion or curiosity) that may wax and wane a bit, but in general remain constant over time. (C) reflects the primary criticism in that people will often act differently depending on the situations they find themselves in. (E) is incorrect because trait theory includes traits that can be viewed as positive or negative, while (A) is a criticism of psychoanalytic theory, (B) of behavioral theory, and (D) of social-cognitive theories of personality.

44. C

Client-centered therapy focuses on the client. The other techniques mentioned in the question are based more on the interpretation aspect of psychoanalysis, in which the therapist is much more in control of the situation.

45. D

Many of our perceptual abilities are rooted in the fact that we use prior knowledge to interpret our experiences in the world. Visual illusions occur because our typically reliable visual system is fooled by some cue that is normally reliable wih respect to a particular perceptual experience. The listed factors besides (D) are cues we use to perceive the world.

46. C

ECT is a procedure in which an electric shock is passed through a client's brain to help alleviate depression. The procedure is rarely used, but it is effective in some cases. The other concepts in the list are either behavioral (A, B, D) or clinical in nature.

47. B

Bandura noted, in the famous "Bobo Doll" experiment, that if a child witnesses an adult acting in an aggressive manner toward a doll and is then reinforced for that behavior, he or she is more likely to act that way toward the doll. The reinforcement does not need to be given directly to the individual for it to be effective. Rather, vicarious reinforcement also leads to an increase in behavior.

48. A

Projection is the defense mechanism of seeing undesirable traits that we possess in others. The other mentioned mechanisms are important, but projection is clearly described here.

49. E

Again, this is another example of the "confusing pairs" kind of question that is common on the AP Psychology exam. In this case, the two similar answers are (A) and (E), and it is important to know the difference. Random sampling refers to a method of studying a small group (the sample) of a larger group (population), and *random* means that all members of the population have an equal chance of being selected for the sample because it is not practical to test the entire population. Random assignment is taking a sample and dividing the subjects into control groups and experimental groups randomly so there are no differences between the two groups, which is required for an experiment to determine cause and effect.

50. A

Jung's concept of the collective unconscious was one of the biggest differences between his theory and that of Sigmund Freud. Skinner studied operant conditioning; Wundt, structuralism; Freud, psychoanalysis; and Piaget, developmental psychology.

51. B

The concept of homeostasis suggests that we need to maintain a balance in our physiological and psychological states to ensure mental health. The other concepts are not related to this idea at all.

52. E

Agoraphobia is a type of anxiety disorder in which a person is afraid to leave his or her safe surroundings. Personality disorders and schizophrenia are much more serious disorders that result in interpersonal impairments. OCD is a disorder of obsessive thoughts and compulsive, anxiety-reducing behavior. Somatoform disorders occur when psychological symptoms are converted to physiological "problems."

53. A

Accommodation occurs when a child develops a new schema to account for differences in experience. Adaptation is the general process of attempting to understand and fit into the environment, organization and equilibration are both processes of "fixing" existing schemas, and assimilation refers to the process of fitting a new experience into an existing schema.

54. E

The democratic leadership style is most effective in that it gives a voice to all members of a group. The other forms remove that input from the equation and can breed malcontent behavior.

55. A

We are social creatures. To create an understanding of the world, we are interested in why people behave the way they do. The role of attribution is to understand motivation for performing behaviors in ourselves and, more particularly, in others.

56. A

Early antipsychotic drugs—chlorpromazine in particular—had very strong effects on the muscles. The drug led to twitching and the development of tics that are reminiscent of Parkinson's disease. Tardive dyskensia is the chemical development of this disorder, caused as a side effect of taking this medication.

57. D

Aphasia refers to a disorder that involves the loss of language (the prefix *a-* here means without), and a loss of language comprehension suggests the damage is in Wernicke's area. Broca's area, (E), is involved with language production, not comprehension. The cerebellum, (A), is involved with coordination and balance, the amygdala, (B), is involved with fear, and the corpus callosum, (C), links the two brain hemispheres together.

58. A

There are many, many forms of psychotherapy. However, for phobias, the treatment of systematic desensitization, developed by Josef Wolpe, appears to be the most experimentally validated treatment plan.

59. D

In the 21st century, neuroscientists have many ways to examine the structure and function of the brain, and you must be sure to know each type. An X-ray, (A), and MRI, (C), can show only the structure of the brain, an EEG, (E), can show function by depicting the brain's overall electrical activity (but not the specific area), and a brain lesion, (B), is simply abnormal tissue. Only PET scans show the activity or function of specific brain areas.

60. C

According the research by Zajonc, if we are in the mere presence of someone, rating of our performance increases. Thus, exposure seems to be the key component to ratings. Also, if we see people, we rate them better than if we don't see them.

61. C

The frequency, localization, and volley theories all are related to hearing. The trichromatic theory was the original theory of vision, suggesting that our retina can only code for three colors. The opponent process model allowed for a more complete understanding of color vision by demonstrating that we use a variety of layers to perceive color.

62. E

The primacy effect suggests that we are really good with the first several items in lists but will often fail on items that come later. This is a good description of this process. The primacy effect is part of the serial position effect, but with the serial position effect, a person would recall both the beginning and the end of the alphabet.

63. B

Developmental research is very difficult to do, because development takes time. Longitudinal studies will follow a group of individuals (called a cohort) across a long span of time. To do the research more quickly, we will often compare a group of people of one age with another, trying to match them as best we can. This is called a cross-sectional design.

64. A

For the other disorders, new drugs have been developed over the past 30 years. However, lithium, originally developed in the 1950s, is still the drug of choice for many patients who suffer from bipolar disorder.

65. B

The general adaptation syndrome occurs when the body prepares itself to deal with stress. We become hypersensitive to stressful situations and struggle with even small annoyances.

66. D

According to Piaget, the ability to recognize conservation is very important. A child who can tell that clay doesn't change mass when it changes shape has made a very big leap in his or her cognitive abilities. This is a child who, according to Piaget, would be in the concrete operational stage of cognitive development.

67. C

According to Baumrind, parents have different styles of raising children. The authoritarian parent exerts a great deal of control; the permissive parent allows everything to occur. The authoritative parent has control yet is willing to allow the child to explore the world and make choices.

68. C

The DSM is important to psychologists and psychiatrists because they are able to use the book to apply a consistent system of diagnosing disorders. There are criticisms of the book, such as dual diagnosis, but in general, the symptoms are clearly set out in the book to allow two independent professionals to see a patient and come to the same diagnosis from the symptoms presented.

69. A

Social loafing occurs when one uses a group to "hide" and not do what is expected. The other responses are social psychological phenomena but do not deal with lack of effort.

70. C

Paradoxical sleep occurs during REM, when our brain waves are very similar to when we are awake. A person in paradoxical sleep is probably dreaming and is typically easily awoken. We seem to need this stage of sleep because if we are denied paradoxical sleep, the next time we sleep, we will go into that stage quicker and remain in it longer than normal. The term *paradoxical* applies because it would appear that we need sleep to rest, yet our brains do not seem to rest during this stage.

71. A

All of the terms involved with experimental design are important for you to know. Remember that the main groups are called the experimental and control groups, and while most examples present just one of each, in the "real world," scientists often use multiple experimental and control groups. The experimental group (D) is always the one that gets the independent variable, while the control group typically gets no treatment or a placebo to mimic the independent variable, as is true in this case.

72. B

Bandura is famous for his work on social learning theory (what is now called social cognitive theory), or vicarious reinforcement. Wundt is known for his work in structuralism; James, for his work on the book *Principles of Psychology*; Watson and Skinner for work in classical and operant conditioning, respectively.

73. E

In this study, chimps were presented with a problem. Food was outside their reach, but they could use the materials in their cages to obtain the food. In most cases, the chimps did not at first have a solution, but after a time, they were able to develop a strategy to obtain the food using what was available to them. Kohler called this *insight*.

74. B

Systematic desensitization is the process of choice for treating such a phobia. The other forms of therapy are also used for such a situation, but desensitization is the only method that has experimentally validated evidence of its effectiveness.

75. C

Watson's work focused almost exclusively on the role of the environment on behavior. Watson argued that we need to reject the notions of consciousness and internal events and instead examine how the environment one's in has an impact on subsequent behavior.

76. D

Vygotsky's theory differs from the other theories listed. Vygotsky's is much less structured and emphasizes the role of experience, language, and culture on learning. According to Vygotsky, a child's ZPD is the area in which a child can solve problems with support. That said, a child who is having trouble in school needs to be evaluated to determine the ZPD and provided with the support necessary to be successful.

77. C

Fraternal twins have the same rate of getting a disorder as any other set of siblings. This is because fraternal twins occur when two eggs are fertilized rather than the typical one. Thus, they are "twins" because they are born at the same time, but they are not identical twins and they don't typically look alike (and they can be different sexes as well).

78. B

The circadian rhythm is the pattern of sleep-wake cycles that people develop if they are on a consistent schedule. If a person is on such a schedule, body temperature, heart rate, and so on will increase or decrease at roughly the same time each day as a way of preparing the body for resting or waking.

79. A

Cognitive dissonance is caused by having two competing beliefs. When a person is working at a job even though he or she hates it, this will cause a great deal of dissonance. To resolve this, the person might either quit or adjust his or her perspective to find there are aspects of the job that are pleasant.

80. C

The fovea is the part of the eye with the greatest degree of visual acuity. Any information that is directed onto the fovea is going to be the information that is most clearly and easily recognized.

81. B

Skinner became interested in behaviorism after reading books by Pavlov, Watson, and Thorndike. However, he believed that the emphasis on classical conditioning was missing many of the behaviors that humans and other animals produce. Thus, he coined the term *operant conditioning* to indicate that he believed the environment "operated" on an organism to produce behavior.

82. A

Endogenous means naturally occurring, and endorphins are the body's natural response to alleviating pain. Thus, the narcotics that serve to dull pain are similar to these naturally occurring chemicals (albeit, more effective).

83. D

Don't let the math scare you. Correlation coefficients are mathematical expressions of the relationship between two variables, such as the relationship between IQ and SAT scores. If the coefficient has a negative sign, that means as one variable increases, the other decreases, while a positive coefficient reflects that the variables move in the same direction. But the question here is about coefficient strength, and you have to know that the strongest correlations are closest to 1 or −1, and the weakest is closest to 0, so in this case it's (D).

84. B

The point of the Milgram study was to demonstrate that participants were willing to give shocks if they were told to do so by an authority figure. Thus, even in situations in which a participant might report they wouldn't do so, Milgram demonstrated that under the right conditions, participants are willing to do things if they are told to.

85. B

Diffusion of responsibility occurs when a group of people all believe someone else is going to deal with the situation. Imagine your power goes out. Everyone might assume that someone else called it in to the electric company. However, it may be that everyone assumes that and no one does. This is another example of diffusion of responsibility.

86. B

A mnemonic is a memory device designed to help us recall things, often in a particular order. One of the oldest techniques is to associate what we are trying to remember with objects in a well-memorized path. Natural language mnemonics are different in that they use the language to create the mnemonic (such as using HOMES to remember the Great Lakes).

87. E

Wolpe is associated with systematic desensitization, Rogers with client-centered therapy, Wundt with structuralism, and Chomsky with language acquisition. Only Freud is associated with psychoanalysis.

88. E

The visual cliff is an ingenious device created by Gibson and Walk in 1960 to determine whether or not infants had yet developed depth perception. The cliff simulated a sharp drop in the crawling surface, and young infants happily crawled across to find their parents. When the participants were a little older, though, they would crawl to the edge of the "cliff" and refuse to cross, indicating that they perceived a deep drop ahead.

89. D

Sperling studied visual sensory memory, Watson and Skinner studied learning and how the environment controls behavior, and Wertheimer studied Gestalt psychology. Wundt's technique of introspection was designed to help us understand the structure of consciousness (hence the name of his theory, structuralism).

90. A

Proactive interference occurs when old information intrudes on your ability to recall newly learned information. Retroactive interference occurs when we are trying to remember old information, but new information gets in the way. Imagine you are trying to remember your old phone number, but you keep remembering your new one. That is an example of retroactive interference.

91. B

According to Jung, we have several archetypes in our collective unconscious. These are patterns of behavior or images that have an impact on our behavior. The persona is the mask that we put on in front of others, the animus is the masculine side of women, the shadow reflects our deep dark secrets, and the self is who we really are.

92. D

Endorphins are released when we experience pain. GABA, dopamine, and serotonin are all neurotransmitters, and Prozac is an antidepressant.

93. B

Negative reinforcement is the process of engaging in behavior that removes aversive stimuli. The result is an increase in the behavior that led to the removal of the stimuli. Positive reinforcement is the process of engaging in behavior that results in the giving of a stimulus that results in the increase in that behavior. Punishment results in a decrease in behavior, and conditioning and UCR are both concepts in classical conditioning.

94. B

Bipolar disorder does result in depression at times, but what differentiates this from clinical depression is the swing between clinical depression and periods of mania.

95. C

In the visual system, two kinds of cells on the retina capture photons of light: rods and cones. Cones are primarily responsible for color, and rods for black and white. Cones are located mostly in the fovea, and rods in the periphery. If it is dark, there is little light available for the cones to fire; thus, black-and-white vision becomes better in such a situation.

96. E

Because vision is primarily processed in the occipital lobe and the occipital lobe is located in the back of the brain, (E) is clearly the best answer.

97. E

Positive reinforcement is marked by a consequence leading to an increase in behavior. It doesn't matter what we think of the consequence. In the described situation, we might believe that a shock is punishment. But because the shock leads to an increase in behavior, it must be positive reinforcement.

98. B

Because we have two eyes, we get two different views of the world. We integrate these views in the brain to give us the perspective of depth. We call this binocular (two eyes) disparity (different views).

99. C

While it was first developed by Wundt, it was Titchener who expanded the method known as introspection. Long before the advent of the fMRI and PET scans, Titchener wanted to know how brains worked, and to do that he asked subjects to report their moment-by-moment sensations. With this data Titchener went on to develop the theory of structuralism, which suggested how the mind is structured from its most basic elements.

100. B

Developmental psychologists study changes over the life span. (A) would be carried out by a cognitive psychologist, (C) by a behaviorist, (D) by a physiological psychologist, and (E) by a social psychologist.

SECTION II

1. Alana recently attended her first fencing match and enjoyed it so much that she began taking fencing lessons. After the first week she threatened to quit because she was so frustrated, and she yelled at her parents a few times when they picked her up from her lessons. First, define each of the following psychological topics, and then give an example for each, including advice that you could give to Alana based on that concept.

   - Procedural memory

   - Displacement

   - Scaffolding

   - Intrinsic motivation

   - Social learning

This question is worth 10 points, one for each definition and one for the correct application to the situation. The following rubric is based on what a typical answer might look like, and rubrics like these are used by AP readers each year to award points when reading essays.

Procedural memory (also known as implicit or non-declarative memory) is used when a person is actively doing something he or she knows how to do, as if the person is following a well-known procedure (1 point). Alana should be informed that because she has not yet learned how to perform fencing movements, she has not developed the procedural memory that she has with other motor movements like walking and catching a ball, but that this will improve over time (1 point).

Displacement is a defense mechanism, a term coined by Sigmund Freud to describe when people take out their anger on others (1 point). Alana is taking her anger out on her parents, who are not causing her frustration, and she should be counseled to channel her frustration in other ways (1 point).

Scaffolding refers to Vygotsky's zone of proximal development, which suggests that teachers should always keep the goal challenging for their students but not so hard that they give up (1 point). One might suggest to Alana that even though she is frustrated, her teacher has set a high standard to keep her challenged, and that the frustration she feels will dissipate as she improves (1 point).

Intrinsic motivation is the internal desire to do a behavior the best one can for its own sake, without the use of external rewards like money or trophies (1 point). Alana has to tap into her intrinsic motivation and work to satisfy her own potential rather than to try to work harder simply to get praise or rewards. Intrinsic motivation creates a more lasting interest than extrinsic motivation (1 point).

Social learning is our ability to change our behavior based on experiences that we see happen to others (1 point). Alana might take time to watch not only her instructor but also the other students, and she may learn to model their behavior in order to improve her own performance (1 point).

2. Dr. Smith is interested in determining the relationship between IQ and success in life. Design a correlational study to examine this issue. Using the following concepts, first define each term and then explain how the term would be used within the context of the study.

- Operational definitions of variables
- Sampling
- Validity
- Ethical principles

This question is worth 8 points. Again, follow what the question asks and be sure to both define and explain how the term would be used in this example.

An operational definition is a definition of the components of a study so that it is clear it can be measured and can be replicated (1 point). IQ can be defined as a score on an IQ test, and success could be defined as income over a five-year span. These would not have to be your answers, but your answers have to be clearly defined and as quantifiable (that is, as easy to put in numbers) as these are (1 point).

Sampling refers to selecting participants who represent the population you are studying and want to generalize about (1 point). For this study we might select 100 participants from the town in which we live to serve as a sample of the population. To do so randomly, we might select names from a phone book or other directory (1 point).

Validity is the extent to which a test measures what it is intended to measure (1 point). In this example, we might be concerned about the validity or accuracy of the results because we want to be able to make claims about the relationship between IQ and success. To do so, we need to make sure we understand that many studies have questioned whether IQ is a valid measure of intelligence, and that there are other measures that might be used to measure intelligence in this study (1 point).

Ethical principles refer to the principles created by the APA that researchers must agree to, and that include getting informed consent, keeping the information we gather confidential, not harming the participants, and debriefing them afterwards (1 point). In this case, we would be sure to get informed consent from the people we are studying, keep their information confidential, and let them know at the conclusion of the study what our findings were. Participants could also leave the study at any time and have their data removed if they chose to do so (1 point).

Practice Test Two Answer Grid

1. Ⓐ Ⓑ Ⓒ Ⓓ Ⓔ
2. Ⓐ Ⓑ Ⓒ Ⓓ Ⓔ
3. Ⓐ Ⓑ Ⓒ Ⓓ Ⓔ
4. Ⓐ Ⓑ Ⓒ Ⓓ Ⓔ
5. Ⓐ Ⓑ Ⓒ Ⓓ Ⓔ
6. Ⓐ Ⓑ Ⓒ Ⓓ Ⓔ
7. Ⓐ Ⓑ Ⓒ Ⓓ Ⓔ
8. Ⓐ Ⓑ Ⓒ Ⓓ Ⓔ
9. Ⓐ Ⓑ Ⓒ Ⓓ Ⓔ
10. Ⓐ Ⓑ Ⓒ Ⓓ Ⓔ
11. Ⓐ Ⓑ Ⓒ Ⓓ Ⓔ
12. Ⓐ Ⓑ Ⓒ Ⓓ Ⓔ
13. Ⓐ Ⓑ Ⓒ Ⓓ Ⓔ
14. Ⓐ Ⓑ Ⓒ Ⓓ Ⓔ
15. Ⓐ Ⓑ Ⓒ Ⓓ Ⓔ
16. Ⓐ Ⓑ Ⓒ Ⓓ Ⓔ
17. Ⓐ Ⓑ Ⓒ Ⓓ Ⓔ
18. Ⓐ Ⓑ Ⓒ Ⓓ Ⓔ
19. Ⓐ Ⓑ Ⓒ Ⓓ Ⓔ
20. Ⓐ Ⓑ Ⓒ Ⓓ Ⓔ
21. Ⓐ Ⓑ Ⓒ Ⓓ Ⓔ
22. Ⓐ Ⓑ Ⓒ Ⓓ Ⓔ
23. Ⓐ Ⓑ Ⓒ Ⓓ Ⓔ
24. Ⓐ Ⓑ Ⓒ Ⓓ Ⓔ
25. Ⓐ Ⓑ Ⓒ Ⓓ Ⓔ

26. Ⓐ Ⓑ Ⓒ Ⓓ Ⓔ
27. Ⓐ Ⓑ Ⓒ Ⓓ Ⓔ
28. Ⓐ Ⓑ Ⓒ Ⓓ Ⓔ
29. Ⓐ Ⓑ Ⓒ Ⓓ Ⓔ
30. Ⓐ Ⓑ Ⓒ Ⓓ Ⓔ
31. Ⓐ Ⓑ Ⓒ Ⓓ Ⓔ
32. Ⓐ Ⓑ Ⓒ Ⓓ Ⓔ
33. Ⓐ Ⓑ Ⓒ Ⓓ Ⓔ
34. Ⓐ Ⓑ Ⓒ Ⓓ Ⓔ
35. Ⓐ Ⓑ Ⓒ Ⓓ Ⓔ
36. Ⓐ Ⓑ Ⓒ Ⓓ Ⓔ
37. Ⓐ Ⓑ Ⓒ Ⓓ Ⓔ
38. Ⓐ Ⓑ Ⓒ Ⓓ Ⓔ
39. Ⓐ Ⓑ Ⓒ Ⓓ Ⓔ
40. Ⓐ Ⓑ Ⓒ Ⓓ Ⓔ
41. Ⓐ Ⓑ Ⓒ Ⓓ Ⓔ
42. Ⓐ Ⓑ Ⓒ Ⓓ Ⓔ
43. Ⓐ Ⓑ Ⓒ Ⓓ Ⓔ
44. Ⓐ Ⓑ Ⓒ Ⓓ Ⓔ
45. Ⓐ Ⓑ Ⓒ Ⓓ Ⓔ
46. Ⓐ Ⓑ Ⓒ Ⓓ Ⓔ
47. Ⓐ Ⓑ Ⓒ Ⓓ Ⓔ
48. Ⓐ Ⓑ Ⓒ Ⓓ Ⓔ
49. Ⓐ Ⓑ Ⓒ Ⓓ Ⓔ
50. Ⓐ Ⓑ Ⓒ Ⓓ Ⓔ

51. Ⓐ Ⓑ Ⓒ Ⓓ Ⓔ
52. Ⓐ Ⓑ Ⓒ Ⓓ Ⓔ
53. Ⓐ Ⓑ Ⓒ Ⓓ Ⓔ
54. Ⓐ Ⓑ Ⓒ Ⓓ Ⓔ
55. Ⓐ Ⓑ Ⓒ Ⓓ Ⓔ
56. Ⓐ Ⓑ Ⓒ Ⓓ Ⓔ
57. Ⓐ Ⓑ Ⓒ Ⓓ Ⓔ
58. Ⓐ Ⓑ Ⓒ Ⓓ Ⓔ
59. Ⓐ Ⓑ Ⓒ Ⓓ Ⓔ
60. Ⓐ Ⓑ Ⓒ Ⓓ Ⓔ
61. Ⓐ Ⓑ Ⓒ Ⓓ Ⓔ
62. Ⓐ Ⓑ Ⓒ Ⓓ Ⓔ
63. Ⓐ Ⓑ Ⓒ Ⓓ Ⓔ
64. Ⓐ Ⓑ Ⓒ Ⓓ Ⓔ
65. Ⓐ Ⓑ Ⓒ Ⓓ Ⓔ
66. Ⓐ Ⓑ Ⓒ Ⓓ Ⓔ
67. Ⓐ Ⓑ Ⓒ Ⓓ Ⓔ
68. Ⓐ Ⓑ Ⓒ Ⓓ Ⓔ
69. Ⓐ Ⓑ Ⓒ Ⓓ Ⓔ
70. Ⓐ Ⓑ Ⓒ Ⓓ Ⓔ
71. Ⓐ Ⓑ Ⓒ Ⓓ Ⓔ
72. Ⓐ Ⓑ Ⓒ Ⓓ Ⓔ
73. Ⓐ Ⓑ Ⓒ Ⓓ Ⓔ
74. Ⓐ Ⓑ Ⓒ Ⓓ Ⓔ
75. Ⓐ Ⓑ Ⓒ Ⓓ Ⓔ

76. Ⓐ Ⓑ Ⓒ Ⓓ Ⓔ
77. Ⓐ Ⓑ Ⓒ Ⓓ Ⓔ
78. Ⓐ Ⓑ Ⓒ Ⓓ Ⓔ
79. Ⓐ Ⓑ Ⓒ Ⓓ Ⓔ
80. Ⓐ Ⓑ Ⓒ Ⓓ Ⓔ
81. Ⓐ Ⓑ Ⓒ Ⓓ Ⓔ
82. Ⓐ Ⓑ Ⓒ Ⓓ Ⓔ
83. Ⓐ Ⓑ Ⓒ Ⓓ Ⓔ
84. Ⓐ Ⓑ Ⓒ Ⓓ Ⓔ
85. Ⓐ Ⓑ Ⓒ Ⓓ Ⓔ
86. Ⓐ Ⓑ Ⓒ Ⓓ Ⓔ
87. Ⓐ Ⓑ Ⓒ Ⓓ Ⓔ
88. Ⓐ Ⓑ Ⓒ Ⓓ Ⓔ
89. Ⓐ Ⓑ Ⓒ Ⓓ Ⓔ
90. Ⓐ Ⓑ Ⓒ Ⓓ Ⓔ
91. Ⓐ Ⓑ Ⓒ Ⓓ Ⓔ
92. Ⓐ Ⓑ Ⓒ Ⓓ Ⓔ
93. Ⓐ Ⓑ Ⓒ Ⓓ Ⓔ
94. Ⓐ Ⓑ Ⓒ Ⓓ Ⓔ
95. Ⓐ Ⓑ Ⓒ Ⓓ Ⓔ
96. Ⓐ Ⓑ Ⓒ Ⓓ Ⓔ
97. Ⓐ Ⓑ Ⓒ Ⓓ Ⓔ
98. Ⓐ Ⓑ Ⓒ Ⓓ Ⓔ
99. Ⓐ Ⓑ Ⓒ Ⓓ Ⓔ
100. Ⓐ Ⓑ Ⓒ Ⓓ Ⓔ

PRACTICE TEST TWO

SECTION I

Time—70 minutes

Percent of total grade—$66\frac{2}{3}$

Directions: You will have 1 hour and 10 minutes to answer 100 multiple-choice questions.

1. Dave has trouble sleeping. Several times a night, he stops breathing and wakes up. Dave most likely suffers from

    (A) narcolepsy.
    (B) cataplexy.
    (C) sleep apnea.
    (D) insomnia.
    (E) somnambulism.

2. If a researcher found that rich people rate themselves as less happy than poor people do, then she could say that wealth and happiness are

    (A) positively correlated.
    (B) negatively correlated.
    (C) independent variables.
    (D) dependent variables.
    (E) causally related.

3. Heuristics are often considered more useful than algorithms because they

    (A) consider all potential solutions to a problem.
    (B) involve conceptual thinking.
    (C) are faster than an algorithm.
    (D) are examples of formal operational thought.
    (E) incorporate mental sets.

4. "I see a bear, my heart beats, I feel scared." This is an example of what theory?

    (A) Set-point theory
    (B) Fight-or-flight response
    (C) General adaptation syndrome
    (D) James-Lange theory
    (E) Cannon-Bard theory

5. Lawrence Kohlberg developed a well-conceptualized view of moral development. Carol Gilligan, however, strongly criticized this theory. The main criticism that Gilligan described was

    (A) sex differences in orientations toward morality.
    (B) vagueness in terms of ages that children reach certain levels.
    (C) no ability to generalize to other cultures.
    (D) the way that Kohlberg assessed morality.
    (E) lack of coherence with other theories of development.

6. Fred did not get a high score on his IQ test. He says that it is because IQ tests are inherently biased—that they do not truly reflect his true abilities. Fred is making what attribution?

    (A) An internal attribution
    (B) The fundamental attribution error
    (C) Actor-perceiver error
    (D) An attribution error
    (E) Poor attribution

GO ON TO THE NEXT PAGE

7. The disorder that is characterized by a flagrant disregard for the rights of others and a lack of remorse for one's actions is called

    (A) paranoid personality disorder.
    (B) histrionic personality disorder.
    (C) schizoid personality disorder.
    (D) schizotypal personality disorder.
    (E) antisocial personality disorder.

8. Which of the following researchers made the argument that intelligence is composed of many more qualities than just traditional math and verbal skills?

    (A) Binet
    (B) Terman
    (C) Gardner
    (D) Wechsler
    (E) Merrill

9. Which of the following is NOT used by cognitive psychologists to measure cognitive processes?

    (A) Eye movements
    (B) Gaze durations
    (C) Latency
    (D) Semantic recognition
    (E) Free association

10. If you look at a flag that has green, black, and yellow colors and then look at a white screen, you will see the American flag with its proper colors. This is due to

    (A) opponent process theory.
    (B) tri-color theory.
    (C) place theory.
    (D) frequency theory.
    (E) gate theory.

11. According to Piaget, at what stage does a child fully understand the concept of conservation?

    (A) Preoperational
    (B) Presensorimotor
    (C) Formal operational
    (D) Concrete operational
    (E) Sensorimotor

12. Maslow's theory of personality involves

    (A) hierarchy of needs.
    (B) belief in a just world.
    (C) locus of control.
    (D) collective unconscious.
    (E) need for achievement.

13. Tammy wanted to remember a list of items she needed to buy at the mall, without writing that list down. Her list had 40 items. While at the mall, she was able to remember the first few items on the list but not the rest. She was demonstrating the effect of

    (A) chunking.
    (B) mnemonics.
    (C) recency.
    (D) primacy.
    (E) organizational drift.

14. Of the following treatments, which would most likely be used with those who suffer from some developmental delays?

    (A) Token economy
    (B) Psychoanalysis
    (C) Cognitive therapy
    (D) Systematic desensitization
    (E) Client-centered therapy

GO ON TO THE NEXT PAGE

15. Which personality disorder has symptoms whereby the patient cannot see shades of gray but rather judges people and issues as being good or bad?

    (A) Schizoid
    (B) Narcissistic
    (C) Schizotypal
    (D) Borderline
    (E) Antisocial

16. Who was the psychologist who developed the first stage theory of cognitive development?

    (A) Sigmund Freud
    (B) Jean Piaget
    (C) Erik Erikson
    (D) Harry Harlow
    (E) Carol Gilligan

17. Wundt

    (A) developed the concept of Gestalt psychology.
    (B) worked at Harvard University.
    (C) developed the first lab in experimental psychology.
    (D) challenged Helmholtz's conception of limen.
    (E) published a text called *Principles of Psychology*.

18. If you were in a car accident and damaged your hippocampus, you would probably experience problems with

    (A) memory.
    (B) sensory processing.
    (C) motor control.
    (D) language.
    (E) vision.

19. In the majority of people, the left hemisphere is dominant for

    (A) vision.
    (B) thought.
    (C) language.
    (D) memory.
    (E) attention.

20. The typical IQ test has a mean of 100 and a standard deviation of 15. If you scored 115, what percentage of others who have taken the test scored lower than you?

    (A) 34 percent
    (B) 48 percent
    (C) 68 percent
    (D) 84 percent
    (E) 98 percent

21. Depth perception is obtained by a variety of cues in the environment. Which of the following cues is based on the different image we get from our eyes because of their location in our heads?

    (A) Interposition
    (B) Linear perspective
    (C) Context
    (D) Localization
    (E) Binocular disparity

22. Not helping someone because you are in a group is due to which of the following concepts in social psychology?

    (A) Diffusion of responsibility
    (B) Groupthink
    (C) Stereotyping
    (D) Just world hypothesis
    (E) Fundamental attribution error

GO ON TO THE NEXT PAGE

23. Which of the following concepts is most associated with Freudian or psychoanalytic therapy?

    (A) Flooding
    (B) Free association
    (C) Unconditional positive regard
    (D) Positive reinforcement
    (E) Punishment

24. I see a bear, my heart starts racing, I start trembling, and I begin to run. From these bodily responses, I understand that I am afraid. This understanding of emotion is consistent with the

    (A) James-Lange theory.
    (B) Cannon-Bard theory.
    (C) opponent-process theory.
    (D) encoding specificity principle.
    (E) availability heuristic.

25. Which of the following is NOT a Jungian archetype?

    (A) Persona
    (B) Shadow
    (C) Anima
    (D) Animus
    (E) Superego

26. A central tenet of the Gestalt school is that

    (A) studying consciousness is essential to understanding psychology.
    (B) mind is what brain does.
    (C) a perception must be studied in its whole or molar form.
    (D) all that is important in psychology is that which is observable.
    (E) biology is the most important element in understanding behavior.

27. A normal distribution is in the shape of a

    (A) bell curve.
    (B) chi square.
    (C) scatterplot.
    (D) bimodal distribution.
    (E) skewed distribution.

28. Victor goes to see a therapist. The therapist says that Victor's anger at his mother is due to his recognizing things about his mother that bother him about himself. This is called

    (A) sublimation.
    (B) projection.
    (C) transference.
    (D) reaction formation.
    (E) repression.

29. Albert Bandura argues that reinforcement does not need to be directly experienced for it to have an impact on behavior. This phenomenon is called

    (A) social loafing.
    (B) vicarious reinforcement.
    (C) operant conditioning.
    (D) classical conditioning.
    (E) attribution theory.

GO ON TO THE NEXT PAGE

30. The idea that we are more likely to prefer something if we have seen it before has been tested by several psychologists. Even if the information is not actually perceived by the participant (it was below threshold), participants still prefer stimuli they have previously been exposed to. This is called

    (A) groupthink.
    (B) halo effect.
    (C) mere exposure effect.
    (D) levels of processing effect.
    (E) spreading activation.

31. Mitch has problems dealing with people. His communication skills are poor, and he often has delusions that he is someone really important and that people are out to get him. Mitch would probably be diagnosed with

    (A) catatonic schizophrenia.
    (B) paranoid schizophrenia.
    (C) multiple personality disorder.
    (D) psychogenic amnesia.
    (E) psychogenic fugue.

32. Stanley Milgram's classic experiment in social psychology is most closely associated with

    (A) persuasion.
    (B) authority.
    (C) leadership.
    (D) altruism.
    (E) attraction.

33. When you are moderately excited, you are most likely going to be most efficient or have your best performance. This is an example of

    (A) Yerkes-Dodson law.
    (B) the Hawthorne effect.
    (C) Weber's law.
    (D) the actor-observer bias.
    (E) Pythagorean theorem.

34. The concepts of introversion/extroversion were measured in a tool created by

    (A) Carl Rogers.
    (B) Hans Eysenck.
    (C) George Kelly.
    (D) Joseph Wolpe.
    (E) Wilhelm Wundt.

35. "Give me a group of infants, and if I could control the world in which they are raised, I could predict which will become doctors and which will become sculptors." This statement is similar to one made by

    (A) Watson.
    (B) Skinner.
    (C) Wundt.
    (D) Rogers.
    (E) Titchener.

36. Two pins are placed so close to each other on a subject's finger that they are perceived as a single point. This is because the pins have not reached the

    (A) absolute threshold.
    (B) just noticeable difference.
    (C) threshold.
    (D) action potential.
    (E) gate theory of pain.

GO ON TO THE NEXT PAGE

37. A department store offers salespeople a bonus if they sell a certain number of items during a month. The bonus serves as a(n)

(A) intrinsic motivation.

(B) conditioned stimulus.

(C) extrinsic motivation.

(D) cognitive dissonance.

(E) positive punishment.

38. Kohlberg's theory of moral development is measured by using which of the following riddles or dilemmas?

(A) Prisoner's dilemma

(B) Heinz dilemma

(C) Sphinx's riddle

(D) Twins problem

(E) Availability heuristic

39. Francine raged at her therapist when she failed to make all A's in her classes as a junior in college. Her therapist remarked in a very relaxed manner how absurd her logic was, because she still had the highest grade point average in her class. The way her therapist responded was most typical of what kind of therapist?

(A) Client-centered

(B) Psychoanalytic

(C) Learning

(D) Cognitive

(E) Eclectic

40. Of the following statistics, which is the most commonly used measure of spread among scores?

(A) Mean

(B) Kurtosis

(C) Mode

(D) Skewness

(E) Standard deviation

41. On the way to the beach, John's car stops running and overheats. He has no water, but he does have several drinks. Eventually, he comes to the realization that he could pour some iced tea into his radiator so he can reach his destination. John is NOT a victim of

(A) a schema.

(B) a script.

(C) an algorithm.

(D) metacognition.

(E) functional fixedness.

42. In most people, the occipital lobe is responsible for

(A) vision.

(B) thought.

(C) language.

(D) memory.

(E) attention.

GO ON TO THE NEXT PAGE

43. A social psychologist finds that he can get students to remember math answers more quickly when they have to compete with each other to give the answer. This is an example of

    (A) the James-Lange theory.
    (B) social comparison theory.
    (C) the Cannon-Bard theory.
    (D) levels of processing.
    (E) social facilitation.

44. Which of the following is a technique used in Freudian therapy?

    (A) Free association
    (B) Free recall
    (C) Systematic desensitization
    (D) Implosion therapy
    (E) Biofeedback

45. The research by Harry Harlow that used wire or cloth surrogate mothers demonstrated the importance of

    (A) contact comfort.
    (B) family resemblance.
    (C) instinctual drift.
    (D) cognitive economy.
    (E) display characteristics.

46. Broca's area is responsible for

    (A) visual acuity.
    (B) language production.
    (C) color vision.
    (D) memory.
    (E) auditory integration.

47. A type II error occurs whenever

    (A) a true null hypothesis is accepted.
    (B) a false null hypothesis is rejected.
    (C) a false null hypothesis is accepted.
    (D) a true null hypothesis is rejected.
    (E) a statistically insignificant result is obtained.

48. A researcher describes his measure as "a score between 5 and 5.2 on the scale." This is called a(n)

    (A) empirical verification.
    (B) controlled observation.
    (C) operational definition.
    (D) statistical generalization.
    (E) hypothesis testing.

49. Paul saw only two Red Sox games, and in both games, the Red Sox lost. Paul concludes that the Red Sox must always lose. This is an example of

    (A) divergent thinking.
    (B) the availability heuristic.
    (C) confabulation.
    (D) spreading activation.
    (E) insight.

GO ON TO THE NEXT PAGE

50. A psychologist might study the connection between aptitude test scores of preschool children and the same children's elementary school grades. If the psychologist finds that there is a strong correlation between the two, then he can say that the aptitude test has _____ because it accurately predicted performance.

    (A) validity
    (B) reliability
    (C) a normal distribution
    (D) standardization
    (E) a large standard deviation

51. The WAIS and WISC are types of

    (A) personality tests based on trait theories.
    (B) intelligence tests.
    (C) normal distribution.
    (D) statistical measures of central tendency and deviation.
    (E) reliability measures for academic tests.

52. The receptive field in the eye with the greatest amount of visual acuity is the

    (A) fovea.
    (B) retina.
    (C) sclera.
    (D) lens.
    (E) cornea.

53. Martin Seligman is most well known for his work on

    (A) operant conditioning.
    (B) cognitive behavioral theory (CBT).
    (C) hierarchy of needs.
    (D) learned helplessness.
    (E) authoritarianism.

54. You are angry at your brother. You learned in psychology class that you can cause him to feel very tired by waking him periodically during sleep. At what stage would you wake him to cause maximum disruption of his sleep?

    (A) Stage 1
    (B) Stage 2
    (C) REM sleep
    (D) Stage 3
    (E) Stage 4

55. The reinforcement schedule that causes behavior to be most difficult to extinguish is

    (A) fixed-ratio schedule.
    (B) variable-ratio schedule.
    (C) fixed-interval schedule.
    (D) variable-interval schedule.
    (E) continuous schedule.

56. In obsessive-compulsive disorder, an obsession is _____ and a compulsion is _____.

    (A) controllable; uncontrollable
    (B) an uncontrollable thought; an uncontrollable impulse
    (C) neurotic; psychotic
    (D) the result of trauma; self-generated
    (E) associated with personality disorders; not associated with personality disorders

GO ON TO THE NEXT PAGE ⟩

57. Of the following individuals, who is responsible for developing the concept of classical conditioning?

    (A) B. F. Skinner
    (B) E. L. Thorndike
    (C) E. O. Wilson
    (D) Ivan Pavlov
    (E) John B. Watson

58. The method of loci is an example of

    (A) the primacy effect.
    (B) the recency effect.
    (C) a mnemonic.
    (D) a heuristic.
    (E) an algorithm.

59. Facial expressions that are associated with particular emotions (such as surprise or fear) are

    (A) very similar throughout the world.
    (B) learned in early childhood.
    (C) different in individualist and collectivist cultures.
    (D) more similar in women than in men.
    (E) more similar in adults than they are in children or adolescents.

60. A client with _____ most likely is suffering from some form of schizophrenia.

    (A) delusions and hallucinations
    (B) eating disturbances
    (C) refusal to go to sleep at night
    (D) the irresistible urge to utter obscenities
    (E) memory impairment at both short-term and long-term levels

61. Electroconvulsive shock therapy (ECT) is a treatment that has received a great deal of bad press. However, it is an effective therapy for a very small group of disorders. Which of the following is one of those disorders?

    (A) Somatoform disorders
    (B) Anxiety disorders
    (C) Personality disorders
    (D) Severe depression
    (E) Sleep apnea

62. In an experiment, participants were asked to remember a lengthy list of words. Several hours later, when asked to recall as many words as they could, many participants wrote down words that were similar in meaning to the actual words. This is an example of

    (A) memory decay.
    (B) state-dependent memory.
    (C) source amnesia.
    (D) implicit memory.
    (E) semantic encoding.

63. When Nancy was in high school, she ate lunch at 10:15 every day. Now, every day at 10:15, she feels hungry. The time of day is a(n)

    (A) unconditioned stimulus.
    (B) conditioned stimulus.
    (C) unconditioned response.
    (D) conditioned response.
    (E) neutral stimulus.

GO ON TO THE NEXT PAGE ⟩

64. If a person is now able to solve complex problems, she is probably in which stage of cognitive development, according to Piaget?

    (A) Sensorimotor
    (B) Presensorimotor
    (C) Preoperational
    (D) Concrete operational
    (E) Formal operational

65. The concept in social psychology that states that people will do things because others are doing them is

    (A) conformity.
    (B) attribution.
    (C) aggression.
    (D) groupthink.
    (E) altruism.

66. In his longitudinal study of gifted children, Lewis Terman found that the children

    (A) were more emotional and less healthy than a control group.
    (B) were healthy and well-adjusted, and did well academically.
    (C) were often bullied and marginalized by their peers.
    (D) felt they had been scarred by being labeled, and refused to participate.
    (E) cared more deeply about saving the planet than a control group.

67. Phil Zimbardo is most associated with which of the following famous studies?

    (A) Obedience study
    (B) Robber cave experiment
    (C) Prison study
    (D) Bystander intervention study
    (E) Nonsense syllable study

68. One main criticism of personality tests is that they

    (A) deal with inherent traits versus learned behaviors.
    (B) focus on specific personality traits.
    (C) focus too heavily on positive personality traits.
    (D) focus too heavily on negative personality traits.
    (E) utilize self-report methods, which are not always accurate.

69. Selective serotonin reuptake inhibitors (SSRIs) operate by

    (A) limiting the reuptake of serotonin in the synapses.
    (B) increasing the amount of serotonin released into the synapses.
    (C) increasing sensitivity to serotonin.
    (D) mimicking the effects of serotonin.
    (E) creating a new connection between synapses.

70. Reliability refers to _____ while validity refers to _____ .

    (A) the ability to measure individuals; the ability to measure groups
    (B) the consistency of the measurements of a test; the extent to which a test measures what it intends to measure
    (C) consistency from text to test; consistency within a given test
    (D) the extent to which a test measures what it intends to measure; the measurements of a test
    (E) the ability of the test administrator; the success of the test

GO ON TO THE NEXT PAGE ▷

71. The psychologist who trained with Wundt and traveled to the United States to set up one of the first labs at Cornell University was

    (A) James.
    (B) Titchener.
    (C) Skinner.
    (D) Bower.
    (E) Watson.

72. Willie spent a year of his life stranded on a desert island. Though he was rescued, he still suffers from anxiety and impaired ability to function normally. Willie would most likely be diagnosed with

    (A) seasonal-affective disorder.
    (B) attention-deficit disorder.
    (C) borderline personality disorder.
    (D) obsessive-compulsive disorder.
    (E) post-traumatic stress disorder.

73. Assume you are interested in helping your dog develop the ability to urinate in the same location every time. To do this, you start by providing many rewards to go outside, and gradually you reward the behavior as it begins to get closer to the desired behavior. This is a process called

    (A) systematic desensitization.
    (B) method of loci.
    (C) operant learning.
    (D) shaping.
    (E) extinction.

74. According to William Sheldon's system of somatotypes, which of the following body types would correspond to an inhibited, intellectual personality?

    (A) Somatomorph
    (B) Mesomorph
    (C) Endomorph
    (D) Ectomorph
    (E) Heliomorph

75. The chemical messengers that provide communication between neurons are

    (A) hormones.
    (B) pheromones.
    (C) neurotransmitters.
    (D) dendrites.
    (E) axon terminals.

76. If two individuals have the same phenotype, they

    (A) have the same genes.
    (B) have the same expressed traits for a particular gene.
    (C) possess the same number of chromosomes.
    (D) are biologically compatible.
    (E) are identical twins.

77. Delusions and hallucinations are most likely to be reported by those who have which of the following disorders?

    (A) Dissociative identity disorder
    (B) Schizophrenia
    (C) Borderline personality disorder
    (D) Major depressive disorder
    (E) Generalized anxiety disorder

GO ON TO THE NEXT PAGE

78. Myelin serves to provide

    (A) faster nerve conduction times.

    (B) slower nerve conduction times.

    (C) rerouting of nerve impulses.

    (D) stronger action potentials.

    (E) closer connection of neurons.

79. The stage during which we typically dream can be described as

    (A) alpha waves.

    (B) beta waves.

    (C) delta waves.

    (D) REM.

    (E) theta waves.

80. Of the following individuals, who is most closely associated with the concept of the imprinting?

    (A) Abraham Maslow

    (B) John Bowlby

    (C) Jean Piaget

    (D) Sigmund Freud

    (E) Konrad Lorenz

81. Which of the following is the most important level of language, according to Chomsky?

    (A) Semantic

    (B) Syntactic

    (C) Lexical

    (D) Morphemic

    (E) Phonemic

82. Which of the following is based on the principles of classical conditioning?

    (A) Token economies

    (B) Differential reinforcement

    (C) Systematic desensitization

    (D) Contingency

    (E) Unconditional positive regard

83. Some psychological tests are designed by comparing a population of those who exhibit a disorder with "normals." Such a test is developed by what is called the empirical method. Which of the following tests would be an example of such a measure?

    (A) Myers-Briggs

    (B) Rorschach

    (C) Thematic Apperception Test (TAT)

    (D) MMPI

    (E) Remote Associations Test

84. A client is encouraged to express his feelings in therapy. During the sessions, the therapist gives the client unconditional positive regard. What type of therapy is this client going through?

    (A) Client-centered therapy

    (B) Group therapy

    (C) Behavior modification

    (D) Psychoanalysis

    (E) Systematic desensitization

GO ON TO THE NEXT PAGE ⇨

85. If you have an extra 21st chromosome, you are likely to suffer from

   (A) XYY syndrome.
   (B) Turner's syndrome.
   (C) Down syndrome.
   (D) Pickwickian syndromes.
   (E) Kleinfelter's syndrome.

86. Which of the following does NOT lead to an increase in behavior?

   (A) Punishment
   (B) Positive reinforcement
   (C) Negative reinforcement
   (D) Shaping
   (E) Vicarious reinforcement

87. "I used to think I wasn't a Red Sox fan. Then I watched the Red Sox win the World Series. Now I think I am a Red Sox fan." This statement is most consistent with

   (A) social comparison theory.
   (B) cognitive dissonance.
   (C) belief in a just world.
   (D) foot-in-the-door phenomenon.
   (E) balance theory.

88. A one-year-old infant says his first word, "Dada." This child

   (A) appears delayed linguistically.
   (B) requires further testing to determine if he is developmentally delayed.
   (C) is displaying appropriate behavior for his age.
   (D) may be delayed, but we cannot tell unless we know what language he is learning.
   (E) is definitely ahead of most normal children.

89. Which of the following terms is not associated with Rogerian, client-centered therapy?

   (A) Empathy
   (B) Unconditional positive regard
   (C) Repression of anxiety
   (D) Positive trusting environment
   (E) Nondirective

90. Of the following correlations, which shows the strongest relationship between two variables?

   (A) −0.79
   (B) +1.1
   (C) 0
   (D) +0.2
   (E) +0.68

91. The concept of learned helplessness was developed by

   (A) B. F. Skinner.
   (B) Albert Bandura.
   (C) Martin Seligman.
   (D) Joseph Wolpe.
   (E) John B. Watson.

92. The scientist who would reject the teachings of the early psychologists and be LEAST likely to study mental processes would be

   (A) Jean Piaget.
   (B) William James.
   (C) Edward Titchener.
   (D) John Watson.
   (E) Wilhelm Wundt.

GO ON TO THE NEXT PAGE

93. The statement "He ran from the police because he is evil" is an example of

   (A) the fundamental attribution error.
   (B) the just-world hypothesis.
   (C) the availability heuristic.
   (D) cognitive dissonance.
   (E) groupthink.

94. When Ms. Jennings analyzed the grades on her last psychology test, she found that the scores had a very small standard deviation. This would suggest that

   (A) only a few students took the test, but most were absent.
   (B) the mean test score was lower than the median score.
   (C) students were confused about the content and left several answers blank.
   (D) the scores tended to be very similar to one another.
   (E) very few students were absent, and most students took the test.

95. The "blind spot" refers to

   (A) the area of the retina that contains only rods and no cones.
   (B) the area of the retina that contains only cones and no rods.
   (C) the area where the optic nerve exits the retina.
   (D) the place in the optic chiasm where the optic nerves cross.
   (E) the area on the cornea where an astigmatism occurs.

96. In an experimental study on how sleep deprivation could affect a person's mental alertness, the _____ in the study is mental alertness.

   (A) dependent variable
   (B) independent variable
   (C) experimental condition
   (D) control condition
   (E) double-blind procedure

97. The concept of _____ suggests that information presented below our ability to perceive influences our attitude or behavior.

   (A) physiological bias
   (B) response contingency
   (C) just noticeable difference
   (D) linear perspective
   (E) subliminal processing

98. The psychologist who started the first experimental laboratory in the United States was

   (A) William James.
   (B) Wilhelm Wundt.
   (C) E. L. Thorndike.
   (D) B. F. Skinner.
   (E) John Watson.

GO ON TO THE NEXT PAGE ▷

99. During development, a fertilized egg can split. If it does, it results in

(A) a developmental delay.

(B) a learning disability.

(C) twins.

(D) fetal alcohol syndrome.

(E) Down syndrome.

100. Which pairing of psychologist and theory is correct?

(A) Skinner: classical conditioning

(B) Pavlov: operant conditioning

(C) Piaget: humanistic psychology

(D) Watson: behavioral psychology

(E) Freud: collective unconscious

IF YOU FINISH BEFORE TIME IS CALLED, YOU MAY CHECK YOUR WORK ON THIS SECTION ONLY. DO NOT TURN TO ANY OTHER SECTION IN THE TEST.

STOP

SECTION II

Time—50 minutes

Percent of total grade—$33\frac{1}{3}$

Directions: You have 50 minutes to answer BOTH of the following questions. It is not enough to answer a question by merely listing facts. You should present a cogent argument based on your critical analysis of the questions posed, using appropriate psychological terminology.

1. Dr. Maxwell wants to investigate the effects of caffeine consumption on mathematical ability in middle school girls. She selects a local middle school and has a computer select 50 of the 250 girls at random to be part of the experiment. The girls are divided into two groups. Each group takes a similar-looking pill and then the girls are given a series of challenging puzzles to solve while Dr. Maxwell keeps track of their scores while solving. At the end of the experiment, Dr. Maxwell concludes that caffeine does boost mathematical performance.

    Define and explain how each of these terms is used in this experiment.

    - Independent variable
    - Dependent variable
    - Random assignment
    - Confounding variables

_____

_____

_____

_____

_____

_____

_____

_____

_____

_____

GO ON TO THE NEXT PAGE ▷

2. Elias is about to begin a training program for new teachers because he is eager to return to school to teach math in a nearby high school where many of the students are struggling with math. For each of the following concepts, first define what they mean, and second, explain how you would use them to help Elias prepare for this challenging career.

- Self-fulfilling prophecy
- Formal operational thinking
- Selective attention
- Content validity
- Learned helplessness
- Mnemonic devices

_____

_____

_____

_____

_____

_____

_____

_____

_____

_____

_____

_____

_____

_____

_____

_____

Practice Test Two: **Answer Key**

1. C	21. E	41. E	61. D	81. B
2. B	22. A	42. A	62. E	82. C
3. C	23. B	43. E	63. B	83. D
4. D	24. A	44. A	64. E	84. A
5. A	25. E	45. A	65. A	85. C
6. C	26. C	46. B	66. B	86. A
7. E	27. A	47. D	67. C	87. B
8. C	28. B	48. C	68. E	88. C
9. E	29. B	49. B	69. A	89. C
10. A	30. C	50. A	70. B	90. A
11. D	31. B	51. B	71. B	91. C
12. A	32. B	52. A	72. E	92. D
13. D	33. A	53. D	73. D	93. A
14. A	34. B	54. C	74. D	94. D
15. D	35. A	55. B	75. C	95. C
16. B	36. B	56. B	76. B	96. A
17. C	37. C	57. D	77. B	97. E
18. A	38. B	58. C	78. A	98. A
19. C	39. D	59. A	79. D	99. C
20. D	40. E	60. A	80. E	100. D

Practice Test Two: **Assess Your Strengths**

Use the following tables to determine which topics (chapters) you need to review most.

Chapter and Topic	Question
Chapter 3: History and Approaches	17, 71, 92, 98
Chapter 4: Research Methods	2, 27, 40, 47, 48, 90, 94, 96
Chapter 5: Biological Bases of Behavior	19, 42, 46, 69, 75, 76, 78, 85, 99
Chapter 6: Sensation and Perception	10, 21, 26, 36, 52, 95, 97
Chapter 7: States of Consciousness	1, 54, 79
Chapter 8: Learning	29, 35, 55, 57, 63, 73, 82, 86, 100
Chapter 9: Cognition	3, 9, 13, 18, 41, 49, 58, 62, 81, 88
Chapter 10: Motivation and Emotion	4, 12, 24, 33, 37, 59
Chapter 11: Developmental Psychology	5, 11, 16, 38, 45, 64, 80
Chapter 12: Personality	25, 28, 34, 44, 68, 74, 83
Chapter 13: Testing and Individual Differences	8, 20, 50, 51, 66, 70
Chapter 14: Abnormal Behavior	7, 15, 31, 53, 56, 60, 72, 77, 91
Chapter 15: Treatment of Abnormal Behavior	14, 23, 39, 61, 84, 89
Chapter 16: Social Psychology	6, 22, 30, 32, 43, 65, 67, 87, 93

Chapter and Topic	Number of Questions on Test	Number Correct
Chapter 3: History and Approaches	4	
Chapter 4: Research Methods	8	
Chapter 5: Biological Bases of Behavior	9	
Chapter 6: Sensation and Perception	7	
Chapter 7: States of Consciousness	3	
Chapter 8: Learning	9	
Chapter 9: Cognition	10	
Chapter 10: Motivation and Emotion	6	
Chapter 11: Developmental Psychology	7	
Chapter 12: Personality	7	
Chapter 13: Testing and Individual Differences	6	
Chapter 14: Abnormal Behavior	9	
Chapter 15: Treatment of Abnormal Behavior	6	
Chapter 16: Social Psychology	9	

ANSWERS AND EXPLANATIONS

SECTION I

1. C

Sleep apnea occurs when a person stops breathing while sleeping. He then wakes up and starts breathing again. Oftentimes, the person does not know that he is waking up, but the episodes do have the effect of causing serious drowsiness. Narcolepsy occurs when one falls asleep at unpredictable times. Cataplexy is a muscle control problem in which a person loses control as if in REM sleep.

2. B

When the question asks about how two variables are related, it's usually a question about the correlation of the two. (An experiment would ask if A caused B, not about the relationship between A and B.) Because wealth and happiness are going in opposite directions—as wealth increases, happiness decreases—the relation must be a negative correlation. Note that knowing that two things are related does not tell us how strong the relationship is, or what causes these items to change.

3. C

A heuristic is a mental shortcut to a solution. An algorithm guarantees a correct solution but often takes more time to implement. So the advantage of using a heuristic is one of time: typically, a heuristic is faster.

4. D

The James-Lange theory of emotion suggests that we feel the physiological response first and then label the emotion. The Cannon-Bard operates in the reverse. The general adaptation syndrome occurs when we lower our resistance to stress because we are already under a great deal of stress in our lives. Set-point theory concerns weight management, and the fight-or-flight response occurs in the face of a stressful situation but does not have anything to do with emotion.

5. A

The biggest issue in the debate between Gilligan and Kohlberg had to do with Kohlberg's idea that women are less likely to reach higher levels of moral reasoning than men. Gilligan claimed that women typically peak with morality, based on consequences of immediacy.

6. C

According to the actor-perceiver error, we make external attributions about our failures. The fundamental attribution error refers to the tendency to attribute others' behavior to internal causes. (A), (D), and (E) are not specific enough to refer to a particular mistake a person is making.

7. E

The hallmark of antisocial personality disorder is the lack of regard for the rights and feelings of others. A paranoid personality disorder demonstrates paranoid behavior without the burden of hearing voices that a schizophrenic deals with. Histrionic personality disorder results in very dramatic, relationship-impairing behavior. Schizoid and schizotypal personality disorders result in poor social functioning and almost cold indifference to social situations.

8. C

John Gardner, in his book on multiple intelligences, argues that traditional intelligence tests do not measure intelligence well. Rather, according to Gardner, each person possesses a bit of seven intelligences (or eight, depending on which source you are reading), each to a varying degree. Binet, Terman, Wechsler, and Merrill all worked on more traditional forms of intelligence tests.

9. E

Free-association is a technique used by practitioners of psychodynamic therapy to attempt to extract information from the unconscious. The other measures are typically used to study internal mental processes, such as memory or reading.

10. A

In the lateral geniculate nuclei of the thalamus are several different classes of cells called center surround cells. These cells fire differentially, depending on the wavelength of light that strikes the retina. The pairings are white–black, green–red, and blue–yellow. When you stare at a picture that has one of the pairings, then remove it and replace it with a white visual field, the firings of the cells alter, and the perception is of the opposite color. The tri-color or trichomatic theory of color vision explains only part of the process, and the other terms are related to audition rather than vision.

11. D

Prior to concrete operations, children do not have the ability to conserve well; they do not have the concept that things can change shape and still maintain quantity. There has been debate that if you measure conservation differently, you will find that children can conserve, but traditional Piagetian theory suggests that the ability to conserve is the first marker that a child has made the transition to concrete operations.

12. A

Maslow's most famous contribution to psychology is the hierarchy of needs, in which he argues that we have basic needs of shelter and food that have to be met before we start to achieve the higher-level needs of love, knowledge, etc. According to Maslow, once we have begun to meet many of the needs at the lower levels, we approach self-actualization.

13. D

The primacy effect suggests that when we try to remember a list, we tend to remember the first few items on the list. The traditional explanation is that we do this because we have the time to rehearse the information to transfer it to long-term memory. The recency effect suggests that we remember information at the end because it is recent. Chunking refers to grouping information to organize it better in STM, and mnemonics are memory aids.

14. A

Typically, people with developmental delays have difficulty with tasks involving high-level cognitive skills. A token economy requires simple processing in that students only need to learn the association between the token and the reward. The other systems would tax the cognitive skills of a developmentally delayed person and probably provide that person with limited benefits.

15. D

The typical borderline personality individual has trouble understanding the differences between someone making a mistake and someone actually being a bad person. Such individuals are unable to tease apart issues such that they can cope with interpersonal relationships appropriately. The schizoid and schizotypal personality disorders result in odd behavior and difficulty in interpersonal relationships. The narcissistic and antisocial personality disorders result in difficulty in dealing with the fact that one's behavior has consequences.

16. B

Piaget is credited with developing the first stage theory of cognitive development. This theory is very well known and is considered essential knowledge for all students of psychology. Freud, Erikson, Harlow, and Gilligan were all psychologists who commented on development, but their theories were not about cognitive development.

17. C

Wilhelm Wundt is credited with starting the first lab in experimental psychology. He began the lab at the University of Leipzig in 1879.

18. A

A great deal of research has demonstrated the role of the hippocampus on memory. Damage to this region results in the inability to form new memories. The other skills are located in different parts of the brain: sensory processing in the parietal lobe, motor control in the frontal lobe, language in the temporal lobe, and vision in the occipital lobe.

19. C

Language seems to be localized for most people in the left temporal and frontal lobes (mostly the temporal). Damage to this region results in a language decrement called an aphasia.

20. D

If each standard deviation is 15 points, then if you scored at 115, you would be 1 standard deviation above the mean. Between the mean and 1 standard deviation, there is 34 percent of the total population. From the mean down, there is 50 percent. So if you score 1 standard deviation above the mean, you scored better than 50% + 34% = 84% of the population.

21. E

The concept of binocular disparity suggests that because we have two eyes, with slightly different views of the world, we are able to see depth. We fuse together the information from the two images to create an image with depth. Interposition, linear perspective, and context all are cues for depth, but they don't require both eyes.

22. A

If we are in a group, we often assume that someone else will help a person. This is called diffusion of responsibility.

23. B

Flooding, positive reinforcement, and punishment are concepts used by psychologists who practice behavioral therapy. Unconditional positive regard is a technique used by Rogerian therapists. Free association is the only concept among the choices that is utilized by psychoanalytic therapists.

24. A

This example is consistent with the notion that physiological change leads to interpretation of emotion. Essentially, the idea is that a physiological response will lead us to think that we are experiencing some emotion.

25. E

(A), (B), (C), and (D) are all part of Jung's theory of archetypes. The superego, however, is a Freudian concept that he explained as being the part of our personality that is our conscience.

26. C

The main idea for Gestalt psychologists is that we need to avoid reductionism. We can't understand complex phenomena by looking at individual pieces, but rather, we need to look at the whole. The idea is that sometimes, things together take on a slightly different form than we might think they do when they are separate.

27. A

A normal distribution is a bell-shaped curve. A chi square is skewed, as is a skewed distribution. A scatterplot will take the shape of the data, and a bimodal distribution has two peaks.

28. B

Projection occurs when we see the issues that bother us in someone else. For example, if it bothers me that my mother always talks to strangers, according to Freud, it is because I don't like that problem in myself. It is easier to be upset with someone else than with ourselves.

29. B

Bandura's work was groundbreaking in that it suggested that reinforcement does not need to be directed at us specifically. If we observe an actor performing a behavior, and that person is reinforced for that behavior, we might take that reinforcement vicariously and, thus, increase the probability that we engage in that behavior as well.

30. C

The mere exposure effect suggests that if we see something, even if we don't prefer it at that point, and we see it again in a different context, we may now prefer that object because of the prior exposure. One interesting study had participants look at shapes below threshold; that is, they couldn't actually see them because they were presented too quickly. Then, participants were presented with pictures that they had to rate. Participants rated "previously seen" pictures higher than pictures they had not seen before, even though they had no idea that they had actually seen the pictures previously.

31. B

The paranoid schizophrenic tends to have the symptoms described. That is not to say that the other disorders don't show some of those symptoms, but this combination of symptoms is typically found only in this disorder.

32. B

In Milgram's research, he found that participants were willing to "shock" a person if they were told to do so, even if it was against their better judgment. The upshot of the experiment was the suggestion that participants will do whatever they are told, if they believe the person telling them to do it is an authority figure.

33. A

According to the Yerkes-Dodson law, we don't perform tasks well at low levels of arousal or very high levels of arousal. Rather, our performance is best when we are at moderate levels of arousal. The Hawthorne effect is close, but this suggests that we do better when we change our environmental context.

34. B

The Eysenck Personality Inventory is a forced-choice tool that yields a score that allows the researcher to determine level of introversion and extroversion. It is a useful scale because it tends to be reliable and provides a measure of dishonesty as a means of evaluating the validity of the instrument.

35. A

In Watson's famous paper in 1913, he claimed that if he had control over the environment, he could create whatever characteristics he desired. That was the beginning of the behavioral movement, which launched the career of Watson and, eventually, Skinner.

36. B

The just noticeable difference is the ability to notice a difference or a change in stimuli. For example, how much sugar in a cup of water does it take for us to notice that the water now has sugar in it? The absolute threshold is our ability to determine the existence of a stimulus, not the ability to notice a change in the stimulus.

37. C

Extrinsic motivation is motivation derived from rewards coming from external sources. Intrinsic motivation refers to motivation that comes from internal sources, or self-motivation. Conditioned stimulus refers to a process in classical conditioning, cognitive dissonance is a concept in social psychology, and positive punishment is a concept in operant conditioning.

38. B

The Heinz dilemma is a famous problem that asks what would happen if a husband were faced with the problem of his wife dying or of him stealing. Kohlberg was not only interested in the answer a person gave but also why that answer was given. According to Kohlberg, that information helps us understand the level of moral reasoning that a person is operating at.

39. D

Francine's therapist is gently but firmly chiding her for her absurd notion that she now is less than smart because she received her first B. The style of a cognitive therapist is to challenge the irrational thinking of one's patients so that they begin to change the way they think, and thus behave. A client-centered, (A), therapist would offer unconditional regard and support, but would not challenge her irrational thinking, nor would a psychoanalyst, (B), or a therapist who took a learning approach, (C). A therapist following an eclectic approach, (E), would use a mixture of several approaches, but not necessarily cognitive.

40. E

The standard deviation tells us how much, on average, each score differs from the mean. The mean is the average, the mode tells us the most frequently occurring score in the distribution, and skewness and kurtosis tell us about the shape of the distribution.

41. E

In this example, the person is able to deduce a solution by thinking about the problem in a unique way. Schemas and scripts are clearly not correct, because they describe thinking about the typical solution to a problem. Algorithm is not correct, because there is a solution that would definitely solve the problem, but that's not the selected solution. Metacognition refers to our ability to describe our thoughts.

42. A

Vision is in the occipital lobe. Thought, memory, and attention are in the frontal lobes. Language is controlled by the left hemisphere in approximately 90 percent of the population.

43. E

Social facilitation theory argues that if we are in competition with another person, we'll perform more quickly than if we are doing the problems by ourselves. (A), (B), and (C) refer to theories of emotions, and (D) is a theory in cognitive psychology.

44. A

Free association is a technique used by practitioners of Freudian psychology to help determine the cause of the anxiety or stress in the unconscious. The belief is that by asking people to say exactly what is on their mind when a certain word is said, the psychologist is able to determine what is happening in the unconscious. (B) is used as a measure in cognitive psychology, and (C), (D), and (E) are all forms of therapy but not Freudian techniques.

45. A

In Harlow's research, it was found that monkeys preferred a mother with both food and comfort associated with her. Given the choice between two surrogate mothers, the animals consistently chose the cloth-covered surrogate.

46. B

Broca's area is located at the junction between the temporal and frontal lobes. Damage to this area results in a decreased ability to produce language clearly. A Broca's patient produces language that is choppy and unclear. Damage to the occipital lobe would result in decreased ability to see clearly or see color, and damage to the frontal lobe would produce problems with memory.

47. D

A type II error occurs when we do not have sufficient statistical power to reject a null hypothesis when, in fact, that hypothesis is incorrect. Type II errors need to be balanced with type I errors when we reject a null hypothesis because of random sampling error.

48. C

Operational definitions are very clearly stated descriptions of the variables we are measuring. The reason we use operational definitions is that at times, we don't have direct access to the variables of interest. Particularly in psychology, if we don't define clearly, we do not provide sufficiently clear definitions for others to measure the same issues we are interested in.

49. B

The availability heuristic happens when we make judgments about the frequency of occurrence of events based on limited or inaccurate information. We need to be careful not to make judgments without having gathered sufficient evidence beforehand.

50. A

The most common method of assessing tests is to ask if the test is doing what it is supposed to. If it is consistent, then it's reliable, and if it measures what it's supposed to, then it's a valid test. Because this test was given to students at such a young age and information was gathered again at the end of elementary school, the psychologist would have plenty of data to compare. If the preschool test accurately predicted elementary grades, then the test would have a high degree of validity.

51. B

The WAIS and WISC tests were developed by psychologist David Wechsler to measure several different kinds of intelligence including block design, basic math, and vocabulary. The WISC is an offshoot of the original WAIS test (and notice the A is for adult and C is for children). These tests can be used not only to provide an intelligence test score, but also to identify issues such as learning disabilities and even ADHD.

52. A

The fovea is a pit in the middle of the retina in which cones are very concentrated. The fovea is the part of the eye with the greatest degree of visual acuity, because when you look at something, that image is falling on the fovea. To see this clearly, we have a dense concentration of cells. The retina is the entire structure that contains the receptor cells. The sclera is the white part of the eye that provides structure. The lens and cornea work together to help focus the image on the retina.

53. D

Seligman's work on learned helplessness showed that if an animal is presented with a situation in which escape is blocked for a sufficient number of trials, it will not try to escape—even in a situation where it could escape.

54. C

If someone is awakened during REM sleep, the next time he goes to sleep, he will slip into paradoxical sleep more quickly and will spend more time in that stage. This is called the rebound effect.

55. B

Of all the schedules, the variable-ratio results in behavior that is the most difficult to extinguish, because no predictable number of behaviors are required prior to the presentation of a reinforcement. Thus, an animal will continue to behave because in the past, behavior has led to reinforcement. Eventually, after many trials of no reinforcement, the animal will slowly begin to develop alternative behavior patterns. Variable-interval is not as good a schedule for maintaining behavior, because it is more difficult to associate time lag with behavior.

56. B

In OCD, the obsession is an uncontrollable thought or anxiety, and the compulsion is what a person does to help stop the anxiety-causing response. An OCD person, for example, might have obsessive thoughts about leaving the stove on. To alleviate that thought, the person will check the stove repeatedly throughout the night to help calm the anxiety.

57. D

Pavlov is the person who developed the concept of classical conditioning, but he did it quite by chance. He was examining digestion in dogs and, by happenstance, found that if he paired the sound of a metronome with the delivery of food, the animal would salivate. Further, he found that the salivation could be controlled by this neutral stimulus. Watson, by the way, did work with classical conditioning, but he borrowed heavily from the work of Pavlov.

58. C

A mnemonic is a memory aid or mental shortcut. To set it up, one needs to have a place that he knows well. Once he has mentally examined that space, he mentally puts himself into that place and puts objects in locations represented in the room. The technique is very effective when one is trying to remember a long list of items or names.

59. A

While Charles Darwin was one of the first to observe the similarities in facial expressions between humans and animals, it was psychologist Paul Ekman who discovered the similarity in human facial expressions all over the world. This is fascinating because up until Ekman's work in the 1960s, emotions and their accompanying facial expressions were thought to be culturally determined.

60. A

Delusions and hallucinations are the two hallmark symptoms of schizophrenia.

61. D

Although ECT is used sparingly these days, it is still an effective treatment for some forms of severe depression. Psychologists do not typically use this approach, but if the patient is suffering and other treatments are not working, ECT is a choice for some people.

62. E

Encoding refers to the way that information enters our body through our senses and then is sent to the brain for further processing. While acoustic encoding refers to information that one hears, and visual encoding to what one sees, semantic encoding is when one remembers the substance of information rather than the exact information itself. Semantic encoding is actually a good sign of memory, in that people are translating the word in their head into a word or term that is more meaningful to them.

63. B

A conditioned stimulus is one that causes a response after training but was initially a neutral stimulus. In this example, 10:15 is not a typical time that one might eat. However, after many pairings of the time with food, the person learns to associate that time with hunger. Thus, the reflex of hunger begins to occur when 10:15 rolls around, regardless of whether or not Nancy is actually hungry.

64. E

Complex logical problem-solving skills are markers that a person has entered the final stage of cognitive development in Piaget's theory: formal operations. Prior to this stage, children may be able to solve simple logical problems. However, after they reach this age, they are able to handle a variety of very complex, abstract problems.

65. A

Conformity is the concept of doing what others are doing, just because they are and you are not. Attribution theory refers to our interpretation of others' actions, aggression is the idea that we sometimes use force to obtain what we desire, groupthink refers to the consistency of a group's opinion after time, and altruism means doing something just because it seems like the right thing to do for someone.

66. B

"Terman's Termites" were followed by the psychologist for more than 35 years. Lewis Terman was determined to do research that would shatter the popular myth that students who were young and gifted would be arrogant, socially awkward, and perhaps even angry as they grew up, and his persistence paid off. The advantage of doing a longitudinal study is that you can get terrific information about how changes take place over time, but a disadvantage is that participants often drop out and it can be expensive to keep up with everyone as they age.

67. C

The Stanford Prison Study was completed in 1971 by Phil Zimbardo and his associates. In this study, 24 students were chosen, with half playing the role of guards and half playing the role of prisoners. The study was set to run two weeks, but Zimbardo had to stop the experiment after only six days because prisoners and guards alike had completely adopted the roles that they had been given and were treating each other badly. The study is an interesting one in that it helps us understand that the power of the situation has a strong influence on our behavior.

68. E

Much of the criticism of personality measures is that they rely heavily on survey methods, which are not always the most accurate measures of behavior. The research on surveys suggests that people will sometimes tell the researcher what they think the researcher wants to hear (demand characteristics). Sometimes, participants don't tell the truth on surveys, either. It is not that they are lying, per se, but rather, it is difficult to know what one might do in a given situation unless one is actually in that situation.

69. A

SSRIs block the reuptake of serotonin, resulting in an increase in the amount of serotonin in the synapse at any given time. This increases the effect of the neurotransmitter (which is inhibitory). These drugs are often used as treatment for depression, suggesting that serotonin may be an important neurotransmitter in the regulation of mood.

70. B

The concepts of reliability and validity are essential in psychological testing. Reliability refers to the extent to which a test measures a construct consistently, and validity refers to the extent to which the test measures what it is supposed to measure. A test can be reliable and not be valid. That is, a test may yield the same score again and again, but it may not be an accurate measure of what it is intended to measure.

71. B

Titchener was one of Wundt's most famous students, and he was enormously influential in developing a lab at Cornell. This is one of those questions you just have to know.

72. E

Sometimes, after a highly stressful event, a person may suffer from post-traumatic stress disorder, in which he may re-experience the anxiety-inducing event (or the emotions that went along with it) for many years after the actual event occurred.

73. D

The process of shaping by successive approximations is often used to train an organism to engage in complex behavior. The example given may start by providing reinforcement when the dog goes out into the backyard. After a while, the dog will continue to go out into the backyard. After that behavior is established, reinforcement would be given for the dog approaching the correct spot in the yard. Eventually, the animal will learn to go in that spot in the yard every time.

74. D

According to Sheldon, the ectomorph tends to be shy and introverted; the mesomorph is more likely to be extroverted.

75. C

Neurotransmitters are the primary messenger system between neurons. Hormones, and some have suggested pheromones, also provide communication in indirect ways. However, the neurotransmitters are the most efficient way that two neurons can communicate with each other.

76. B

A phenotype is an expressed gene. That is, a phenotype is an expressed physical characteristic. There are lots of people who are over six feet tall. This would mean that they have the same expressed gene, that of tallness.

77. B

Delusions and hallucinations are hallmarks of most individuals with schizophrenia. Remember that delusions are false beliefs such as thinking that you are someone else—the queen of England, for example—while hallucinations are false sensory experiences that can be visual (seeing stimuli that are not present) or auditory (troubling noises or voices). Auditory hallucinations tend to be far more common and patients may hear voices that command them to do certain tasks.

78. A

Myelin wraps itself around axons to produce faster action potentials. Myelin is most common in the cortex, where fast-acting neural transmission is essential for the higher-level cognitive functioning that occurs in that region of the brain. It is also essential for fast-twitch muscle control. The disorder of multiple sclerosis is a demyelinating disease in which muscle control is lost due to loss of myelin.

79. D

REM sleep (rapid eye movement) is also called paradoxical sleep. The reason for this is that during sleep, our brain waves typically slow down dramatically. However, during REM sleep, our brain waves fire as quickly as they do when we are awake. Thus, during dreaming, we are most easily awoken as it doesn't take much for our brain waves to switch to being awake.

80. E

Konrad Lorenz did a great deal of work looking at inborn behaviors. He found that ducklings will imprint or bond with the first organism that they see after birth. The classic picture is of Lorenz walking with his ducklings following.

81. B

According to Chomsky, syntax is what provides language with a great deal of its meaning. That is, the placement of a word in a sentence helps us determine the part of speech and, eventually, the meaning of the word. The semantic level is the level of meaning of the sentence, the lexical level is the word meaning, the morphemic level is the smallest unit of meaning in a language, and phonemic level is the smallest unit of sound in a language.

82. C

Systematic desensitization is a process that relies on pairing the stress-inducing situation with relaxation. Eventually, instead of inducing stress, the formerly stress-inducing situation will produce relaxation. (A), (B), and (D) rely on operant conditioning principles, and unconditional positive regard is a concept in humanistic psychology.

83. D

The MMPI (Minnesota Multiphasic Personality Inventory) was developed by comparing the results of "normals" who visited the hospital to those who were committed for a variety of disorders. The questions that yielded the biggest differences between the two groups were retained and became part of the instrument.

84. A

Client-centered therapy focuses on helping the client recognize that she is of value. The therapist will listen to the issues as explained by the client, and help her to see that she is a valuable person with many strengths. This therapy is called client-centered because the client sets the direction of the therapy. In the other forms of therapy mentioned, the therapist leads the session, with the client filling in when asked questions.

85. C

Down syndrome results from having an extra 21st chromosome. The other disorders are genetic in nature, but the genes involved are not the 21st.

86. A

Punishment is designed to decrease the probability of a behavior occurring. According to Skinner, punishment should not be used unless there is no other choice, as it has possible side effects. Also, Skinner argued that unless punishment is consistent and severe enough to be punishing, it will not be effective.

87. B

In cognitive dissonance, behavior and cognitions need to be consistent. In the described situation, the behavior of watching the Red Sox is inconsistent with the person not liking the team. Thus, either the behavior or the cognitions need to change to make things consistent for the person and alleviate the anxiety caused by the inconsistency.

88. C

The typical child says his first word sometime around the first year. It is not uncommon for this to be delayed, but typically by around the first year, the child has said something that the parents have responded to as a word.

89. C

According to Rogerian psychology, all but (C) are important in therapy. Repression of anxiety is a concept most commonly associated with Freudian psychoanalysis.

90. A

Don't be fooled by the negative sign. The correlation coefficient tells us two things: (1) the number tells us the strength of relationship, and (2) the sign tells us the direction of the relationship. The bigger the number, the more the two variables are related. The sign tells if the relationship is in one direction (as one variable changes, the other changes in the same direction) or inverse (as one variable changes, the other changes in the opposite direction). Although (B) seems to be a bigger number than −0.79, correlations cannot be larger than 1, so this answer is impossible.

91. C

Learned helplessness occurs when an organism has been placed in a situation from which it cannot escape. After several attempts that are unsuccessful, the animal will stop trying to escape. Later, even if it is very clear the animal can escape, it will not try because it has learned that it "cannot."

92. D

Watson introduced the United States to behaviorism and the belief that the only thing that mattered was the way behaviors were reinforced or punished. Watson's famous "give me a dozen healthy infants" line was merely a boast, but remembering it will help students recall Watson's emphasis on shaping behavior and ignoring the "black box" of the mind. All of the other choices are psychologists who were very much interested in how the mind is structured (Titchener and Wundt), functions (James), and changes over time as we grow (Piaget).

93. A

The fundamental attribution error states that we typically attribute other people's behavior to dispositional features. In this case, the notion of being evil is an internal attribution that is being made about another.

94. D

There are two primary ways to describe data, and students tend to be familiar with measures of central tendency and measures of variation. Three main measures of central tendency are mean, median, and mode, which are called central tendency measures because they describe where the middle of the data is. Less familiar is the concept of variation, which includes range and standard deviation, a formula for explaining how far data "drift" from the center. The smaller the standard deviation is, the closer the data is to the mean and the more similar the scores are to each other.

95. C

The blind spot is in the back of the eye where the optic nerve exits the eye. At that point of the retina, there are no receptor cells, and thus, we have no visual information being gathered. We compensate for this by "filling in the blank" during normal visual processes.

96. A

Recall that in an experiment a researcher wants to use one variable—the independent variable—to see what effect it has on another variable—the dependent variable. In this example the researcher would deprive participants in the experimental group of sleep (the independent variable) for a certain number of hours and then do tests to check for their alertness (the dependent variable). These tests will use scores which can be used to measure the amount of lack of alertness the sleep deprivation is responsible for. Experimental, (C), and control conditions, (D), as well as the double-blind procedure, (E), are components of experimental design but are not involved with the dependent variable.

97. E

Subliminal processing suggests that we are influenced by information that is not consciously processed by us. That is, we don't actually have a memory of experiencing the event, yet our behavior is still altered.

98. A

Although Titchener is often credited, James actually started a lab in his basement in the mid-1870s. The lab was a demonstration lab, but many of the techniques developed laid the groundwork for experimental techniques later on in psychology.

99. C

When a fertilized egg splits, the result is identical twins. This does not happen very often, and it is not the only way that twins can occur. Twins can occur if two eggs are fertilized simultaneously.

100. D

Skinner studied operant conditioning; Pavlov studied classical conditioning; Piaget studied developmental psychology; and Freud studied the unconscious, not the collective unconscious (that was Jung).

SECTION II

1. Dr. Maxwell wants to investigate the effects of caffeine consumption on mathematical ability in middle school girls. She selects a local middle school and has a computer select 50 of the 250 girls at random to be part of the experiment. The girls are divided into two groups. Each group takes a similar-looking pill and then the girls are given a series of challenging puzzles to solve while Dr. Maxwell keeps track of their scores while solving. At the end of the experiment, Dr. Maxwell concludes that caffeine does boost mathematical performance.

Define and explain how each of these terms is used in this experiment.

- Independent variable
- Dependent variable
- Random assignment
- Confounding variables

This question is worth 8 points, one for each definition and appropriate application to this question.

The independent variable is that factor that an experimenter wishes to investigate in an experiment, and it is given to one or more experimental groups (1 point). In this example, the independent variable would be the consumption of caffeine (1 point).

The dependent variable is being studied by the experimenter to see what effect the independent variable has on it. The dependent variable has to be operationally defined in such a way that it can be quantified (1 point). In this example the dependent variable would be the girls' scores for solving the math puzzles (1 point).

Random assignment means to place each of the participants in either a control or experimental group in a manner in which each participant has an equal chance of being in any group (1 point). In this case, a computer could be used to place participants in each group to reduce any bias on the part of the experimenter (1 point).

Confounding variables are factors in an experiment other than the independent variable that might influence the dependent variable and throw off the reliability of any data that is gathered. There should be only one difference between an experimental group and a control group—the independent variable—and any other difference would be a confounding variable (1 point). In this example, there are many potential confounds. If one group was given the puzzles early in the day and the other group got them in the afternoon, then time of day would be confounding, or if all of the members of the school's chess team were placed in one group, this would again be a confounding variable because it could be chess experience, not caffeine, that results in success (1 point).

2. Elias is about to begin a training program for new teachers because he is eager to return to school to teach math in a nearby high school where many of the students are struggling with math. For each of the following concepts, first define what they mean, and second, explain how you would use them to help Elias prepare for this challenging career.

- Self-fulfilling prophecy
- Formal operational thinking
- Selective attention
- Content validity
- Learned helplessness
- Mnemonic devices

This question is worth 6 points for accurately providing an appropriate example. (NOTE: You do not need to define the term explicitly, but it must be clear from your answer that you know what it means.)

Elias must be made aware of the self-fulfilling prophecy to be sure that he does not come into the school thinking that these children are failures at math. If students perceive that he thinks they are not smart or not good at math, then they may act that way, thus reinforcing his belief and making it come true (1 point).

Piaget's theory of cognitive development said that formal operational thinking might not appear until early adolescence if at all, so Elias should be prepared for the idea that all of his students might not be comfortable with logical thinking and hypothetical situations (1 point).

All of us only have a finite amount of attention, and a student who is busy texting or playing on the computer in class is not paying full attention to the teacher, which will negatively impact learning. Elias might counter this by frequently shifting topics or moving students around the room to reduce the chances of them zoning out or playing with technology (1 point).

When giving tests, Elias has to be sure that his test questions accurately reflect what he has taught in order for it to be a fair test. To ensure content validity, he might ask a veteran teacher to go over the test with him and verify that the questions selected include a fair representation of what was covered in class (1 point).

If students repeatedly experience failure in a math classroom, they may give up and refuse to really participate in class and learn new concepts. Elias should know that even when he gives students new tools and strategies for solving problems, some may shut down and say, "This will never work"—just like the dogs in Seligman's experiments who could have escaped the shock but had given up trying (1 point).

A great way to teach students to learn anything is by teaching them about mnemonics and helping them to create some of their own. If Elias can help students to come up with catchy sayings or abbreviations, they may more easily be able to remember the formulas required in his class (1 point).

GLOSSARY

Accommodation A process described by Piaget of creating a new schema because an experience does not fit into an existing schema or adapting schema to fit new experiences

Action potential The all-or-none firing of a message from one neuron to another

Actor-perceiver bias An attribution error we make when we believe that others' behavior is due to the environment and our behavior is due to our own efforts

Adaptation According to Piaget, the goal of development is to adapt to one's surroundings.

Alfred Adler A colleague of Freud, he argued that the unconscious controls much of our behavior (introversion, birth order)

Algorithm A problem-solving strategy that is guaranteed to lead to the correct solution

Anxiety disorders Excessive anxiety that causes disruptions in dealing with everyday life; these include generalized anxiety disorder, phobic disorder, and obsessive-compulsive disorder; often treated with medication such as Xanax or Paxil

Applied behavior analysis (ABA) A form of therapy or research that focuses on understanding the context in which behavior occurs and attempting to control the context to alter the behavior

Assimilation A process described by Piaget of fitting a new experience into an existing schema

Attachment An emotional bond between parent and child that forms early in life and sets the pattern for future emotional bonding

Attribution theory A theory that states we often infer the reasons that someone might engage in a behavior by observing that person

Axon The part of the neuron that carries information from one part of the cell to another cell

Bandura, Albert A psychologist well known for his work on social learning theory

Behaviorism A school of thought that suggests that the environment controls all aspects of human behavior

Biological approach An approach that suggests that we can understand behavior by examining the brain and the central nervous system

Bystander effect The idea that if we witness something happen, we often believe someone else will help and, thus, we do not

Cataplexy Falling into REM sleep while conscious; a person suffering from cataplexy will lose muscle control and fall down

Cerebellum	A part of the hindbrain responsible for control of motor coordination and some autonomic responses, such as breathing and heart rate
Chomsky, Noam	A linguist who revolutionized our theories on how we acquire and utilize language
Chromosomes	The genetic code that gives rise to our biological characteristics
Classical conditioning	Suggests that some behavior is controlled by learned associations between neutral stimuli and reflex-causing stimuli; developed by Ivan Pavlov in his work on the digestive system in dogs
Cochlea	The structure in the inner ear that transduces sound from physical waves to neural impulses (via the basilar membrane)
Cognitive confirmation bias	The idea that we look for information that confirms out beliefs about a person, group, or situation
Cognitive psychology	Branch of psychology concerned with the study of how people think, remember, and pay attention
Concrete operational stage	The third stage in Piaget's theory in which a child can use some logical thought but hasn't yet advanced to using abstract cognitive thought
Conditioned response	A learned response to a previously neutral stimulus
Conditioned stimulus	A previously neutral stimulus that now gives rises to a reflexive response
Conformity	The tendency to do things because others are doing it (as shown in the studies by Asch)
Confounding variable	A term used in research methods to describe a situation in which an unexpected variable caused a change in a dependent variable in such a way that it is not possible to determine what caused the outcome
Conscious	According to Freud, the part of our consciousness that we are currently aware of
Consciousness	The active processing of information in our brain
Cornea	The outer layer of the eye in the front. The cornea bends light so that it focuses on the retina.
Correlation	A statistic that provides information on both the strength of a relationship and the way the two variables are related (either directly or inversely)
Cortex	The outer shell of the brain, divided into four regions (occipital lobe: responsible for vision; parietal lobe: responsible for receiving sensory information; temporal lobe: responsible for language and hearing; frontal lobe: responsible for higher-level cognitive functions, such as thought and emotion)

Defense mechanisms (or ego defense mechanisms)	Developed by Anna and Sigmund Freud, defense mechanisms are designed to protect the ego from harm; these include repression (pushing information deep into our unconscious), projection (seeing the anxiety-causing behavior in others), reaction formation (engaging in antagonistic behavior to a desire), sublimation (replacing an anxiety-inducing desire with something that is acceptable), and displacement (directing anxiety responses toward something other than the issue causing the anxiety)
Dendrite	A part of a neuron that receives information from other cells
Dependent variable	An outcome measure in an experiment
Descartes, René	Philosopher who was most well known for his work on the mechanical nature of human behavior (mind-body dualism)
Development	The relatively predictable set of changes people go through as they grow, including changes in social, cognitive, and physical skills
Dissociative disorders	A break in the connection between reality and perception of reality; these include psychogenic fugue, amnesia, and dissociative identity disorder (sometimes called multiple personality disorder)
Divided attention	The ability to divide our mental effort among a variety of tasks at one time
Ego	According to Freud, the part of personality that tries to satisfy the demands of the id within the context of the superego ("reality principle")
Encoding	The process of taking information into the information-processing system
Episodic memory	Memory for events that are autobiographical
Equilibration	The process of periodically restructuring schemas to provide a better fit of experience to knowledge
Experiment	A method of research in which a variable or variables are manipulated to determine the impact they have on an outcome measure
Extrinsic motivation	Motivation that is derived from an outside obtainable goal (like positive reinforcement from an outside source)
Forebrain	The convoluted part of the brain that is said to contain the parts of the brain that make us different from other species
Forensic psychology	The study of how psychology and the law interact; forensic psychologists are concerned with using what we know about psychology to solve crimes, hire better police, and learn how better to adjudicate justice
Formal operational stage	The highest level of cognitive development, according to Piaget, in which a child can conduct complex logical thought
Freud, Sigmund	Considered the "father" of psychoanalysis; he believed that the unconscious controlled our behavior
Functionalism	A school of thought founded by James that suggests that the goal of psychology is to understand the function and purpose of consciousness

Fundamental attribution error	The belief that we make attributions about others' behavior as being caused by internal rather than external factors
Genetics	The study of how our biology codes for our physical characteristics
Gestalt	A principle of perception that states that we use a variety of cues to help us organize the world around us (Pragnanz and closure are two examples). Also, an early form of psychology that stated that our experience is more than the physical stimulation that we receive.
Health psychology	The branch of psychology concerned with applying the results of psychological research to promoting healthy lifestyles and understanding issues such as stress
Heuristic	A shortcut we use when we are solving problems
Hindbrain	The area of the brain that controls mostly autonomic functions, such as breathing and heart rate
Humanism	A school of thought that suggests that human behavior is purposeful and goal driven and that we have free will to determine our own paths; also sometimes called *phenomenological psychology*
Hypothalamus	The part of the brain responsible for motivation
Id	According to Freud, the part of our personality that demands immediate satisfaction of its needs ("pleasure principle")
Impression formation	In social psychology, we often form impressions of people based on a variety of shortcuts; we use these impressions to determine appropriate actions toward those people in the future
Independent variable	A variable that is manipulated by an experimenter to determine the effect it has on an outcome (or dependent) variable
Industrial/organizational psychology	The branch of psychology concerned with applying the findings of psychology to improve the workplace environment
Inferential statistics	A set of techniques that allows us to draw inferences about how our sample corresponds to the population at large. (t and F are common inferential statistics.)
Insomnia	Inability to sleep or stay asleep for long periods of time
Institutional Review Board (IRB)	The organization charged with evaluating research to determine if it meets the ethical standards of the institution
Intrinsic motivation	Motivation that comes from within a person
Iris	The colored part of the eye; a muscle that controls the pupil
James, William	Considered the founder of American psychology; led a school of thought called *functionalism*
Jung, Carl	A colleague of Freud who believed that we have both an unconscious and a collective unconscious and that these areas of mind controll much of our behavior

Language	A complex communication system that involves the use of a limited set of abstract symbols to convey an unlimited number of messages
Lateral hypothalamus	The part of the hypothalamus that controls the motivation for eating
Learning	A relatively permanent change in behavior due to experience
Lens	A malleable structure inside the eye that changes shape to help us focus light on the retina
Levels of processing	A theory proposed by Craik and Tulving that suggests that memory is a by-product of perception and the more effort is involved in perceiving a stimulus the better memory will be
Limbic system	A part of the brain that is responsible for emotional response to stimuli
Linguistic universals	A set of theoretical constructs concerning properties that all languages share
Long-term memory	Our memory for information that is no longer active but is accessible
Mean	A measure of central tendency that is the average of all the scores in a sample
Median	A measure of central tendency that is the middlemost score in a sample
Midbrain	The part of the brain that serves as a pathway of sensory cells as sensory information passed from one region of the brain to the other
Milgram, Stanley	A psychologist famous for his experiment on obedience, in which he ordered people to continue giving "shocks" even when they appeared to be painful to the person receiving them
Mode	A measure of central tendency that is the most commonly occurring score in a sample
Mood disorders	An inability to control or stabilize mood; these include clinical depression and bipolar disorder. Often treated with medications such as Prozac, Wellbutrin, or Zoloft
Morpheme	The smallest unit of meaning in a language
Motivation	The drive to begin or maintain behavior
Myelin	A coating around an axon that speeds up action potentials
Narcolepsy	The sudden, unavoidable urge to fall asleep
Naturalistic observation	Observation in which the participants are monitored in the natural environment in which the behavior typically occurs
Neo-Freudians	Psychoanalytic theorists who modified Freud's theory but still believed that the cause of anxiety was unconscious
Neuron	A cell in the brain and central nervous system that is responsible for communication between different parts of the body
Neurotransmitter	A chemical message between neurons (GABA, acetylcholine, serotonin)
Night terrors	Visions that some people have just after falling asleep; these are not dreams; the person will wake up screaming and terrified; more common in boys under age 12; can occur in stage 4

Obedience	Doing what one is told to do, often because responsibility is felt to lie in the person who is the authority; the work of Stanley Milgram helped us understand this
Oedipus complex	According to Freud, children will at one point during their psychosocial development suffer from unknown anxiety as they feel attraction to the opposite-sex parent and jealousy of the parent of the same sex; most children successfully navigate this stage
Operant conditioning	A theory that suggests that behavior is controlled by the consequences of that behavior; if the behavior increases, it is being reinforced; if the behavior decreases, it is being punished; developed by B. F. Skinner
Operationalism	A theory of research that suggests that some behavior may be able to be measured directly, so we need to state the way we intend to measure that behavior clearly and concisely
Ossicles	The three small bones in the middle ear that translate sound into the inner ear (malleaus, incus, stapes)
Pavlov, Ivan	A physiologist who developed the theory of classical conditioning
Perception	The interpretation of sensory information via experience
Personality	A pattern of behavior that remains somewhat consistent across time
Personality disorders	Pervasive patterns of behavior involving difficulty in interacting with others; these include borderline personality disorder and antisocial personality disorder
Phoneme	The smallest unit of sound in a language
Piaget, Jean	A developmental psychologist famous for his stage theory of cognitive development
Pinna	The part of the outer ear that we see
Preconscious	According to Freud, the part of our consciousness that we are not currently thinking about but could if we wanted to
Premack principle	The idea that we can use a highly desirable activity to reinforce the completion of a less desirable task
Preoperational stage	The second stage of Piaget's theory in which the child develops simple cognitive skills
Probability	The basis of all statistics. Probability is the potential chance of any outcome occurring in any given situation.
Prosocial behavior (or altruism)	We engage in behavior that leads to a good outcome.
Psychoanalysis	Freud's approach to therapy, often called talk therapy; Freud used a variety of techniques to treat his clients, including dream analysis, hypnosis, and free association

Psychoanalytic approach	Suggests that our behavior is controlled by forces outside of our conscious awareness; this approach was founded by Freud
Psychological disorders	Patterns of behavior that cause a person to suffer from lack of ability to engage fully in society
Psychology	The science that studies the behavior and mental processes of organisms
Psychosocial stages of development	According to Freud, we all go through stages of psychosocial development where the source of pleasure varies; if we don't successfully navigate each stage, we may become fixated at that stage and will suffer from that later in life
Punishment	A consequence designed to stop a behavior (Positive punishment is the application of an aversive stimulus, while negative punishment is the removal of a desirable stimulus, both with the goal of decreasing behavior.)
Pupil	The part of the eye that opens and closes to allow the correct amount of light into the eye
Rapid Eye Movement (REM sleep)	Stage of sleep during which our brain waves are similar to when we are awake. During this stage, we tend to be dreaming; this happens 4–6 times each night
Reinforcement	Any consequence that leads to an increase in the probability of a behavior occurring again. (positive reinforcement is when something is given, and negative reinforcement is when something is removed. Both lead to an increase in behavior)
Retina	The part of the eye at the back that contains photoreceptors (rods for black and white, cones for color)
Retrieval	The process of getting information out of long-term memory for additional processing
Scaffolding	A process of learning new responses by utilizing support to develop higher-level skills
Schedules of reinforcement	Intermittent reinforcement; not giving reinforcement for every instance of a behavior (fixed-interval: after a fixed amount of time has passed; fixed-ratio: after a fixed number of behaviors has occurred; variable-interval: after time has passed, but the amount of time between reinforcers varies; variable-ratio: after behavior has occurred, but the number of behaviors required for reinforcement varies)
Schema (or scheme or schemata)	Any unit of knowledge
Schizophrenia	A class of disorders that include a break with reality, often marked by auditory hallucinations and poor communication skills; these include paranoid schizophrenia, disorganized schizophrenia, and catatonic schizophrenia Often treated with drugs such as chlorpromazine, Zyprexa, or Risperdal.
Sclera	The white part of the eye that provides structure

Selective attention	The ability to focus our mental energy on one topic at a time
Self-fulfilling prophecy	The idea that you will ascribe certain attributes to a person based on information obtained prior to meeting the person, without taking into account performance
Semantic memory	Memory for general facts or knowledge
Sensation	The process of receiving information from the environment through the senses
Sensorimotor stage	The initial stage of cognitive development, according to Piaget, in which the child obtains knowledge only from the senses and produces a motor response
Sensory memory	The ability to store information in its sensory form for a few hundred milliseconds so that it can be processed after we have processed other information
Short-term memory	Our memory for events that we are currently thinking of; it is limited in capacity to about 7±2 bits of information at any given time
Signal detection theory	A theory designed to help measure our perceptual processes
Skinner, B. F.	Considered by many to be the most important psychologist of the 20th century; he went against the traditional approach of studying psychology by claiming that all we need to know about behavior is the consequences of behavior, and if we understand that, we can predict and control future behavior; his approach was called operant conditioning
Social facilitation	Evidence suggests that when we compete, we perform better than we would if we were engaging in behavior alone
Sociocultural approaches	Suggest that human experience within the context of the social culture determines human behavior
Somatoform disorders	With such a disorder, an individual suffers from a form of a physical ailment, though there is no ailment that a physician is able to diagnose; these include conversion disorder and hypochondriasis
Somatosensory cortex	A strip across the very front of the parietal lobe that receives information from different parts of the body; there is a relationship between the amount of cortex devoted to a region and the level of sensitivity of that area; for example, a great deal of cortex is devoted to the fingertips because those areas are much more sensitive than, say, the back
Somnambulism	Sleepwalking; typically, this happens during stage 4 of sleep; it is *not* dangerous to wake up someone who is sleepwalking
Sports psychology	The area of psychology concerned with applying the field to improving sports performance

Spreading activation model of memory	A theory that posits that memory is organized around themes and we activate nodes (or ideas), which leads to activation of related concepts via links (or connections)
Stages of sleep	During the night, we pass through stages of sleep; each is marked by slower and slower brain waves, respiration, and heart rate; as the night progresses, the amount of time we spend in these stages changes
Standard deviation	A measure of spread among scores that represents how much, on average, each score differs from the mean
Statistics	A theory of information that is used to evaluate relationships between variables
Stereotypes	Beliefs about an individual based on generalized beliefs about a group of which that person is a member
Strange situation	An experimental procedure designed to measure attachment
Structuralism	A school of thought founded by Wundt that suggests that the goal of psychology is to understand the structure and organization of consciousness
Superego	According to Freud, the part of our personality that serves as our conscience
Synapse	The gap between dendrites and axons
Syntax	The organizational principles of a language
Teratogens	Outside substances that can be taken in by the mother that have negative influences on a developing fetus
Threshold	Limits on our perception; also, absolute threshold, the least amount of information required for a stimuli to register in our perception
Titchener, Edward B.	A student of Wundt; he traveled to United States and founded the first lab in a college at Cornell University
Trait theorists	Personality theorists who believe that we can understand personality by examining the separate characteristics that a person displays
Tympanic membrane	The eardrum; a structure that vibrates when sound hits it
Unconditioned response	The response to a stimulus, such as a reflex
Unconditioned stimulus	A stimulus that leads to a response in the world naturally
Unconscious	According to Freud, things that are too painful to experience are pushed into our unconscious; this information is not accessible to our consciousness, but it does cause anxiety if not dealt with appropriately
Ventromedial hypothalamus	The part of the hypothalamus that controls motivation for satiety (or feeling full)
Vygotsky, Lev	A developmental psychologist who argued that language and culture influence development above and beyond what the biological perspective might allow
Watson, John B.	An early behaviorist who believed that classical conditioning explains a great deal of human behavior

Wundt, Wilhelm   Considered the founder of experimental psychology at the University of Leipzig in 1879; he founded a school of thought known as Structuralism

Zone of proximal development (ZPD)   The gap between the abilities of children that they are capable of dealing with and that they can deal with if provided with support